India and Israel

India and Israel contextualises the varied aspects of the partnership between the two countries, with a specific focus on the dominant driver—the defence engagement that was forged in the context of mutual complementarities.

India's broad-spectrum relationship with Israel transformed into a strategic partnership in 2017, a quarter century after the establishment of full diplomatic ties. India and Israel have successfully steered the relationship forward, despite the baggage of fraught and convulsive neighbourhoods. The contributors to this volume include policy makers and military leaders who played an important role in the growth of the relationship, as well as academics who have closely followed its trajectory, shedding important light on the transformation of the India–Israel bilateral relationship into a strategic partnership over the course of past tumultuous 25 years. Chapters highlight Israel's increasing engagement with India's diverse federal polity, the de-hyphenation of the India–Israel ties from India's relationship with Palestine, as well as the role played by US non-state (pro-Israel US-based interest groups) and sub-state (US Congressmen) actors in shaping India–Israel ties. The concluding chapter examines Israel's relationship with the People's Republic of China (PRC), given that both the PRC and India established diplomatic ties with Israel almost simultaneously.

India and Israel will be of great interest to scholars of strategic studies, international relations, Middle Eastern Studies, Asian Studies, as well as those working in diplomacy, government, and the military.

The chapters were originally published as a special issue of *Strategic Analysis*.

Jayant Prasad was Director General of the Manohar Parrikar Institute for Defence Studies and Analyses, India, from September 2015 to September 2018. He was India's Ambassador to Afghanistan, Algeria, Nepal, and the UN Conference on Disarmament, Geneva.

S. Samuel C. Rajiv is Associate Fellow at the Manohar Parrikar Institute for Defence Studies and Analyses, India. He has published on issues related to India's foreign and security policies in *Strategic Analysis*, *Foreign Policy*, and *The Jerusalem Post*, among others.

India and Israel

The Making of a Strategic Partnership

Edited by
Jayant Prasad and S. Samuel C. Rajiv

Routledge
Taylor & Francis Group

LONDON AND NEW YORK

First published in paperback 2024

First published 2020
by Routledge
4 Park Square, Milton Park, Abingdon, Oxon OX14 4RN

and by Routledge
605 Third Avenue, New York, NY 10158

Routledge is an imprint of the Taylor & Francis Group, an informa business

Publisher's Note
The publisher has gone to great lengths to ensure the quality of this reprint but points out that some imperfections in the original copies may be apparent.

Disclaimer
Every effort has been made to contact copyright holders for their permission to reprint material in this book. The publishers would be grateful to hear from any copyright holder who is not here acknowledged and will undertake to rectify any errors or omissions in future editions of this book.

British Library Cataloguing-in-Publication Data
A catalogue record for this book is available from the British Library

ISBN: 978-0-367-46504-9 (hbk)
ISBN: 978-1-03-283933-2 (pbk)
ISBN: 978-1-00-302913-7 (ebk)

DOI: 10.4324/9781003029137

Typeset in Times New Roman
by codeMantra

Contents

Citation Information

The chapters in this book were originally published in *Strategic Analysis*, volume 41, issue 4 (2017). When citing this material, please use the original page numbering for each article, as follows:

Chapter 1
Editors' Introduction
Jayant Prasad and S. Samuel C. Rajiv
Strategic Analysis, volume 41, issue 4 (2017) pp. 311–313

Chapter 2
India–Israel: Retrospective and Prospective
Chinmaya R. Gharekhan
Strategic Analysis, volume 41, issue 4 (2017) pp. 314–324

Chapter 3
A Perspective on India–Israel Defence and Security Ties
N. A. K. Browne
Strategic Analysis, volume 41, issue 4 (2017) pp. 325–335

Chapter 4
Israel and India: Looking Back and Ahead
Efraim Inbar
Strategic Analysis, volume 41, issue 4 (2017) pp. 369–383

Chapter 5
Assessing US Influence over India–Israel Relations: A Difficult Equation to Balance?
Nicolas Blarel
Strategic Analysis, volume 41, issue 4 (2017) pp. 384–400

Chapter 6
Redefining 'Strategic' Cooperation
P. R. Kumaraswamy
Strategic Analysis, volume 41, issue 4 (2017) pp. 355–368

Chapter 7

India–Israel Defence Engagement: Land Forces' Cooperation
Alok Deb
Strategic Analysis, volume 41, issue 4 (2017) pp. 336–340

Chapter 8

India–Israel Defence Engagement: A Naval Perspective
Prakash Gopal
Strategic Analysis, volume 41, issue 4 (2017) pp. 341–347

Chapter 9

India–Israel Defence Trade: Issues and Challenges
Amit Cowshish
Strategic Analysis, volume 41, issue 4 (2017) pp. 401–412

Chapter 10

India–Israel: The View from West Asia
Sanjay Singh
Strategic Analysis, volume 41, issue 4 (2017) pp. 348–354

Chapter 11

Israel–China Ties at 25: The Limited Partnership
S. Samuel C. Rajiv
Strategic Analysis, volume 41, issue 4 (2017) pp. 413–431

For any permission-related enquiries please visit:
http://www.tandfonline.com/page/help/permissions

Contributors

Nicolas Blarel is Assistant Professor at the Institute of Political Science at Leiden University, the Netherlands.

N. A. K. Browne (Air Chief Marshal) (Retd), Chief of Air Staff, Indian Air Force (IAF) from July 2011 to December 2013, was the first Defence Attaché in Israel from April 1997 till July 2000.

Amit Cowshish is Consultant at Manohar Parrikar the Institute for Defence Studies and Analyses, India.

Alok Deb (Maj. Gen.) (Retd) was Deputy Director General at the Manohar Parrikar Institute for Defence Studies and Analyses, India, from November 2016 to November 2019.

Chinmaya R. Gharekhan (Ambassador) was Special Envoy on the Middle East Peace Process of the UN Secretary General and also the Indian Prime Minister.

Prakash Gopal is a former Indian Navy officer, currently pursuing his PhD at the University of Wollongong, Australia.

Efraim Inbar is President of the Jerusalem Institute for Strategy and Security (JISS).

P.R. Kumaraswamy (Professor) teaches contemporary Middle East at Jawaharlal Nehru University (JNU), India.

Jayant Prasad (Ambassador) was Director General of the Manohar Parrikar Institute for Defence Studies and Analyses, India, from September 2015 to September 2018.

S. Samuel C. Rajiv is Associate Fellow at the Manohar Parrikar Institute for Defence Studies and Analyses, India.

Sanjay Singh (Ambassador) was Secretary (East) at Ministry of External Affairs (MEA), India.

Editors' Introduction

Jayant Prasad and S. Samuel C. Rajiv

India's burgeoning relationship with Israel since January 1992 is an exemplar of India's post-Cold War foreign policy practice. From a relationship described as 'stillborn for 40 years'[1] to the broad-spectrum partnership a quarter century later, India–Israel relations ties have developed well, pushed by a rapid expansion of defence ties. The growth of the India–Israel partnership is a testimony to the sagacity shown by Indian and Israeli leaders in steering the relationship forward, despite the baggage of a fraught and convulsive neighbourhood.

This process gained from the non-partisan support for the relationship across the political spectrum—and the vicissitudes of internal political change, inevitable in democracies, had little adverse impact on it.

In the case of India, the Narasimha Rao-led Congress coalition took the first big step in normalising diplomatic ties. Subsequently, both the Congress and the Bharatiya Janata Party (BJP)-led coalition governments added greater ballast to the relationship. Successive Israeli governments, on their part, committed to Israel's growing partnerships in Asia, including with China and India. As P. R. Kumaraswamy contextualises in his contribution to this Special Issue, unique challenges propelled Israel's pursuit of new partners, including continued hostility to its existence within its extended neighbourhood.

The Special Issue places in perspective the varied aspects of the India–Israel partnership and chronicle the complimentary factors that propelled it during, the past quarter century. The 'overlapping strategic interests' for Efraim Inbar, included, among others, the arms and technology transfers, low intensity conflict, and the challenge of Islamism. Inbar in his contribution to this Issue as well as in his earlier scholarship also insists that India and Israel face similar kinds of threats—'radical offshoots of Islam in the greater Middle East'.[2] Kumaraswamy, however, avers that both countries 'have been careful not to present themselves in alliance against militant Islam'.[3]

Alliance or not, it is apparent, however, that India and Israel are on the same side of the strategic divide when it comes to pushing back against Islamist terrorist groups. Incidents like 26/11, wherein Israeli citizens were actively targeted by the Pakistan-based Lashkar-e-Taiba (LeT), underline the universal nature of the threat posed by such terrorist groups and their sponsors. Israel faces challenges posed by Palestinian groups. Israel's kinetic responses in Gaza in recent times though have been the subject

Jayant Prasad is Director General, Institute for Defence Studies and Analyses (IDSA), New Delhi. S. Samuel C. Rajiv is Associate Fellow at IDSA, New Delhi.

of much international scrutiny, given the hugely disproportionate loss of lives caused by its military interventions.

Defence trade has been the defining aspect of the bilateral partnership, as brought out in the contributions to this Issue. From the Indian viewpoint, the mutual benefit came from the modernisation needs of its armed forces, and from the Israeli perspective, from its expertise in niche areas relating to surveillance and anti-missile defences. Incidentally, these were precisely areas in which India found itself deficient in developing indigenous capabilities. These complementarities resulted in mega deals like the Phalcon Airborne Warning and Control Systems (AWACS) and the Barak-I ship-borne point-defence systems.

Surface-to-Air Missile (SAM) systems being currently co-developed for the Indian Navy (IN) and the Indian Air Force (IAF)—and soon for the Indian Army—are a prime example of the nature of ongoing cooperation in the defence sector. Amit Cowshish writes that there needs to be a greater focus on such co-development, co-production projects, with an associated emphasis on exports to third countries. At the same time, in order for India to take full advantage of such high-tech defence cooperation with countries like Israel, Cowshish calls for strengthening elements of the country's procurement processes and greater clarity and transparency about the needs of the armed forces.

Air Chief Marshal (ACM) N. A. K. Browne (Retd), India's first Defence Attaché in Israel, in an important contribution infused with never-before published accounts of critical aspects of the India–Israel defence cooperation, chronicles the growth of the relationship forged in the context of India's wars. His essay brings to attention the fascinating example of how Rafael's Litening Laser targeting pods were operationalised by the IAF to effectively counter Pakistani Man Portable Air Defence Systems (MANPADS) on the icy heights of Kargil.

As for potential areas of further cooperation, Major General Alok Deb (Retd) highlights the fact that Indian and Israeli militaries have never carried out institutionalised joint training or exercises, which is the norm between countries with a significant strategic component in their bilateral relationship. ACM Browne posits that aerospace power potential could be further enhanced with joint bilateral exercises and associated training between the respective services. Commander Prakash Gopal advises that joint exercises between the two navies are the way to go forward 'to test the waters'. While the scale and complexity of such exercises may be progressively enhanced, Gopal writes that the focus initially could be on non-contentious issues like Search and Rescue (SAR), Humanitarian Assistance and Disaster Relief (HADR) and Non-combatant Evacuation Operations (NEO), among others.

Major General Deb writes that the most important takeaway for India's military in the long term should relate to the domain of ideas and innovations, of which crack Israeli Defence Force (IDF) outfits like Unit 8200 are prime examples. Many of the country's leading start-ups have been established by alumni of such elite units, who developed their unique skills in the harsh operational environment while securing their country.

On other aspects of the bilateral ties, Kumaraswamy states that greater economic cooperation with state governments would continue to be the fulcrum of Israel's engagements with India. Such an approach, he notes, would harmonise with the development-oriented policies of the current Indian federal government. This approach, according to him, also ensures that the political opposition to Israeli policies vis-à-vis the Palestinians, which colour the approach of the Ministry of

External Affairs (MEA) or urban elites is somewhat attenuated. While being an important insight, it is important to note that the MEA's responses to Israeli military interventions in Gaza have been consistent—they have been critical of the 'disproportionate' use of force by Israel while at the same time acknowledging the cross-border 'provocations' that led to Israeli actions.[4]

As for the Palestinian issue, Inbar writes that pro-Palestinian feelings are widespread in India at the expense of Israel. Given the broad range and depth of India–Israel ties, this may not be entirely valid. While India supports the Palestinian cause diplomatically and economically, this has not been at the expense of rising cooperation with Israel, and vice-versa, as so cogently brought out by Chinmaya R. Gharekhan, former Special Envoy of the UN Secretary General and the Prime Minister on the Middle East Peace process.

On West Asian reactions to India–Israel ties, Sanjay Singh writes that Israel's evolving position in the regional geo-political framework and the region's view of India, and the promise of the positive role it can play in West Asian affairs, colour their appreciation of India–Israel ties. He notes that Arab diplomatic support to causes India holds dear has been intermittent. Singh writes that India–Israel relations stand on their own merit and have become de-hyphenated from both the Palestinian issue, and even more importantly, from US–India relations.

Nicolas Blarel, in his comprehensive analysis of the US factor in India–Israel ties, writes that the US involvement in the bilateral relationship has been constant, albeit neither consistent nor direct. He sheds light on the key role played by non-state and sub-state actors in shaping India–Israel ties, including Congressmen Emmanuel Celler in the 1940s and Stephen Solarz in the 1980s, and pro-Israel US-based interest groups such as the Anti-Defamation League (ADL) and the American Jewish Committee (AJC), in shaping the nature of India-Israel ties.

S. Samuel C. Rajiv in his article examines Israel's relationship with the other big Asian power, the People's Republic of China (PRC), given that both PRC and India established diplomatic ties with Israel at about the same time. He argues that despite the varied nature of their bilateral ties, three limiting factors continue to cast their shadow on the Israel–China partnership. These are the conundrum of defence trade and security ties, China's Palestine policy, and China's massive economic stake in West Asia. Nevertheless, the 'comprehensive innovation partnership' that both countries are pursuing gives China access to cutting-edge Israeli innovation with dual-use applications. This could play out to Israel's disadvantage in critical areas like Unmanned Aerial Vehicles (UAVs) and surveillance technologies, where Israel has niche expertise and products.

We hope the contributions in this Special Issue will be of interest to policymakers, the intelligentsia, and the informed public interested in a deeper understanding of the varied aspects of the India–Israel partnership, especially in the context of Prime Minister Narendra Modi's upcoming visit to Israel.

Notes

1. Arthur Rubinoff, 'Normalisation of India-Israel Relations: Stillborn for Forty Years', *Asian Survey*, 35(5), May 1995, pp. 487–505.
2. Efraim Inbar, 'The India-Israeli Entente', *Orbis*, 48(1), Winter 2004, p. 93.
3. P. R. Kumaraswamy, 'India and Israel: Emerging Partnership', *Journal of Strategic Studies*, 25(4), 2002, p. 202.
4. For an examination of these aspects, see S. Samuel C. Rajiv, *Indian Responses to Israel's Gaza Operations*, Mideast Security and Policy Studies No. 119, BESA Centre, Ramat Gan, Israel, May 2016.

India–Israel: Retrospective and Prospective

Chinmaya R. Gharekhan

Mr. Minister, for us in Israel, India is not just a country, it is a civilisation.
Shimon Peres to Eduardo Faleiro, New York, 1992

Shimon Peres' (then Foreign Minister of Israel) meeting with Eduardo Faleiro (then Indian Minister of State for External Affairs) on the sidelines of the United Nations General Assembly (UNGA) in New York in September 1992 was among the first ministerial-level contacts between India and Israel after the establishment of diplomatic relations in January of that year. Peres, whom I was to meet many times in the ensuing years in my various capacities, left a deep impression on me. As I discovered later, he formulated his spoken words as if he was drafting, rather crafting something for publication—fine, chiselled and most apt words without the slightest apparent effort at articulation.

Early history

It took India nearly 42 years from recognition of the state of Israel in 1950 to the establishment of diplomatic relations in 1992. And it had taken two and a half years to accord recognition to the new state after it announced its own birth on May 14, 1948. There were sound ethical and political reasons for these delays. Two of the most important leaders of India's freedom movement—Mahatma Gandhi and Jawaharlal Nehru—followed the course of the Zionist movement, the latter more intently. In an interview with the *Jewish Chronicle*, published in London on October 2, 1931, Gandhiji said:

> My attitude towards the Jews is one of great sympathy. I have very many Jewish friends ... I am sometimes asked whether I regard the Jews as the Chosen People, and I say well in a sense "yes". But then all peoples consider themselves to be chosen ... Zionism meaning re-occupation of Palestine has no attraction for me. I can understand the longing of a Jew to return to Palestine, but he can do so if he can without the help of bayonets, whether his own or those of Britain.[1]

Expressing deep sympathy for the persecution suffered by the Jews, Gandhiji concluded:

Ambassador Chinmaya R. Gharekhan was Special Envoy on the Middle East Peace Process of the UN Secretary General and also the Indian Prime Minister.

My remedy is twofold. One is that those who profess to be Christians should learn the virtue of toleration and charity, and the second is for Jews to rid themselves of the cause for such reproach as may be justly laid at their door.[2]

Nehru viewed the Palestine issue from the prism of struggle against colonialism and imperialism. Involved as he was in the war, albeit a non-violent one, against the British colonial power, he sympathised with the Arab struggle for independence against the same colonial authority. Delivering the Presidential Address at the Conference on Peace and Empire organised by the India League and the London Federation of Peace Councils on July 15, 1938, Nehru observed, *inter alia*:

... Right through two thousand years, there has never been any real conflict between the Arabs and the Jews in Palestine ... It is fundamentally a problem created by British Imperialism in Palestine, and unless you keep that in mind, you will not solve it. Nor is it likely to be solved by British Imperialism ...[3]

Most significantly, Nehru observed:

It is essentially a struggle for independence. It is not a religious problem ... British Imperialism played its hand so cleverly that the conflict became the conflict between Arabs and Jews and the British Government cast itself in the role of umpire.[4]

It is prescient to note that Nehru's solution, advocated way back in 1938, is similar to the one being advocated by everyone today, 78 years later—(a) 'that you cannot solve this problem by trying to crush the Arab people'; and (b) 'that it will not be settled by British Imperialism but by the two main parties coming together and agreeing to terms'.[5] Nehru was consistent in his conviction that the Palestine issue would be resolved only by the two parties coming together, without the intervention of the British. He believed that it was Britain which was responsible for the situation to start with, and its mediation would make matters worse. He was also convinced that violence, by the Jews or the Arabs or Britain, would not yield a satisfactory solution acceptable to both sides.

India and the establishment of the Jewish state

While Kumaraswamy in his admirably researched book *India's Israel Policy* analyses the arguments and circumstances which led India to vote against UN Resolution 181 of 1947 which partitioned Palestine into two states, he seems to have overlooked an important element while scrutinising and criticising India's stand.[6] Israel was and is the only state in recent times that was created by systematically and forcibly importing a large number of Jewish immigrants into the territory. Israel is a land of immigrants like the US, with the difference that the land was already settled by a large Arab population and that many of the Jews who migrated there were goaded and even financially helped to do so. Notwithstanding the famous slogan of the Zionists—'land without people for a people without land', more than 600,000 Arabs were already residing in Palestine when Jewish immigration commenced in the early part of the 20th century.

It is important to consider other critical ingredients which led to the establishment of the Jewish state. The Zionist movement which started towards the end of the 19th century in Europe gained in momentum after Britain issued the Balfour Declaration in

1917, which conceded in effect the Zionist demand for a state in Palestine while talking only of civil and religious rights for the Arabs. Balfour sowed the seeds of the unending conflict between the Jews and the Arabs. But it was the horrors of the holocaust that nailed the creation of Israel. It is not a given that the Zionists would have achieved their dream in the absence of Hitler's horrors, for which the Arabs were in no way responsible and which made the Western nations feel guilty, compelling them to concede the demand for a Jewish state. In the process of rendering justice to the persecuted Jews, the international community, which effectively meant the Western world at the time, caused immense injustice to the Palestinian people. India therefore saw that the Palestinian case merited more consideration.

India was opposed to the partition plan. Nehru was most reluctant to give up on his proposal for a federal state despite the fact that the UN had already adopted Resolution 181 and that Israel had proclaimed its independence in May 1948. His clear preference was for a federal state with two entities enjoying widest possible autonomy, with special status for Jerusalem. However, as Kumaraswamy mentions, there were few takers for the idea. It is interesting to note that Nehru did not give up hope for India's proposal months after the First Arab–Israeli War had started. Thus, in a letter to the chief ministers dated July 15, 1948, he observed, *inter alia*:

> In a military sense, probably the Arabs are stronger. But the fact that American and Russian prestige are involved in maintaining the new state of Israel, it will not be easy for the Arabs to win through ... Both sides feel passionately about their position and are hard fighters ... I still think the position we took in the UN was the correct one.[7]

Again, in a letter to Vijayalakshmi Pandit dated September 29, 1948, Nehru wrote:

> We have all along been opposed to partition. We still feel a federated state, with the widest possible regional autonomy in the areas occupied respectively by the Arabs and Jews would be the best solution.[8]

Despite all the reservations, India recognised the state of Israel in September 1950. It made good sense to wait for until such time as the First Arab–Israel War came to an end and the various truce agreements were concluded; in other words, when Israel became an established fact of international life. Why did Nehru not announce the establishment of diplomatic relations with Israel at the same time as the recognition of the state of Israel? After all, all other major powers, including the Soviet Union, had done so. There was probably a mix of reasons.

Perhaps the most important reason was the sentiments among the Muslim community in India. Muslims all over the world had sympathy for the Arabs. In India, they were a significant minority. After the breakaway of some Muslim majority areas to form Pakistan (Nehru preferred describing the division of India as 'secession' rather than partition), Indian leaders were sensitive to Muslim opinion. Pakistan had come out strongly in support of the Palestinian people, and India could do no less for fear of alienating the Arab states. The birth of Israel had coincided with the trauma of the sub-continent's partition and the First Arab–Israeli War had more or less coincided with the first India–Pakistan war over Kashmir. India had taken the question of Pakistan's aggression to the United Nations Security Council (UNSC) where the same Western countries were very hostile to India. These included Britain which had dumped the Palestinian issue in the lap of the UN. Given the unfavourable atmosphere in the UNSC, India could not afford to adopt an openly friendly attitude towards Israel.

Once the decision regarding diplomatic relations was delayed, it kept getting further delayed for one reason or another. In addition to what has been stated above, Maulana Abul Kalam Azad, a close associate of Nehru, played his part in persuading India's first prime minister against establishing diplomatic relations. President Gamal Abdel Nasser, who was Nehru's partner in the Non-Aligned Movement (NAM), may also have been influential in this matter. During the Suez Crisis of 1956, India had come out strongly in favour of Egypt; it was hardly the time for establishing normal relations with the aggressor nation. A few years later, there was the June War in 1967 between the Israelis and the Arabs. During all these years, Pakistan was solidly in support of the Arabs. The Soviet Union had also come out in support of the Arabs during the Cold War. India thought it had very little choice but to continue with its pro-Palestine stance.

In a warmly worded letter to Israel's then Foreign Minister, Moshe Sharett, dated June 5, 1954, Nehru stated that India had no basic objection to establishing diplomatic relations and that he was convinced that the problem could only be solved by some settlement between Israel and the Arab countries. Nehru wrote: 'It is possible that at an appropriate moment, we might be of some service in this matter ... If we established diplomatic relations with Israel at the present juncture, this would not facilitate our task.'[9]

It was only in 1992, after the end of the Cold War following the collapse of the Soviet Union, and after China had done so, that the government of Narasimha Rao decided to take the significant step of establishing diplomatic relations with the Jewish state. As it happened, the Muslims of India took this decision in their stride. Is it the case that Indian politicians misread the sentiment among the Muslim community all along? It is worth noting that during the years when full relations were absent, Israelis, including very senior officials and even ministers, as well as various experts, visited India and held talks with senior Indian personalities.

An Israeli delegation attended the Asian Relations Conference in 1947, even before either country had become independent. In February–March 1952, as Kumaraswamy notes, the Director General of the Israeli Foreign Ministry visited Delhi and was entertained to lunch by Nehru, besides meeting several ministers.[10] Israel too was forthcoming and complied with our requests for sending experts in various fields despite lack of diplomatic relations.

Israel's revisionist historiography

Israel has an excellent, even enviable tradition of academic freedom. Several academics and columnists have written what are known as 'revisionist' accounts of the widely and deeply believed narrative of the history of Jews and of the coming into being of the state of Israel. The most prominent 'new' historians are Benny Morris, Ilan Pappe, Avi Shlaim and Simha Flapan. Their sources were official Israeli Government papers de-classified 30 years after the creation of Israel. Flapan in his book *Birth of Israel: Myths and Realities* identified seven 'myths' and presented well-researched refutations of each of those myths.[11] One of the most common myths would have the world believe that the newborn state faced the onslaught of the Arab armies as David faced Goliath—a numerically inferior, poorly armed people in danger of being overrun by a military giant.

Flapan argues that the facts and figures pointed to a different situation altogether. He quotes David Ben-Gurion as admitting that the war of self-defence lasted only until June 11, 1948 when huge quantities of arms reached Israel whose better trained armed forces then attained superiority on land, sea and air. Another 'myth' is that the Arab leaders rejected the hand of friendship extended by Israel. The fact, according to Flapan, is that Israel turned down successive proposals made by Arab states and neutral mediators that might have brought about accommodation.

Without doubt, the most controversial of the 'new' historians is Shlomo Sand whose books *The Invention of the Jewish People* and *From the Holy Land to Homeland* created a storm of outrage in Israel and the US.[12] His central thesis is that the Jews of Europe, the Ashkenazim, are largely the descendants of peoples who converted to Judaism in the distant past and that the claim that all Jews descended from the ancient Israelites is false. He insists that the Bible should not be taken as history. He suggests that just as Muslims and Christians are the progeny of converted people, Jews likewise are descendants of converts. He argues that Judaism too was a proselytising religion.

Sand's conclusion is that, consequently, the contention that the European Jews are reclaiming ancient rights to their homeland in what is now Israel is false. Moreover, the peoples now known as 'Palestinians' are in all likelihood much more closely descended genetically from the ancient Israelites but who converted to Islam or Christianity, and who have a just claim to the land. Sand stoutly defends Israel's right to exist but favours a bi-national state in which the Jews and the Arabs live as equal citizens. Despite Sand's almost heretical thesis, his books are best sellers in Israel. This shows the vibrancy of the academic and intellectual life and the freedom historians enjoy in Israel.

The challenges of the Arab–Israeli peace process

The history of the Arab–Israel peace process is as old as the state of Israel. One of the earliest efforts at reconciling the conflicting claims of the two sides was the Peel Commission of 1939. Starting with the peace proposals of Count Bernadotte in 1948, other efforts to bring the two sides together have included the Jarring Mission, Allon Plan, Rogers Plan, Camp David Accords, Fahd Plan, Reagan Plan, Arab Peace Plan, Oslo Accords, Geneva Initiative, Beilin-Abu Mazen Plan, Quartet Plan, Road Map, Clinton Parameters and Taba Plan, among others. The peace process has gone through many highs and lows, mostly lows. Perhaps the most promising period was when Yitzhak Rabin was the prime minister of Israel.

Rabin had earned a reputation in Israel for his 'iron fist' policy towards the Palestinians, which made him, in a way, best qualified to take risks and to offer concessions. The Oslo Accords were made possible because of Rabin's recognition that Israel could not hang on to the Gaza strip where the scattered Jewish settlements were surrounded by hostile Palestinians and who had suffered casualties during the first intifada of 1987. On the Palestinian side, Yasser Arafat, Chairman of the Palestine Liberation Organisation (PLO), was the only one who could agree to the Accords, for which he was criticised by many within and without the occupied territories. Arafat told this author several times that he missed his 'partner' Rabin. Arafat, Israel's 'terrorist', received the Nobel Peace Prize in 1994, along with Rabin and Peres. When Benjamin Netanyahu became prime minister in June 1996, all hopes of a settlement vanished.

Unlike the common perception, Camp David II in 2000 was always going to fail. The then President Bill Clinton convened the talks against Arafat's desire and at the insistence of the then Israeli Premier Ehud Barak. The Americans invariably consulted the Israelis before submitting any formula to Arafat. Arafat was isolated and denied the opportunity to consult other Arab leaders which he absolutely had to do in view of the vital interest of the Muslim Umma particularly as regards the question of Jerusalem. The Palestinians, being the weaker party, needed a third party to mediate the negotiations and the only country with influence was the US. Dennis Ross, the American mediator, whom Arafat privately called 'Dennis the Menace', was biased in favour of Israel. As in the real estate business, there is no such thing as 'honest broker' in international relations.

More recently, former Secretary of State John Kerry made a determined effort in 2014 to find common ground between the parties. He set a self-imposed time limit of 9 months and clocked thousands of miles and huge effort, but could not succeed. Perhaps he was encouraged to invest so much personal energy and prestige because Netanyahu had, rather unexpectedly, stated in a speech in Bar Ilan University in 2012 that he accepted the two-state solution.[13] His real position was revealed in March 2015 when he made it clear that 'there would be no Palestinian state as long as I am the prime minister'.[14]

President Donald Trump during a joint press conference with Netanyahu in Washington in February 2017 stated that both the Israelis and the Palestinians will have to make concessions for any forward movement. Netanyahu's response was dismissive of his host's approach. He stated his position loud and clear when he said that the two conditions on which he would absolutely insist were that the Palestinians must recognise Israel as a Jewish state and Israel must have total security control over all the land from the sea to the Jordan river, which means the whole of a future state of Palestine, its land as well as its air space.

Netanyahu will in all likelihood retain his position for some years to come— despite the swirling charges of corruption that have recently engulfed him. The opposition is divided among several parties. The 'Peace Now' movement, though still alive, is not vocal or effective. The Israel Labour Party lacks dynamic leadership, and the right and far right are with Netanyahu. The Palestinian national movement is fragmented, with Hamas ruling in Gaza since 2007 and the Fatah in the West Bank riddled with large-scale corruption. President Mahmoud Abbas, now 82 and holding on to office, does not seem to be in a hurry to relinquish power, perhaps because there is no obvious successor. There are not many leaders who could command respect of the people and who could take over. The one name on which the Palestinians would perhaps readily agree is that of Marwan Barghouti, but he is in Israeli prison under-going two successive life terms. The Palestine National Authority (PNA) in the West Bank suffers from the same problems which plague non-democratic regimes. The division in the Palestine national movement, between Hamas and Fatah, as well as the internal struggle for power in the PLO suits Israel.

The international community is too preoccupied with its own problems of eco-nomic slowdown, influx of refugees and civil war in at least four Arab countries (Libya, Syria, Yemen and Iraq). Egypt is grappling with serious internal problems consequent on the overthrow of the Muslim Brotherhood regime in 2013 and is facing severe economic crisis. Cairo is still, however, capable of and anxious to play a role in bringing about reconciliation between the two Palestinian factions. However, President Abdel Fatah al-Sisi's priority clearly is to be on the right side of President Trump. Many of the other Arab states are too busy fighting in the civil war in Syria and Yemen and in any case have no love lost for the Palestinians and are anxious to make up with Israel. Indeed, Saudi Arabia and Israel have become allies against their common enemy Iran. The terrorist attacks in Israel have diminished, with the result that there is no great incentive among the Israeli public to change things.

Whither the two-state solution?

The international community is committed to the two-state solution. The Palestinians too have made a strategic decision in favour of two states. Reasonable elements in Israel also support the two-state solution. The question is how to get there and what kind of Palestinian state is to be established. Kerry in his 72-minute swansong on December 28, 2016 outlined the parameters of the two states, which seem logical and fair.[15] It was noteworthy that he made repeated references to the Arab Peace Initiative first put forward by Saudi Arabia in 2002 which offered normal relations between the Arabs and Israel in return for full withdrawal from occupied territories, something that the Americans had not done so categorically previously.

President Trump, in the same joint press conference with Netanyahu referred to above, stated that he could accept a one-state or two-state solution provided the two sides agreed to it. He also directly told his guest, to the surprise of many, to stop building settlements for a while. Netanyahu gave no commitment in this regard and is in fact going ahead with building more settlements and creating facts on the ground. I remember President Hosni Mubarak telling Prime Minister Rajiv Gandhi in Cairo in 1985: 'Soon, there will be no land left on which to establish a Palestinian state.'

Trump has welcomed both Netanyahu and Abbas to the White House, and also met them on his first trip abroad in May 2017. He has asserted that the Arab-Israeli dispute can be resolved within his lifetime. Trump may be underestimating the complexity of the issues involved. He has however been in no hurry to implement his campaign threat to shift the US Embassy from Tel Aviv to Jerusalem. If and when that happens, there will be a strong reaction in the Islamic world. Palestine has declared that it will withdraw its recognition of Israel. It might even lead to a third intifada among the Palestinians. It is, however, doubtful if there is any real appetite among them for another violent campaign, given the certainty that Netanyahu will deal with it most ruthlessly, with the international community remaining quiescent. In any case, the two Palestinian entities in Gaza and the West Bank are unlikely to form a common front in the foreseeable future.

It is entirely probable that the Palestinians might achieve their objective, substantially if not fully, by adopting the Gandhian method of non-violence. The late Edward Said mentioned this to me, and Sari Nusseibeh, who was the president of the Al Quds University for many years, is also convinced that it is the only hope for the Palestinians. I personally believe that non-violent struggle might succeed against Israel.

At some point in time, the Israelis will have to come to terms with demographic realities. The non-implementation of the two-state solution will mean one state or three states—the third one being Gaza. Perhaps the best avenue open to the

Palestinians is to disband the PNA and compel Israel to absorb the three million Palestinians into Israeli society with all the consequences that would entail. How will Israel deal with such a scenario? It will mean scores of Jewish settlements surrounded by resentful and hostile Arab populations, without the present convenient arrangement whereby the PNA is responsible for maintaining law and order. As Kerry reminded Netanyahu in his December 28, 2016 speech, Israel will have to choose between becoming a Jewish state or a democratic state; it cannot be both.

India's stakes

It might be worth speculating what the situation would have been today if India's proposal for a unified, federal state in Palestine had been accepted in 1947, before Resolution 181 was adopted. Isn't it conceivable that in that case, the two communities would over time have learnt to live together in relative peace and harmony? Where does all this leave India now? Our formal position is that India supports the two-state solution, with Israel and Palestine living side by side as good neighbours. This is also the consensus view among the international community. India must pursue its national interests. This translates, or should translate, into maintaining good relations with Israel as well as keeping up its traditional and principled policy of supporting the Palestinian cause and further developing relations with the Arab world. While the regimes in Arab countries might have lost interest in the Palestine issue, they still have to reckon with the Arab 'street' where support for the Palestine cause remains firm, though perhaps not as fervent as before mainly because of the current turmoil in the region.

We have huge interests in the Arab countries particularly in the Gulf, collectively more than in Israel, given the size of the Indian diaspora in those countries and our dependence on them for energy sources. At the same time, our relations with Israel have prospered, especially, but not only, in the defence sector. Successive Indian governments have managed to maintain a balance between these two competing considerations. It is, in fact, not a zero-sum game, and it is perfectly possible to develop close relations with both sides without negative impact on either of them. The total value of two-way trade with Israel in 1992 was about $200 million. In 2008–2009, it was more than $3.5 billion, going up to nearly $5 billion in 2015–2016. If the Free Trade Agreement (FTA) is signed, the negotiations for which started in 2002, the trade is expected to grow to $10 billion in 5 years. These figures are exclusive of the defence sector.

Defence industry is extremely vital for Israel as it is a crucial source of employment. Israel is the 10th largest producer and sixth largest exporter of arms in the world, with India providing the largest export market. Thus, India is extremely important for the Israeli defence industry. This ought to give India some leverage *vis-à-vis* Israel, but in practice it seems to give diplomatic advantage to Israel. We are mindful of the fact that Israel provided some much needed military supplies to India at the time of the Kargil Conflict.

On the diplomatic side, the balance has been well maintained. If an Israeli head of state has visited India (former President Ezer Weizman in 2007), so has the head of state of Palestine. Indeed, Arafat came to India several times and President Abbas has been our guest more than once and paid another visit in May, 2017. India has also extended quite generous aid to Palestine over the years amounting to nearly $30 million. We are financing the construction of what could be the parliament building of the future Palestine State in a locality called Abu Dis in East Jerusalem. We were the first non-Arab country to recognise the Palestine state and have built for them the residence and embassy of Palestine in Delhi's posh Diplomatic Enclave. M. J. Akbar, Minister of State for External Affairs, on a visit to Ramallah (which serves as the capital of Palestine pending the conclusion of final status talks) in November 2016, reaffirmed India's continued support for Palestine and announced increased aid as well as the establishment of an IT park in Palestine.[16]

There is a widespread perception that India has diluted its diplomatic support to the Palestinian cause over the past 20 years or so. While the rhetoric on the Palestine issue has been toned down a great deal, there is not much change in India's voting pattern in UN forums. The UNGA adopts every year a bunch of resolutions regarding Palestine. India used to support and co-sponsor most of them in the beginning. Gradually, we have stopped sponsoring five or six of them since 1993. A recent example was our vote in July 2015 when India abstained from voting on a resolution in the UN Human Rights Council in Geneva condemning, *inter alia*, Israel's disproportionate aerial bombing on Gaza in 2014 which killed 2300 civilians. The government justified the vote on the ground that the resolution contained a reference to the International Criminal Court to which India is not a party. External Affairs Minister Sushma Swaraj declared in the parliament that there was no change in India's traditional policy of supporting the Palestine cause.

Prime Minister Modi too has reiterated our principled support to Palestine. The Arabs are speculating whether or not Modi will visit Ramallah when he visits Israel. News reports indicate that he will pay a standalone visit to Israel in early July 2017. If that were to be the case, he would have come to the conclusion that it would not have any adverse impact on our relations with the Arab states. The fact that whatever incidents have taken place in India in the past couple of years involving violence against Muslims has not come in the way of our expanding relations, economic and otherwise, with the Gulf countries, as evidenced by the state visit of the Crown Prince of the Emirates, would seem to support the government's assessment.

There is no reason for India to be on the defensive regarding its growing relations with Israel. During my several visits to Palestine as Special Envoy, it was made clear to the Palestinian interlocutors that India was following its national interests, just as an independent Palestinian state would do once it emerged on the international scene. Facts and ground realities were explained to the Palestinians. It was also mentioned that many in India were not appreciative of Palestine's unreserved support to anti-India resolutions sponsored by Pakistan in the Organisation of Islamic Cooperation. The Palestinians understand such frank and interest-based policy. But they suspect that India's recent pronounced pro-Israeli tilt has an ideological element.

Many in India applaud Israel's firm riposte to the rocket and missile attacks from the Gaza strip, but mistakenly interpret it as anti-Islamic action whereas for Israel, it is a response to terrorist attacks directed against its territory. Israel is considered by many Indians as an example to follow in dealing with cross-border terrorist attacks, forgetting that Israel is dealing with an extremely weak adversary, unlike Pakistan which is a strong military power and has a nuclear arsenal. While no survey has been undertaken, it does appear though that the Muslim community in India is not overly concerned at the government's increasingly pro-Israeli stance, preoccupied as it is with more urgent problems of jobs, education, safety, etc. However, if Israel were to make any move to alter the status quo regarding the Al Aqsa mosque or if the US were to shift its embassy from Tel Aviv to Jerusalem, it could have strong negative repercussions among the Muslims of India.

Similarly, there is no need for India to be on the defensive with Israel about our support for the Palestinian cause. If Mr Modi were to spend a few hours in Ramallah, which are what most leaders even from the West and the US do—and which is what President Pranab Mukherjee did, the Israelis are not likely to protest. There is no contradiction between developing mutually beneficial relations with Israel and continuing to support the Palestinian cause which is precisely what successive governments have done.

In closing

India is interested in political stability in the region. India has huge interests there which are well known and do not need to be spelt out here. The region will not be stable without a just solution to the Palestinian issue. The region presently is engulfed in violent and intractable civil and sectarian strife. President Trump's full-throated support to the Saudi-led Sunni coalition against Iran, which was on display during his May 2017 visit to Riyadh, will further inflame the region. Iran, together with its partners of convenience such as Russia, will never tolerate a situation wherein they see their national interests seriously threatened. In this milieu, the Arab world seems to have very little time for the Palestinians. It is, therefore, not unnatural to regard the issue as of not much consequence. But things never remain the same for too long. President Trump's predictable unpredictability might make the region more volatile. His attack on a Syrian air base on April 6, 2017 with 59 Tomahawk cruise missiles in response to the alleged use of Sarin gas by the Damascus regime has made the situation, already highly complex, even more complicated. His action, for which he has received high praise domestically as well as from Saudi Arabia and Turkey, has been condemned by Iran and Russia who have reiterated support for President Assad.

The US and Russia were supposed to cooperate in Syria to defeat the Islamic State, but now that cooperation seems unlikely. The allegation of the regime being responsible for the chemical weapons bombardment in Idlib province is not too convincing since Assad had everything going for him of late, including military successes and even statements from Washington that the priority was the defeat of the Islamic State and not Assad's removal. Thus, it did not make sense for Assad to do something which would negate all these political and diplomatic advantages.

Obama's 'pivot' to Asia had indicated reduced interest in West Asia, but the turmoil in the region, which is not going to end any time soon, will ensure America's continuing deep engagement. Any attempt to alter the status quo on the Al Aqsa mosque or the shifting of the American Embassy to Jerusalem will provide a powerful tool to the extremists such as the Islamic State to radicalise elements of Muslim populations everywhere, including in India. Russia has re-inserted itself forcefully into the region and has China's backing for its efforts. Russia cannot take China's support for granted, as was evident when China abstained from the UNSC resolution related to the Idlib chemical attack on April 12, 2017, which was vetoed by Russia.

India has done well by not getting involved in this murky situation so far. India needs to keep in touch with these powers as well as with Egypt and Iran, regarding the rapidly evolving developments in West Asia. India should have a realistic appreciation of what role, if any, it can play in the prevailing situation in the region. India's own geo-strategic profile has seen an increase in recent times as evidenced in the increased frequency of the Indian Navy's visits to the region and the number of high-level political visits both ways. The Gulf countries seem open to India playing a bigger, more substantive role, including in the security sphere. The cooperation between them and us in the common fight against terrorism has taken on a strategic dimension. We need to take a long-term view of the situation and maintain close relations with both sides, as all successive governments have done.

Acknowledgements

The author thanks S. Samuel C. Rajiv for his research assistance.

Disclosure statement

No potential conflict of interest was reported by the author.

Notes

1. Gandhi's interview to the *Jewish Chronicle*, London, October 2, 1931, at http://www.jewish virtuallibrary.org/interview-to-the-jewish-chronicle-london-by-gandhi-october-1931 (Accessed March 15, 2017).
2. Ibid.
3. Dorothy Norman (ed.), *Nehru: The First Sixty Years*, Volume I, Asian Publishing House, New Delhi, 1965, p. 569.
4. Ibid.
5. Ibid., p. 570.
6. P. R. Kumaraswamy, *India's Israel Policy*, Columbia University Press, New York, 2010.
7. Nehru Memorial Museum and Library, *Nehru Papers*, File 11, Part I, p. 201.
8. Nehru Memorial Museum and Library, *Nehru Papers*, File 13, part II, p. 413.
9. Ravinder Kumar and H. Y. Sharada Prasad (eds.), *Selected Works of Jawaharlal Nehru: June 1, 1954–September 30, 1954*, Vol. 26, Oxford University Press, New Delhi, 2002, pp. 527–528.
10. P. R. Kumaraswamy, No. 6, p. 132.
11. Simha Flapan, *Birth of Israel: Myths and Realities*, Pantheon Books, New York, 1988.
12. Shlomo Sand, *The Invention of the Land of Israel: From Holy Land to Homeland*, trans. Geremy Forman, Verso, London and New York, 2014; Shlomo Sand, *The Invention of the Jewish People*, trans. Yael Lotan, Verso, London and New York, 2012.
13. 'Full Text of Netanyahu's Foreign Policy Speech at Bar Ilan', *Haaretz*, June 14, 2009, at http://www.haaretz.com/news/full-text-of-netanyahu-s-foreign-policy-speech-at-bar-ilan-1.277922 (Accessed February 10, 2017).
14. Barak Ravid, 'Netanyahu: If I'm Elected, There Will Be No Palestinian State', *Haaretz*, March 16, 2015, at http://www.haaretz.com/israel-news/elections/1.647212 (Accessed February 10, 2017).
15. John Kerry, 'Remarks on Middle East Peace', The Dean Acheson Auditorium, December 28, 2016, at https://2009-2017.state.gov/secretary/remarks/2016/12/266119.htm (Accessed February 10, 2017).
16. 'Official Visit of H.E. Mr M. J. Akbar, Minister of State of External Affairs of India, November 7–9, 2016', Representative Office of India, Ramallah, Palestine, November 10, 2016, at http://roiramallah.org/press.php?id=65 (Accessed February 10, 2017).

A Perspective on India–Israel Defence and Security Ties

N. A. K. Browne

Historical links

India's defence and security ties with West Asia has not been a recent phenomena but dates back to more than a century. Indian cavalry soldiers scripted a brave saga of courage and sacrifice in what perhaps may be described as the last cavalry charge in history. This unique cavalry action on September 23, 1918 comprising the Jodhpur, Mysore and Hyderabad Lancers (as part of the 15th Imperial Service Cavalry Brigade) was tasked with capturing the port city of Haifa in present day Israel. The Brigade was part of the Fifth Cavalry Division of the Desert Mounted Corps with the overall objective of folding up the Turkish Seventh and Eighth Armies (Ottoman Empire).

Since 1516, Haifa was considered the last fortified stronghold of the Ottoman Army. In the ensuing battle, the cavalry charge led by the Jodhpur and Mysore Lancers under some very heavy machine gun fire resulted in the Regiment capturing Haifa with over 700 prisoners and heavy weapons. The Commanding Officer (CO) of the Jodhpur Lancers Major Thakur Dalpat Singh, however, lost his life in the operations. He was awarded the Military Cross while Capt. Aman Singh Bahadur was awarded the Indian Order of Merit (IOM) for this action. The Indian causalities included one officer, seven other ranks and the loss of 60 horses with six officers and 28 other ranks wounded.[1]

Interestingly, after Independence the three Lancer Regiments were merged to form the 61st Cavalry—the only mounted horse cavalry in the world. To date, September 23 is celebrated as its Raising Day or 'Haifa Day'. Given that the victory and liberation of Haifa contributed in large measure to the growth of present day Israel, the sacrifices of Indian officers and soldiers continues to be fondly remembered by Haifa residents. The Teen Murti Memorial raised in 1924 near South Avenue in New Delhi is testimony to the valiant action of the Indian Regiments and cavalry troops who fell in the line of duty. More importantly, 2017 not only marks the centenary year of the Haifa battle but also coincides with the 25 years of establishment of diplomatic relations between India and Israel.

Initial policy hesitations

India–Israel interactions over the past seven decades not only reflect instances of congruence of interests shaping a mutually beneficial relationship but also include

Air Chief Marshal N. A. K. Browne (Retd), Chief of Air Staff, Indian Air Force (IAF) from July 2011 to December 2013, was the first Defence Attaché in Israel from April 1997 till July 2000. He also served as the Indian Ambassador to Norway from August 2014 to August 2016.

policy contradictions and limitations. This was most evident in their early formative years as independent nation-states. Both countries unburdened themselves of the yoke of British colonialism within a short span of nine months—while India gained independence on August 15, 1947, Israel did so on May 14, 1948. In a sense, India and Israel's rapprochement and development as functional democracies amidst varied security challenges emanating from their immediate neighbourhood can be considered as 'miracle stories' in the post-World War II scenario. And yet, it was only in September 1950 that India agreed to grant Israel de jure recognition with the opening of a consular office in then Bombay to facilitate immigration of the Indian Jewish community to Israel.

Some of India's policy compulsions maybe attributed to its need for pursuing energy and economic security with the Gulf Arab states; Cold War realities and its dependence on the Soviet Union; a perceived pre-eminent role in the Non-Aligned Movement (NAM); and sensitivity of policymakers to its large Muslim constituency coupled with the traditional unwavering support to the Palestinian cause. Notwithstanding this policy construct, following an arms embargo placed by the US, UK and France, Israel proceeded to supply through other sources, limited quantities of heavy 160 mm mortars to the Indian Army during the 1965 and the 1971 Indo–Pak conflicts.[2] These equipped two Artillery Regiments and proved highly effective with their steep trajectory and heavy calibre charge especially in mountainous terrain. It is pertinent to note that eight of these heavy mortars guns saw action during the 1999 Kargil Conflict as well.

Post-Cold War dynamics

The collapse of the erstwhile Soviet Union concomitant with the fall of the pro-Soviet regimes in Eastern Europe in 1989—which collectively represented the traditional sources for 70 per cent of Indian military equipment—coupled with the decline in rupee trade, led to a transformed and unstable international order with major associated fault lines in the global balance of power. All these developments impacted India adversely. This also marked the period when Pakistan-sponsored insurgency commenced in great earnest in Jammu and Kashmir. Thus a twin-pronged strategy was adopted: the first to diversify India's military equipment base with access to Western technologies; and the second to seek new avenues and partners to establish joint research and development (R&D) projects in critical sectors. Israel was a prime candidate to cater to both the criteria, though a calibrated shift was required for the realisation of the policy goals in all its dimensions.

The real credit for this major West Asia 'policy change' and a reassessment of India's foreign policy can be attributed to former Prime Minister Narasimha Rao and his highly professional and astute then Foreign Secretary J. N. Dixit. These two personalities worked in tandem to impart a new trajectory to India's foreign policy interactions in light of the changed geopolitical circumstances. This was most evident in the context of normalising full diplomatic relations between New Delhi and Tel Aviv. Politically, the policy decision was made simpler as a result of the direct Israeli–Palestinian peace process negotiations in Madrid in October 1991.

Another factor to be considered was that China was actively considering establishing full diplomatic relations with Israel, which it eventually did on January 24, 1992 —five days prior to India doing so. Moreover, this move could also be a driver favourably impacting India–US relations given the influence the Jewish lobby wields in Washington. Taken together, and as a consequence, India established full diplomatic relations with Israel on January 29, 1992 while its embassy was opened in May of the same year. But it would take another five years before a defence wing could be established. The import of these developments was indeed historic and needs to be viewed in the context of not only changed dynamics in the international order but domestic compulsions as well. This was amply reflected in J. N. Dixit's own assessment: 'I consider our establishing relations with South Africa and then with Israel as the most significant among developments in India's foreign policy, which occurred during my period as Foreign Secretary.'[3]

Establishment of defence wing in Tel Aviv

To take the process forward, then Prime Minister Rao and then Foreign Secretary Dixit in early 1994 held discussions with the then Air Chief Marshal (ACM) S. K. Kaul to explore options for engaging the Israel defence establishment formally. It was proposed that the Air Chief would lead a four-member Indian Air Force (IAF) delegation to Israel in April 1994 (other members of the delegation included an Air Vice Marshal, a Group Captain and, the junior-most, a Wing Commander). Maj. Gen. Herzle Bodinger, Israeli Air Force (IsAF) Chief was the official host and there were specific instructions for both sides to keep the visit under total wraps. More importantly, the delegation carried a letter from Rao to Yitzhak Rabin, the then Israeli Prime Minister and also Defence Minister.

The first impressions were highly encouraging as the delegation was warmly welcomed and ushered by Rabin himself into his Hakirya office in the Ministry of Defence (MoD). He further went about reading aloud the prime minister's letter in his trademark heavy baritone voice. The delegation was assured of all possible assistance and in a broad sense, provided a useful opportunity to project the IAF's immediate and long-term specific requirements with the potential for mutual cooperation in defence modernisation, joint research and production. Thus, it was in April 1994 that the first formal engagement on defence and security issues commenced with the Israelis.

Tragically, Rabin was assassinated the following year. Meanwhile, back in New Delhi, Rao in 1995 approved 'in principle' the establishment of a Defence Wing for our mission. However, the timing was to be decided at a later date. It was only in December 1996 following the visit to India of then Israeli President Ezer Weizman that creation of the Wing was finally cleared. As the junior-most member of ACM Kaul's delegation, I was privileged to open the Defence Attaché's office in Tel Aviv on April 7, 1997. A similar arrangement followed the Israeli Defence Attaché's (IsAF Col.) positioning in New Delhi.

Accessing strategic technologies

An interesting facet of this bilateral relationship was the access provided to India by Israel's highly developed R&D industry and the engineering and technological support of their various institutions. This was all under the watchful eye of Israeli state-owned agency MAFAT (Hebrew acronym for the Administration for the Development of Weapons and Technological Infrastructure) and its close partnership with India's Defence Research and Development Organisation (DRDO). Given the technology denial environment of the early 1990s—especially so in the aftermath of the sanctions regime following the nuclear tests in May 1998—this new-found access to strategic technologies provided a unique opportunity to the Indian defence scientific community. Dr A. P. J. Abdul Kalam, during his tenure as the Scientific Advisor to the Defence Minister, spearheaded this endeavour under an inter-governmental arrangement called the Indo–Israeli Management Committee (I2MC).

The effort involved a broad mandate for research into common projects relating to sensors and weapons systems with joint funding and a long-term objective of producing these niche technologies by domestic defence industries. These efforts have yielded positive results. The induction of the Green Pine multi-functional radar and development of air defence missile systems, including the Indian Navy's Long Range Surface-to-Air Missile (LRSAM) and the IAF's Medium Range SAM (MRSAM), amongst others, have validated the conceptual framework of this approach.

India's quest for technology and Israel's need for economising defence research have therefore become complimentary.[4] Dr Kalam remained a highly respected figure with the Israeli defence research community. 'I have come to pray for peace in the Holy Land', he once remarked after visiting the famous Al Aqsa mosque in the heart of Jerusalem. He was greatly admired for his sharp intellect and yet was seen as a man with a very simple approach to life. Dr Kalam last visited Israel in February 2008 when he delivered a lecture at the 48th Israel Annual Conference on Aerospace Sciences.[5]

AWACS and the US factor

The US factor has played a significant role, though not directly, in influencing Indo–Israeli defence ties. As part of the annual defence and economic assistance package of approximately $3 billion (of which approximately $1.6 billion is earmarked for defence), Israel is highly dependent on the US for access to critical dual-use technologies requiring end-user clearances. It is also allied to the US for seeking strong political and economic support at multilateral forums. These conditionalities imply that the US can successfully block a new programme or freeze an ongoing project irrespective of the costs imposed on either the customer or the supplier. As a result, we watched with great interest when the US pressurised Israel to block the sale of the Israel Aircraft Industries (IAI)-developed Phalcon Airborne Early Warning and Control (AEW&C) project to China in 2000. This phased-array radar system mounted on a modified Russian IL-76 platform was already undergoing flight tests at the Ben Gurion airport when the project was cancelled. It was reported that the Chinese plans to upgrade the Harpy anti-radiation attack drone was also scuttled.

It was quite evident in those early years that the strategic aspect of the relationship would have to be carefully managed at 'different levels' to avoid a situation witnessed with China vis-à-vis India. To the credit of our interlocutors and dramatis personae in New Delhi and Tel Aviv, a similar contingency did not arise, except for a short period following the May 1998 nuclear tests. For the record, a trilateral memorandum of understanding (MoU) between India, Israel and Russia—with adequate safeguards incorporated—ensured that the IAF's strategic Airborne Warning and Control Systems (AWACS) project on three similar IL-76 modified platforms was successfully completed and delivered during 2009–2011. It also indicated that few Israeli specialists and defence companies continued to maintain close working ties with their Jewish counterparts in Eastern Europe and the former Soviet Union. Following the dramatic events of the late 1990s, these specialists and contacts were now available to be tapped by Israeli defence establishment. The AWACS project demonstrated the fulfilment of a long-term operational need for acquiring an 'eye in the sky' for India well before similar systems could be developed indigenously by the DRDO.

Pokhran II and Israeli reactions

As events unfolded in May 1998 following the Pokhran tests, Israel was, significantly, one of the few countries that did not condemn the tests. The then Israel Defence Forces (IDF) Chief of Staff Gen. Amnon Lipkin Shahak was scheduled to visit India the week after the tests. As expected, we were informed that the visit would be re-scheduled due to the 'changed circumstances'. Nevertheless, a small incident worth recounting reflects on the pragmatic and real-politik nature of Israeli interests and policy. Back in New Delhi, one of the fallouts of the May tests was that barring a few, the foreign study tour of the National Defence College (NDC) stood cancelled by most foreign countries.

A request was therefore made to the Director General (DG) of the Israeli MoD if they could accept the visit with additional students. The response was not only positive but they went out of their way to accord a warm welcome to two busloads of visitors! On the last day before winding up discussions with the DG, one of the senior students queried as to what had compelled the hosts to accept the visit. DG Ilan Biran diplomatically evaded the embarrassing question. But as the visitors moved out of the hall, he took me aside and explained in his very simple but rustic style:

> Our experience is that when two elephants fight, only small animals get hurt. Within two years when you people make up with each other, then where does that leave tiny Israel? We have worked so hard to reach this point in our relationship and if we also turn our back on India now, then you will never forgive us.

Those simple words in a sense summed up Israel's reaction, for it clearly portrayed a sound understanding of geopolitics and self-interest. Clearly, the quest for strong bilateral ties was indeed a strategic priority. Diplomatically, it all turned out to be prophetic in the challenging days that lay ahead.

Kargil conflict and the IAF

Viewed from a different perspective, it has also been surmised that the protracted dialogue over the nuclear question and gradual improvement of Indo–US relations would only enhance and facilitate Indo–Israeli ties.[6] India's 'temporary isolation' following the nuclear tests, as imposed by certain powers, only worked to Israel's advantage and this was most evident shortly thereafter during the Kargil War in 1999. Reports note that Israel supplied the Indian Army 'around 40,000 rounds of 155 mm and 30,000 rounds of 160 mm mortar ammunition'. Further, it also supplied 'laser guided bombs and UAV's [unmanned aerial vehicles]'.[7] The quick response to India's request for military assistance increased Israel's credibility as a reliable arms supplier even during a crisis and helped to bolster the relationship.[8]

An interesting aspect of the Kargil War which has not received due attention is the pivotal role of a piece of equipment in IAF's inventory that was operationalised for the first time as the conflict progressed. It turned the tables on Pakistani defences on the icy mountainous heights of the Saltoro ridge. But first, as background, in the

1980s, the IAF's precision strike capability in the form of Laser Guided Bombs (LGBs) and its associated Laser Designator Pods was limited to the Mirage fleet and that too, only by day. With intent to acquire an integrated weapon system for day/ night operations, the IAF selected the Israeli Litening Pod in 1997 to equip the Mirage and Jaguar fleets. The targeting pod was still in its development phase and, throughout 1998, the integration process on the Mirage 2000 at Gwalior and at Aircraft and Systems Testing Establishment, Bangalore, was turning out to be a slow and laborious affair.

However, the onset of hostilities in the Kargil sector by end May 1999 changed the ground situation almost overnight. Under the stringent rules of engagement of not crossing the Line of Control (LoC), the IAF had to recast its strategy for conducting precision strikes against Pakistani Man Portable Air Defence (MANPAD)-defended high altitude targets located between 15,000–17,000 feet. This demanded LGB weapon release solutions closer to 30,000 feet—an exercise which had not been practised earlier. Further, the pod designers at Rafael Industries (north of Haifa) had not envisaged the challenging operating environment and had to incorporate major software/hardware modifications as the conflict progressed.

The problem was further compounded since the Mirages with prototype pods were deployed at their forward operating base; the Litening Test benches were in the factory at Haifa and at Bangalore while the original Mirage Test benches were in Gwalior. The entire cyclic process had to be coordinated between Air Headquarters, the Defence Attaché's office at Tel Aviv and various other agencies; while the software changes were being 'tweaked' on a daily basis. The results showed, despite the distances involved, the severe time crunch during actual operations and a time zone difference of 02:30 hrs.

Notable among 240 attack missions flown by Mirages were the airstrikes on Muntho Dalo (16,500 feet), Tiger Hill (17,000 feet) and Point 4388 in the Drass sector. On June 16, a major supply and logistics depot at Muntho Dalo in the Batalik sector was spotted by a Mirage on the Litening pod; the following day, this target was hit and destroyed by four Mirages. Also on June 24, the Battalion Headquarters on top of Tiger Hill was hit by a Mirage LGB and soon followed by four other LGB attacks on Tiger Hill by day and night. These airstrikes were instrumental in the Indian Army recapturing Tiger Hill on July 4. Writing in his blog on Kargil Conflict and the Pakistan Air Force (PAF), Group Captain Kaiser Tufail, a veteran PAF pilot surmised:

> By June 16, [the] IAF was able to open up the laser guided bombing campaign with the help of Jaguars and Mirage 2000 [...] The Mirage 2000 scored at least five successful laser guided bomb hits on forward dumping sites and posts.[9]

While the real heroes of this short but very challenging campaign would remain the brave young officers, jawans and the pilots/ground crew for their quick adaptation, the significant role of the software engineers and other 'backstage boys' responsible for operationalising this weapons system in record time under some very trying conditions, truly deserves an acknowledgement. This was endorsed to me by a senior IsAF test pilot who thanked the IAF since it too had acquired the same Litening pod and was in the process of validating its performance. In this case however, the IAF had simply short-circuited the entire process and operationalised a critical piece of equipment in real time.

Space cooperation

As part of growing bilateral ties and close cooperation with the scientific community, Israel was interested in partnering with the Indian Space Research Organisation (ISRO) for joint programmes. Shimon Peres, then Deputy Prime Minister and Foreign Minister, visited ISRO in January 2002. Following this visit, then head of Israel's Space Research Programme Col. Aby Har-Even and then ISRO Chairman Dr K. Kasturiarangan signed an agreement on space cooperation in November 2002.[10] These protocols, supported by strong political will on both sides, became the real enablers for further expanding the envelope. As a result, in January 2008, ISRO launched an Israeli Synthetic Aperture Radar (SAR) surveillance satellite, TecSAR. This was followed by India's launch of the Israeli-made SAR imaging satellite RISAT-2 on board a domestically built Polar Satellite Launch Vehicle (PSLV) from the Sriharikota Space Centre.[11] Given the complementarities and the niche capabilities available on both sides of the spectrum, space cooperation is an area which continues to showcase the technological prowess of both countries. The coming decade is likely to witness enhanced cooperation in associated programmes of other space applications as well, including the cyber domain.

Counter terror cooperation

On a different note, Judaism was one of the first foreign religions to arrive in India in recorded history (AD 68). While on the other side, the Sufi saint Baba Farid came to the Holy Land in the 13th century and meditated in the Holy city of Jerusalem where the Indian Hospice is now located. More importantly, Indian Jews are a religious minority, but unlike many other parts of the world, they have lived in India without any instances of anti-Semitism or discrimination. While the majority of Indian Jews migrated to Israel after 1948, new Jewish communities were established in Mumbai, New Delhi and Bangalore in the beginning of the 21st century. These communities were established by the Chabad-Lubavitch movement which had sent Rabbis to serve the religious and social needs of Jewish business people, visitors and Israeli backpackers (who number approximately 40,000 per year) touring India. The largest centre is the Nariman House in Mumbai.

It was this very Nariman House in Colaba which came under terrorist attacks during 26/11. The building was taken over by two Lashkar-e-Taiba (LeT) terrorists (total 10), and several residents were taken hostage. In the ensuing security action, both terrorists were killed but not before they had murdered Rabbi Gavriel Holzberg and his six-month pregnant wife Rivka and four other hostages. The attack on Chabad House (amongst other locations in Mumbai which led to the horrific killing of 166 civilians) demonstrated a clear intent of Pakistani jihadi elements to target Indian and Israeli interests. In this context, it is worth recalling then National Security Advisor (NSA) Brijesh Mishra's address in 2003 at the American Jewish Committee (AJC) underlining the potential for cooperation between India, Israel and the US in fighting extremism. Mishra noted that 'such an alliance would have the political will and moral authority to take bold decisions in extreme cases of terrorist provocation'.[12]

In addition to formulating a Joint Working Group (JWG) on counterterrorism (which received strong impetus following 26/11), Israel offered Homeland Security (HLS) assistance in 2009, with the Maharashtra government sending a delegation for hands-on experience.[13] Viewed in perspective, both India and Israel face considerable national security challenges. Given the common threat perceptions of Islamist terror (though from different sources) and challenges of border management to thwart infiltration, it is envisaged that intelligence sharing, HLS cooperation and training and development of counter terrorism strategies are likely to constitute an important element of future Indo–Israeli security ties.

Strategic interactions: incremental growth

The last two decades have indeed witnessed an incremental change in the levels, scope and dynamics of defence ties between the two nation states. Both countries' defence establishments have adopted a pragmatic approach with a strong underpinning of political support devoid of any polarised positions. For India, following the collapse of the Soviet Union, it was crucial to achieve technological progress and self-sufficiency, but it was not in a position to do so on its own. It urgently required external assistance and participation. For its part, Israel enjoyed certain unique advantages over other arms suppliers. These included its experience with weapons and systems of both the former Cold War blocs, the no-questions-asked policy that governs its arms trade, its reputation as a reliable supplier coupled with its expertise in technological innovation and upgradation skills.[14]

Moreover, Israel needed new defence markets to sustain the financial viability of its defence industries. This requirement has therefore found expression in the form of Israeli defence industries establishing joint collaborative ventures with Indian firms and other public sector undertakings (PSUs) keen to widen the aperture by forging 'production and manufacturing partnerships' and to leverage domestic market opportunities. At the same time, the Israeli Government has actively encouraged the commercialisation of technologies with dual-use (in the defence industry) by funding these ventures.

With growing confidence following a broad understanding to find viable solutions, the processes have also been institutionalised via a JWG between the respective Ministries of Defence and a Sub-Working Group (SWG) on Defence Procurement Production and Development between DG, Acquisition, MoD and his Israeli counterpart, Director SIBAT (Hebrew acronym for International Defence Cooperation Directorate). Functional engagement in the form of Staff Talks between the Service Headquarters also provides a useful tool to share domain knowledge expertise in the areas of training, safety and inter-operability issues.

It is interesting to note that the increased induction of US origin platforms in the IAF's inventory (C-130J Special Operations aircraft, C-17 strategic airlift aircraft, Apache attack helicopters, Chinook heavy lift helicopters with associated weapon systems and communication protocols) coincidentally provides a certain degree of commonality with IsAF platforms. It is envisaged that in the not-too-distant future, aerospace power potential could be further enhanced with joint bilateral exercises and associated training between the respective services. Furthermore, considering recent geopolitical developments highlighting the importance of the Indian Ocean Region (IOR) to India's security calculus, any move for bilateral cooperation between the two navies also requires closer examination.

Besides developing its highly effective and potent airpower capability, Israel's strategic community has been advocating expanding the range and potential of its existing navy. Generally, the Israeli strategic community is increasingly interested in the sea, both to provide depth and for the deployment of a submarine-based nuclear second-strike force.[15] The Israeli Navy's Saar-5 Corvettes, which are able to stay at sea for long periods of time, have been seen in the Indian Ocean. Indeed, Israel has plans to triple its submarine force and to build additional Saar-5 Corvettes. In this context, the strategic convergence of both countries to secure access to the energy corridors transiting through the IOR and the capacity to deal with the growing unstable character of certain littorals on its periphery demands a greater degree of inter-operability, cooperation and access to the region. Overall, these developments would be watched with great interest, not only in the extended West Asian region but also in the Asian sub-continent, especially in India's immediate neighbourhood.

Broad-based relationship

And yet, a number of strategists and policy pundits have taken great pains to articulate that 'the evolving relationship is definitely not a military alliance'. As per P. R. Kumaraswamy, 'Neither side wants to be drawn into the regional conflict of the other. Both emphasise that their defence ties are meant only to enhance national defence capabilities and stability and are not directed against any third party.'[16] Within the rubric of this construct, it is easy to decipher the compulsions as also limitations and therefore the need to harmonise specific activities based on their core interests. An official visit to Israel in January 2013—this time as Chairman Chiefs of Staff Committee (COSC) and IAF Chief, confirmed this belief. I was privileged to not only witness the growing ties through a realist lens but also experience the rapid transformation of this evolving relationship in the intervening years, in the context of an altered West Asian landscape. While the geo-political environment posed significant challenges, it also offered mutually beneficial opportunities. Fortunately, the past two decades have provided the necessary ballast and have laid the foundations for a stable, enduring and, most importantly, a consistent defence and security policy to steer this important relationship.

Defence ties have, however, not been unidimensional, as delineated above. The bilateral engagement has encompassed not only defence and security agendas but has included other strong pillars of trade and commerce, agriculture, science and technology, education and cultural ties. Notably, from a humble beginning of only $200 million in 1992, bilateral trade now exceeds $5 billion. Perhaps the largest benefit accruing from these relations is the progress in the field of agriculture. There is an active 'action plan' for 2015–2018 with forays into new sectors such as dairy and water management. Many centres of excellence in agriculture have been commissioned in different states such as Haryana, Rajasthan and Gujarat, among others. In addition to partnerships and joint funding, India has also benefitted from Israeli expertise in horticulture mechanisation, micro-irrigation and post-harvest management. In addition, high-level political contacts have continued to sustain the momentum of growing relations. President Pranab Mukherjee's historic visit in 2015 (where he also addressed the Knesset), followed by a reciprocal visit by Israeli President Reuven Rivlin in November 2016, External Affairs Minister Sushma Swaraj's visit in early 2016 and the forthcoming visit of Prime Minister Narendra Modi in July 2017 bear testimony to the shared interests of both countries.

In closing

Finally, as two relatively young democracies but with ancient civilisations, influenced by a complex interplay of geo-political and geo-strategic interests, India and Israel continue to skilfully manage this very fascinating relationship. Shorn of any Biblical reference, the rapid pace of progress and development in the past 25 years almost reflects on the need to make up for lost time in the 'four decades spent in the wilderness'.[17] Both have re-defined and shaped their priorities with relative ease in the post-Cold War era. That there has been a level of consistency and predictability in the growing relationship highlights the bipartisan efforts of successive governments and the effective role of career diplomats and defence officials.

The year 2017 marks the 25th anniversary of the establishment of full diplomatic relations between India and Israel, which as indicated earlier also coincides with the centenary year of Haifa's liberation by the Indian cavalry. One is reminded of a 'thank you' letter written in April 1994 by ACM Kaul following his very successful first visit to Israel. It was addressed to his host, the IsAF Commander Maj. Gen. Bodinger, whose family, incidentally, lived in Mumbai during the 1940s. The IAF Chief quoted the opening lines of a poem written by well-known Indian poet Nissim Ezekiel, a Jew from Mumbai:

I am alone
And you are alone.
So why can't we be alone together?[18]

Back then, in the early summer of 1994, those few lines made eminent sense.

Disclosure statement

No potential conflict of interest was reported by the author.

Notes

1. 'Battle of Haifa, September 23, 1918', NDTV, September 26, 2010, at http://www.ndtv.com/article/india/battle…1918-54867 (Accessed November 20, 2016).
2. Rajendra Abhyankar, 'The Evolution and Future of India–Israel Relations', Research Paper No. 6, March 2012, Tel Aviv University, at http://www.tau.ac.il/humanities/abraham/india-israel.pdf (Accessed November 20, 2016).
3. J. N. Dixit, *My South Block Years: Memoirs of a Foreign Secretary*, UBS Publishers' Distributors Ltd, New Delhi, 1996.
4. P.R. Kumaraswamy, 'India and Israel: Emerging Partnership', *Journal of Strategic Studies*, 25(4), 2002, p. 202.
5. Rajendra Abhyankar, No. 2.
6. P. R. Kumaraswamy, No. 4, p. 203.
7. Rahul Bedi, 'Moving closer to Israel', *Frontline*, 20(4), February 2003.
8. Y. S. Shapir, 'Israel's Arms Sales to India', *Strategic Assessment*, 12(3), 2009, p. 29.
9. Kaiser Tufail, 'Kargil Conflict and Pakistan Air Force', January 28, 2009, at http://kaiser-aeronaut.blogspot.in/2009/01/kargil-conflict-and-pakistan-air-force.html   (Accessed November 30, 2016).
10. A. Barzilai, 'Israel, India Sign Space Programme Cooperation Agreement', *Haaretz*, November 11, 2002. Cited in Efraim Inbar and Alvite Singh Ningthoujam, *Indo-Israeli Defense Cooperation in the Twenty-First Century*, December 22, 2011, at http://www.rubincenter.org/2011/12/indo-israeli-defense-cooperation-in-the-twenty-first-century/   (Accessed November 30, 2016).
11. Neeta Lal, 'India's Eye in the Sky Takes Aim', *Asia Times*, April 21, 2009, at http://www.worldsecuritynetwork.com/India-Israel-Palestine/Lal-Neeta/Indias-eye-in-the-sky-takes-aim (Accessed November 20, 2016).
12. Efraim Inbar, 'The Indian-Israeli Entente', *Orbis*, Winter 2004, p. 103.
13. Ritu Sarin, 'From Israel, Lessons of fighting Terror', *Indian Express*, July 21, 2009, at http://archive.indianexpress.com/news/from-israel-lessons-on-fighting-terror/492051/   (Accessed November 25, 2016).

14. P. R. Kumaraswamy, No. 4, p. 202.
15. Efraim Inbar, No. 12, p. 100.
16. P. R. Kumaraswamy, 'Beyond the Veil: Israel-Pakistan Relations', JCSS Memorandum 55, Jaffee Centre for Strategic Studies, Tel Aviv, 2000.
17. The non-relations phase in India–Israel ties (from 1950–1992) could be compared to the 40 years the people of Israel are supposed to have spent while in 'Exodus' in the Sinai desert after their release from captivity in Egypt and their journey towards the 'promised land' in the Biblical narrative.
18. Poem / Lyrics "Acceptance" by Nissim Ezekiel published in Asian Jewish Life-India Issue December 2010, pg. 13 (https://issuu.com/asianjewishlife/docs/ajl-aut2010-whole-final)

Israel and India: Looking Back and Ahead

Efraim Inbar

Abstract: The article begins by reviewing the Zionist attempts to turn India into a friend. The Zionist movement viewed India as important almost from its formation. Attitudes shaping behaviour prior to the formation of both the states are assessed, as is the icy relationship that prevailed between the two states prior to January 1992. The factors that brought about the change in the relationship to ambassadorial status are analysed, along with the two countries' burgeoning strategic partnership. Finally, a few thoughts are offered concerning the future of the relationship.

The Zionists and India

The Zionist movement (Jewish nationalism) has been, ever since its beginning at the end of the 19th century, preoccupied with a search for legitimacy and recognition. Apart from creating facts in the ancient homeland, the Land of Israel, the early Zionists also conducted an intensive diplomatic campaign to secure international support for the Zionist cause. This was the establishment of a national home for Jews in what was known at the time as Palestine. It was primarily directed at the main powers of consequence in Europe and the Ottoman Empire that ruled over Palestine. Initially, Asia was not on the radar of Zionist diplomatic efforts. Many Asian countries, including in West Asia, were under colonial rule. With the exception of Japan, the Asian states generally played a minor role in the international arena. Moreover, in contrast to Europe and the US, the Jewish communities on the Asian continent were small and had little political clout.

Since the 1930s, however, India attracted greater attention. The country was under British rule that was increasingly opposed by a nationalist movement. This movement, led by Mohandas Gandhi, became a global *cause célèbre*. Zionist leaders saw parallels in their own struggle for self-determination and were very sympathetic to the Indian quest for independence.[1] David Ben Gurion, the future Prime Minister of Israel, showed great respect for Gandhi, calling him 'a great leader' heading an unprecedented struggle for freedom against the mightiest empire on earth. His emphasis on non-violence also elicited Ben Gurion's admiration.[2] Zionist leaders of all political hues continued to express such views even after Gandhi's negative opinion of Zionism became public.[3] Gandhi's autobiography was published in Hebrew in 1945, while Jawaharlal Nehru's was translated in 1941. Other books about India appeared in the same period, suggesting interest in the country among the public at large.

Efraim Inbar is Professor Emeritus of Political Studies at Bar-Ilan University and Founding Director of the Begin-Sadat Center for Strategic Studies.

The Zionist movement made efforts to approach Gandhi, Nehru and other leaders of the Indian National Congress (INC) to sensitise them to Jewish aspirations. These attempts met with little success. Jews were perceived by the Congress leadership as a religious group possessing no national rights, a similar prism to that employed with regard to the status of Muslims in India. That leadership, with its limited knowledge of Jews and Judaism, ignored the historic links between Jews and their homeland.

Despite their self-perception as progressives, the Zionists were often considered tools and allies of British colonialism. In contrast, the Arabs in Palestine were seen as a native people, a partner in the struggle against British imperialism. Moreover, the Zionist preference for partition in the Land of Israel between Jews and Arabs was not acceptable within the Indian political context. Therefore, most of the Indian political class, which was heavily influenced by Gandhi and Nehru, developed hostility towards Zionist aspirations in Palestine.[4]

In addition, the political realities on the ground dictated caution in dealing with the Zionists. The Hindu leadership, as well as the British Government in India and in London, believed that the Muslim population in India was very sensitive to developments in Palestine. This inclined the Indian national movement against Jewish nationalist aims. India, like much of Asia, lacked a cultural attachment to the Bible, and had little sympathy for the Zionist desire to establish their state.

Zionist efforts to change the position of India towards Zionism intensified after India became a member of the United Nations Special Committee on Palestine (UNSCOP). Yet India led the minority report against partition and the establishment of a Jewish state next to an Arab one. Partition along 'religious' lines was not politically correct in India at that time. Nehru instructed the Indian delegation to the UN to vote against the UN partition resolution in November 1947 that was ultimately passed by the UN General Assembly (UNGA)—33 to 11. In response, the Arabs of Palestine and the Arab states rejected the UN partition resolution and started a war against the nascent state of Israel.[5]

The early and rooted Indian animosity to Zionism persisted for years, to the dismay of Zionist leaders, and scarcely changed after Israel was established in 1948 —just 1 year after Indian independence. The Zionist movement failed to convince the Indian leadership that its image as a culturally Western phenomenon that was politically linked to Western interests was not the entire story.

Israel and India

India was more hostile to Jewish aspirations than other important countries such as Japan or China. In June 1949, India voted against acceptance of Israel to the UN. India awarded de facto recognition to Israel only in the fall of 1950, after China, the Philippines and Burma had done so (Japan was under American occupation until 1952). The fact that two Muslim states, Turkey and Iran, lent de facto recognition made it easier for India to do the same.[6] India allowed Israel to open a consulate in Bombay (today Mumbai) in 1953, a situation that continued until the opening of the embassy in 1992. For many years, the Indian Government severely constrained the diplomatic activity of the consulate. The limited interaction between the two countries was conducted mostly in Washington, at the UN in New York and in London.

India's reluctance to have full diplomatic relations was obviously related to the fact that the Arab states were numerous, while Israel was just one small country. For example, Arab opposition blocked the inclusion of Israel into the Afro-Asian bloc at the UN and later at the Non-Aligned Movement (NAM). India was one of the leaders of those international bodies, but it ignored Israel's geographic location in the Middle East. Furthermore, the dispute with Pakistan over Kashmir became a major factor in deterring India from becoming more receptive to Israeli overtures. India needed the support of the Arab states at the UN and feared that better relations with Israel could jeopardise such support.

The 1956 Suez Campaign, where Israel allied itself with France and Great Britain, two declining colonialist powers, in attacking Egypt, a leader of NAM, reinforced Israel's image as a tool of Western power. At the same time, the campaign portrayed Israel as a powerful country—a useful image in an international arena that is usually animated by *realpolitik*. Moreover, one of its military-diplomatic achievements was the removal of the naval blockade at the Tiran Straits, which opened a naval route to Asia for Israeli trade.

After 1956, Israel scored diplomatic successes in Africa, but Asia remained a difficult arena. Israel, however, persevered. Moshe Sharett, Israel's Foreign Minister (1948–1956), was convinced that Israel should reinvigorate its efforts in Asia. He was even ready to take the post of Ambassador in Delhi, if India would allow the establishment of an embassy.[7] In his view, Israel was linked by destiny to the Asian continent.[8] Similarly, Ben Gurion attached great importance to Asia and believed that the two most populous states in the world, China and India, were destined for global greatness. Moreover, he believed Asian states could adopt Israeli models in the areas of nation-building, agriculture, and water management, challenges which little Israel was grappling with successfully.[9] Regarding India, he was very sceptical about the potential for improvement in bilateral relations as long as Nehru remained in power.[10] Nor had the atmosphere between the countries grown any more encouraging. India for instance initiated anti-Israel initiatives at the UN.

The estrangement from Israel did not change, despite Israel's supplying military equipment upon demand (primarily mortars and ammunition) during India's wars with China (1962) and Pakistan (1965, 1971) and the low-key cooperation between the intelligence services over the years. While India's brass generally appreciated Israel's willingness to help and showed professional respect towards their Israeli colleagues, the politicians and diplomats continued to be critical of any potential rapprochement with the Jewish state. Gradually, Israel became identified as an American ally in the 1960s, which further hindered good relations with India as it was deeply suspicious of American foreign policy.

The 1973 oil crisis increased India's dependency upon Arab oil-producing nations, reinforcing the policy of keeping Israel at arm's length. At the UN, India continued to support sanctions and acts of punishment against Israel while awarding the Palestine Liberation Organisation (PLO) observer status. Following years of interaction, India lent diplomatic recognition to the PLO in January 1975, despite its Covenant's call for the destruction of the Jewish state.[11] In November 1975, it sponsored the infamous UNGA Resolution 3379 that compared Zionism to racism.

The loss of power by the Congress Party in early 1977 to a coalition of parties (mainly Janata Party and Jan Sangh) did not drastically change Indian policy towards Israel. This was despite the coalition's expressed support for normalisation of relations and the peace process with Egypt that had resulted in the 1979 Egyptian–Israeli peace treaty. (Israel did, however, note a change in tone.[12]) When Indira Gandhi returned to the post of prime minister in January 1980, the Nehruvian policy towards Israel was continued. The 1982 Israeli invasion of Lebanon and the outbreak of the Palestinian *intifada* in December 1987 turned into major impediments for normalisation.[13]

From Israel's perspective, despite its desire to overcome its regional isolation and achieve overall legitimacy, Asia remained a secondary arena for diplomatic activism. Israel was consumed by its conflict with the Arab states and the need to assure political and military support from a great power. This meant that Israel's diplomatic attention for most of the 20th century was focused on Paris and then on Washington.

Establishing diplomatic relations

The end of the Cold War provided an opportunity to change the anachronistic Indian policy towards Israel.[14] The year 1991 was the turning point. After the collapse of the Soviet Union, which had been India's main diplomatic and strategic ally during the Cold War, India was 'forced to reorient its foreign policy to accommodate the changing international milieu'.[15] The issue of relations with the Jewish state was also addressed. The diplomatic benefits of downgrading relations with Israel and maintaining a consistent pro-Arab voting record at the UN were evaluated and juxtaposed against an appraisal of the role of Israel in West Asia and the possible benefits to be accrued by becoming closer to Jerusalem.[16]

The decision to upgrade relations with Israel was also the product of the disappearance of several inhibiting factors. First, a change in trends in the political economy of energy sources lessened the leverage of the Arab bloc, and the oil-producing states in particular. By the end of the 1980s, fears of energy crises had subsided substantially. The oil market became a buyers' market, diminishing the weight of Arab objections to the enhancement of relations with Israel. India also realised that efforts to divert Arab support for Pakistan on the Kashmir issue were ineffective.

Moreover, the Arab–Israeli peace process, reactivated by the Americans in the aftermath of the 1991 Gulf War, further marginalised the objections of Israel's regional enemies to third-party ties with Jerusalem. The October 1991 peace conference in Madrid, a formal gathering with Israel to which almost all Arab countries sent senior diplomatic delegations, served as a convenient pretext for hitherto reluctant states to develop a closer relationship with Israel. In the wake of the PLO support for Saddam Hussein, the PLO and the Palestinian issue it represented received less support from Arab states and others, affecting also the traditional India support for the Palestinian cause that hindered a reassessment of relations with the Jewish state.[17]

Indeed, India signalled to Israel its willingness to gradually upgrade its relations. Yet, Israel rejected incremental steps and insisted on full diplomatic relations particularly before India could participate in the multilateral framework initiated at the Madrid Peace Conference. New Delhi had many interests in the Middle East (oil, foreign workers, radical Islam) and showed great interest in the multilateral track of the Madrid Conference, particularly in the Arms Control and Regional Security Committee. China decided to upgrade relations with Israel to secure its presence at the process generated by the American diplomacy and India did not want to fall behind.

The domestic political dynamics also played a role in the upgrading of Indo-Israeli relations. The decline in the fortunes of the Congress Party and the ascendance of the Bharatiya Janata Party (BJP) in the Indian political system helped remove hesitations about Israel. The BJP's nationalist and Hindu outlook made the Jewish state not so much of a diplomatic burden, but a potential ally against Pakistan and radical Islam. Indeed, the BJP convention of October 1991 introduced for the first time a clause calling for full relations with Israel. Normalisation was also the result of the economic liberalisation initiated by then Prime Minister Narasimha Rao of the Congress Party, which depended heavily on economic and technological interactions with the West. Israel was perceived as a well-integrated part of the new globalised economy that India wished to join.[18]

India was also sensitised to the political power of the Jewish organisations. Isi Liebler, the then Vice President of the World Jewish Congress, conducted a series of talks with senior government officials. In parallel many American Jewish organisations had intensive dialogues with Indian representatives.[19] As India attempted to secure a $2–5 billion loan from the World Bank and the International Monetary Fund, Washington became even more important. In fact, some of the Indian interlocutors who favoured better relations with Israel invited pressure from the US on the issue of diplomatic upgrade with Israel to help them overcome the diplomatic inertia of their country.[20]

The official announcement of full diplomatic relations came on January 29, 1992. It was specifically linked to the upcoming visit of Prime Minister Rao to the US. New Delhi believed that announcing full diplomatic relations with Israel was conducive to a better atmosphere in the US due to the closeness between Washington and Jerusalem. For Israel, upgrade of relations with India together with similar steps by Russia, China, Turkey, Nigeria and additional Afro-Asian states in the early 1990s was an end to relative international isolation. This post-Cold War trend allowed for a gradual increase in emphasis on nourishing good relations with Asia, a continent of rising importance.

The new era

New Delhi soon realised that there was little cost to establishing full diplomatic relations with Jerusalem, neither at home nor abroad. Moreover, the two countries learned that they shared a similar outlook on their regional disputes and a common strategic agenda.[21] Both India and Israel display extremely high levels of threat perception. Both states are continuously challenged by low-intensity conflict and terror. The two states are involved in protracted conflict within their respective regions, characterised by complex ethnic and religious components not always well understood by outsiders, and have waged several major conventional wars against their neighbours.

For India and Israel, the conflict over Kashmir and the one between Israelis and Palestinians are perceived to have major destabilising spill over effects primarily in the immediate region of each state, which create incentives for external intervention. Such extra-regional involvement is not always welcome. Indeed, the two states display similar attitudes towards the international community, which seems incapable of understanding their conflicts with their neighbours. Both face weapons of mass destruction (WMD) in the hands of their rivals. The two countries feel beleaguered in their own region. Generally, the two states espouse affinities in their strategic cultures, entertaining similar notions about behaviour during conflict.

While Israel's strategic situation has improved considerably since the end of the Cold War due to the evolving Arab–Israeli peace process and favourable changes in the international system,[22] existential fears have not evaporated. Israel still meets profound hostility in the Arab world, parts of which still want its demise. This means that Israel's quest for legitimacy and influential friends such as India has not ended.

One current source of threat to the two nations is similar—the radical offshoots of Islam in the greater Middle East. It was over the issue of radical Islam that the threat perceptions of India and Israel clearly converged. India regarded parts of the Arab world as hubs of Islamic extremism. The threat was felt closer to home regarding Saudi-Pakistani relations, which India viewed with suspicion. For Israel, the Islamic radicals in the Arab world and in the Islamic Republic of Iran constituted a constant security challenge. Moreover, religious extremism energised the residual Arab enmity towards the Jewish state. The combination of Iran's fanatic hatred and nuclear potential con-stituted a clear existential threat.[23] The Pakistani nuclear arsenal is similarly viewed in New Delhi as being in danger of falling into the hands of Islamic radicals.

The two states differ, however, in their global orientations. India's vulnerability increased after the end of the Cold War as its patron, the Soviet Union, collapsed, thus reducing a main source for diplomatic support and military technology. Nevertheless, despite the recent improvement of relations with Washington, India still harbours suspicions of American foreign policy and prefers a multi-polar world in which it can have greater latitude and perhaps play a larger role in international affairs. In contrast, for Israel, the demise of the Soviet Union, an ally of the Arab enemies of the Jewish state, was a clear bonus.

Israel is strategically interested in American hegemony. The US, due to its domestic political system, is also more susceptible to Israeli sensitivities in the formulation of its Middle East policies. The retreat of American power, particularly during the Obama presidency, created much concern in Jerusalem.[24] Moreover, the existential dangers to Israel did not disappear in the post-Cold War period and any rising competitor of Washington is likely to take the Arab side.

The common strategic agenda is an important element in the bilateral relationship that flourished in the defence area.[25] The Indian defence establishment has always been less hostile of Israel than its political masters. It followed with interest Israeli achieve-ments in the battlefield and in weapons production, developing a professional apprecia-tion of Israel's strategic predicament and military performance. India gradually overcame its inhibitions and engaged also in security cooperation with Israel. In March 1995, Israel's air force commander paid an official visit to India, which was reciprocated by his Indian counterpart in July 1996. Influential scientist and then Chief of the Indian Defence Research and Development Organisation (DRDO), A. P. J. Abdul Kalam, paid a visit in June 1996. By April 1997, New Delhi also sent the first military attaché, an air force officer, marking a new era in the bilateral relationship.

India–Israel strategic engagement took off after the Kargil War (1999), when Israel promptly provided laser guided bombs for India's Mirages, Unmanned Air Vehicles (UAVs) to collect timely intelligence and a variety of ammunitions. Indeed, the then influential Home Minister, Lal Krishna Advani, during a well-publicised visit to Israel (June 2000) called for strengthened cooperation in all fields. The historic September 2003 visit of Ariel Sharon to India, the first ever by an Israeli Prime Minister, marked the new Indo-Israeli collaboration. The visit was an opportunity to enhance understanding of the other at the highest levels and to further promote bilateral defence and trade ties.

Some of the pertinent overlapping strategic interests are enumerated as follows:

Arms and technology transfers

India's quest for the latest military technologies and Israel's need to broaden the market for its military products are complementary. The Russian failure to deliver the promised weapons at the expected price and/or schedule also pushed New Delhi to seek other sources. Difficulties in the Indian development of weapons systems at home indicated a need for outside technological help that have led to the purchase of Israeli products. The success of the American forces fighting Russian-made Iraq weaponry reinforced Indian military planners caution about depending heavily on Russian arms,[26] and search for Western equipment including those made by Israel.

Israel emerged by the beginning of the 21st century as New Delhi's preferred military technology source and has become the second largest defence supplier after Russia, with France ranking third. India turned into a very important arms market for Israel and a partner in developing advanced military technology. Israeli defence industries need to export most of its products to survive economically and welcomed partnerships in weapons development.

During the first years of interaction, India turned to Israeli companies primarily to upgrade some of its ageing Soviet platforms as the Israelis developed an excellent record at retrofitting old military equipment of all kinds and sources. For example, Israeli firms supplied advanced avionics for India's Mig-21 fighters, and state-of-the-art fire control systems and thermal imagers for the Indian T-72 tank fleet, as well upgrades for Soviet 133mm artillery pieces.

The Israeli defence industries were successful in expanding sales. The best-known Israeli products purchased by the Indian military were UAVs,[27] and the naval Barak point-defence system. Israeli advanced radar and communication equipment were also purchased by New Delhi. Indian military planners were reported to ask their government to buy electronic warfare equipment only from vendors that do not sell such equipment to Muslim countries.[28] This often gave Israel an advantage over American and French competitors.

India, which has been trying to procure effective air defences particularly since Pakistan's 1998 nuclear tests, approached Israel regarding the airborne Phalcon radar to be mounted on the Russian built IL-76 transport aircraft, and the long range Green Pine radar. The sale of the Phalcon required American approval, which was finally secured by Israel in May 2003. India signed a contract for the purchase of two additional Phalcon/IL-76 Airborne Warning and Control Systems (AWACS) valued at $1 billion during the November 2016 visit of Israeli President Reuven Rivlin to India.[29]

An important stage in defence cooperation is co-production, playing to the strength of Israeli firms in research and design and to the strength of Indian firms in manufacturing. Moreover, it confirms with the Indian requests for technology transfer and emphasis on domestic production. A long list of Israeli military items, such as ammunition, UAV parts, and even missiles (Spike anti-armour, the Python-4 air-to-air, Barak-8 surface-to-air) are being produced in India.

Terror and infiltration

In February 1992, the then Indian Defence Minister Sharad Pawar admitted cooperation with Israel on counter-terrorism (CT).[30] Both states have a long history in CT activities. Their cooperation in this area is conducted away from the public's eye. It involves exchange of information on terrorist groups, their finances, recruitment patterns, training and operations. It also involves comparing national doctrines and operational experience.[31] After September 11, 2001, CT gained a higher priority on the strategic agenda of many countries and the need for international cooperation became more urgent. The November 2008 Mumbai terrorist attacks underscored the need for better CT preparations in India and elicited greater cooperation with Israeli agencies.

Israel and India face also a serious challenge of low intensity conflict at their borders. They exchange views on their respective record and compare notes on equipment and doctrine. Facing the challenge of Muslim fundamentalist terrorism springing from camps inside Pakistan, the Indian military aims at developing the ability for quick deployment of troops inside enemy lines for specific missions. As India strives to close its borders to infiltration of terrorists, it needs good border monitoring equipment of the type that Israel has developed over the years to meet its own infiltration challenges. Israel has also supplied India with portable battlefield radars and a wide assortment of human movement detecting sensors, hand-held thermals, night warfare vision equipment and electronic fences.[32]

Radical Islam

India and Israel face the challenge of radical Islam at home as well as in their immediate neighbourhood. For India, the 1979 Shiite Revolution in Iran has given legitimacy to the Islamisation efforts of General Zia Ul Haq, who took over Pakistan in 1977. It was his regime and the developments in Afghanistan that energised the radical Muslims in India's region. Pakistan has encouraged the activities of extremists when it suited its foreign policy goals in Afghanistan and in India. While the Pakistani 'secular' military still calls the shots, the country is gradually being radicalised and has the potential for being taken over by radical Islamists.

Although Pakistan is relatively far away, Israel observes the developments in this country with concern. It is wary of radical Muslim movements that are theologically opposed to the existence of the Jewish state. Moreover, Pakistan is a nuclear state. Therefore, Jerusalem's fears are two-fold—the seepage of nuclear technology from Pakistan (with governmental authorisation or as a rogue operation) to the Arab world and Iran and a nuclear-armed Islamic regime in Islamabad.

Both countries understand the political repercussions entailed by the rise of radical Islamist forces in the Middle East on their immediate strategic environment. The more recent Islamic State in Iraq and Syria (ISIS) phenomenon has ramifications beyond the battlefields of Iraq and Syria. Its offshoots threaten the stability of Egypt and Jordan, Israel's neighbours, and are increasingly a source of concern in South and South-East Asia.

India and Israel also share fears of Saudi Arabia's role in the spread of Islamic fundamentalism in many places of the world.[33] Despite the better tacit relations between Riyadh and Jerusalem because of growing Iranian clout in the Middle East, Israel understands that Saudi Arabia has not desisted from supporting radical Islamists. The Islamic Republic of Iran became Israel's arch enemy since the 1990s. Its inflammatory Islamic rhetoric, support for terrorist activities, coupled with its missile and nuclear programmes have become more feared than before. The 2015 nuclear deal with Iran was not linked to Iran's foreign behaviour and missile programme, hardly soothing Israel's fears. On this issue, India does not concur, while understanding Israel's concerns.

India and Israel both have Muslim minorities and if even small parts of them become radicalised, this could have serious domestic security consequences. India has a minority of 170 million Muslims, being the second largest Muslim community in the world (after Indonesia). A large part of this community, however, is well integrated in Indian society. Israel's Arabs constitute about 20 per cent of its population. While most of them are law-abiding citizens, Israel is worried about the growing appeal of Muslim organisations among them, and their links to their Palestinian counterparts. In recent years, we have witnessed a significant increase in the numbers of Israeli Arabs involved in terrorist activities, which overall, is a small-scale phenomenon.

Indian Ocean

The Indian–Israeli nexus has various Indian Ocean implications. It goes without saying that India is an important international actor in the Indian Ocean. The Indian Ocean has become, however, an area of growing interest for Israel, because of its growing apprehensions about Iran and Pakistan and its burgeoning strategic relationship with India. And India strengthened its military presence in the Indian Ocean in response to China's ongoing 'string of pearls' power projection strategy.

Historically, Israel has seen the Indian Ocean as the transit area for its links to countries in the East, particularly because it could not use land routes, which were blocked by its hostile Arab neighbours. Jerusalem was particularly interested in one of the Indian Ocean choke points, the Bab El Mandeb Straits, through which all its exports to South and East Asia pass. Israel's overtures to Ethiopia and afterwards to Eritrea had these Straits in mind. Kenya and South Africa, also states on the Indian Ocean littoral, have similarly attracted the attention of Israeli strategy.

Israel's main strategic concern after the removal of the Iraqi threat (2003) is the Islamic Republic of Iran abutting the waters of the Indian Ocean. In response to the existential threat posed by Iran, Israel's strategic reach by air and sea has been increased. Israel has developed since the beginning of the 1990s a capability to project air and naval power to distances of above 1500 km. Israel also expanded its air refuelling options to extend its military reach.[34] In parallel to air power, Israel built an ocean-going navy with Iran in mind. Israeli Saar-5 corvettes are able to stay for a long period of time at sea and were seen in the Indian Ocean and larger ships are on order from Germany.

The Israeli submarines were equipped with long-range cruise missile launching capability. One such missile was tested in the Indian Ocean, generating reports about Indian–Israeli naval cooperation.[35] India's interests are not averse towards a greater Israeli presence in the Indian Ocean. Generally, there is a growing interest within the Israeli strategic community in the sea as much needed strategic depth and for the deployment of a submarine-based nuclear second-strike force. Israel builds such capabilities in case Pakistan becomes more active against the Jewish state. A larger navy is needed by Israel also to secure its gas fields in the Mediterranean.

Central Asia

India has long standing strategic and cultural links to energy-rich and newly accessible Central Asia, which is viewed as its 'extended strategic neighbourhood' where it competes with its regional rivals China and Pakistan for influence.[36] Israel similarly takes an interest in this area that has become part of the Greater Middle East. Like India, Israel sells military equipment to Central Asian states and has a modest diplomatic and business presence. Israel, as well as India, aims at limiting the influence of the Iranians and the Saudis, which contribute to the spread of radical Islam. Similarly, they are concerned about the Islamic colouration of Turkish foreign policy (since 2002) and its presence in the region.

Both states also want stability in that region to allow uninterrupted flow of oil and gas. While there may be differences over the direction of the planned pipelines, India and Israel are in accord over the preference for low energy prices. India's economy needs it, while Israel's perspective is more political. India has some concerns about China's 'One Belt, One Road' initiative along the historic Silk Road, which will enhance Beijing's influence. Israel has been sensitised more recently to Chinese projects in the Greater Middle East and in its own country. Its pro-American orientation colours its attitudes to Chinese deeds with suspicion.

The Washington dimension

The growing American–Indian relationship, particularly after September 11, will not bring India under the American fold and some differences will inevitably remain.[37] While New Delhi is a major player in the international system and is able to manage an independent mutually beneficial relationship with Washington, the links with Jerusalem have the potential to smooth over some of the difficulties in dealing with the US. As noted, the upgrading of relations with Israel was believed in New Delhi to have a positive effect on the American dispositions towards India.

The power of the Jewish lobby in America is often exaggerated, but it is generally effective. In the 1990s, the American Jewish organisations were politically astute enough to understand the importance of India for the US and for Israel, as well as the potential advantages of nurturing good relations with the burgeoning Indian community in America, whose congressional power is on the rise. Cooperation between the two diaspora has the potential to magnify the voices of two communities that are small—about 5 million Jews and 2 million Indians—but highly educated, affluent and attached to democratic homelands facing what they increasingly view as a common enemy.

The official Israeli lobby—the America-Israel Political Affairs Committee (AIPAC)—and Jewish organisations such as the American Jewish Committee and the Jewish Institute on National Security Affairs (JINSA) nourish ties with India and with the Indian lobby in Washington. Many members of the Indian lobby US-India Political Action Committee (USINPAC), which was formed only in September 2002, expressed their desire to emulate American Jewish groups and showed interest in building a long-term relationship.

The two communities are working closely together on domestic and foreign affairs issues, such as hate crimes, immigration and anti-terrorism legislation, as well as backing pro-Israel and pro-India candidates. The Jews and the Indians worked together to gain the Bush administration's approval for Israel to sell Phalcon AWACS to India. Moreover, in July 2003, they were successful in adding an amendment (to the bill giving aid to Pakistan) that called on Islamabad to stop Islamic militants from crossing into India and prevent the spread of WMD.[38] In the fall of 2008, Jewish support was important in passing in US Congress the Indo-US nuclear deal that allowed India access to nuclear technology for civilian uses, despite not being a party to the Non-Proliferation Treaty (NPT). This allowed for greater cooperation between New Delhi and Washington.

Another area of Indian–Israeli congruence is US-sponsored international arms control regimes. Both states resisted American pressures to comply with the NPT, which is viewed in both capitals as flawed and ineffective. The two states are cooperating against American initiatives in that area that were revived during the Obama presidency.

The future

The significant overlapping strategic concerns reviewed above are likely to continue. While the evolving relationship between India and Israel intensified over the years and became quite intimate, it is not a military alliance. Neither side wants to be drawn into the regional conflict of the other. Both emphasise that their defence ties are meant only to enhance national self-defence capabilities and stability, and were not directed against any third party. Israel does not want to be identified by Pakistan as an enemy,[39] and displays considerable caution in its relations with China. Similarly, India has many political and economic interests in the Arab world, as well as emotional support for the Palestinians, and a growing Indian diaspora in the Gulf. Its views on Iran, Pakistan's neighbour, differ from Israeli perceptions of Tehran.

Two strategic developments of the 21st century seem to strengthen the strategic glue between India and Israel—the decline of the US and the rise of China. In the Middle East, the Obama administration has projected weakness and encouraged Iran's quest for hegemony. This weakness of the US inevitably has ripple effects in other parts of the globe. Indeed, Asian states view the declining American role with concern. Despite the Obama administration's rhetoric about pivoting to Asia, it did little to reassure its allies. Indeed, many of them now fear the rise of China, which is aggressively pursuing ambitious goals. In East Asia, Chinese assertiveness and the growing North Korean nuclear threat are believed to be receiving an inadequate American response. American credibility is now under question, and allies elsewhere may determine that it would be wise to hedge their bets. The Philippines, under the colourful President Rodrigo Duterte, appears to wish to substitute its American orientation with a Chinese one.

India and Israel watch such developments with concern. Israel's good fortunes have been linked to American primacy in world affairs. For India, China presents a serious national security challenge. China's growing assertiveness in its region and growing influence in the Indian Ocean constitutes a problem for India, exacerbated by Beijing's growing trade and defence relations with India's South Asian neighbours. It is not clear whether the new American President, Donald Trump, will adopt a more assertive foreign policy than his predecessor and how he will confront China, as he displayed isolationist impulses during his election campaign.

Israel's military and defence industries are very pleased with the developing bilateral ties. They are aware of the common strategic agenda, the magnitude of Indian military requirements and the willingness of India to spend money on defence needs. In 2016, a senior officer in the Israeli Air Force remarked that military cooperation with India was extremely important, adding: 'India is a very significant country, its air force is large and it operates a variety of western and eastern platforms.'[40] In 2015, the then Chairman of Rafael (Israel's Weapon Development Authority), Itzhak Gat, had stated the following at the opening of the Israeli pavilion, on behalf of the Israeli industries:

> India is a superpower that offers a technological opportunity for the (Israeli) defense industry. We must be attentive to their needs. Unless we adapt, we will not be able to develop over here.[41]

Defence industry officials hope for less red tape in the Indian bureaucracy to significantly shorten the processes and timetables for tenders, which sometimes last for years, thereby expediting major deals. Cooperation in space can be strengthened. Israel is interested in Indian space launching capabilities, while its small satellites have attracted Indian attention. Over the years, Israel has enhanced its diplomatic presence in India by increasing the number of its diplomats stationed there and by adding a consulate in Bengaluru. The post of Ambassador to India became prestigious in the Foreign Service reflecting the growing importance of India for Israel.

Israel is cognisant of the relative decline of Europe in global affairs and the parallel rise in importance of Asian states. India no doubt is a rising Asian and global power. Already in January 2002, Shimon Peres, the then Israeli Foreign Minister, said in New Delhi: 'We regard India to be one of the most important countries in the world'.[42] Prime Minister Benyamin Netanyahu, during President Pranab Mukherjee's visit in October 2015, remarked: 'We are very deeply part of the West in many, many ways, but we look to the East ... We appreciate Europe, but we admire Asia.'[43] Moreover, Europe is beleaguered by anti-Semitism, while the Asians are culturally much less infected by that social disease. India has been particularly tolerant of Jews. Israel hopes that India will change its voting pattern in international organisations that has been not friendly towards Israel. A few signs of change are already visible as India has been recently opting to abstain instead of voting automatically with the Arab bloc.

Since 1992, economic relations have progressed rapidly. From $200 million in 1992, comprising primarily of diamonds, civilian trade has diversified and stood at nearly $5 billion in 2015. India has been buying Israeli technology in several areas, including agriculture, water treatment, waste management and recycling, prompting several Israeli companies working in these areas to expand into India. For Israel, India is a huge civilian market which is hardly tapped. The two countries are negotiating a trade agreement, something that is expected to significantly increase trade.

The early interest of the Zionists in India has persisted in Israel's society. It is primarily reflected in the tens of thousands of young Israelis that spend some time in India after their military service. Upon their return, many of them become India's ambassadors to the Israeli society amplifying the interest in India, its people and culture. Since normalisation, the frequency of Indian cultural shows and academic forays in Israel has increased, although much more can be done.

In contrast, Israel still has to overcome feelings of suspicions among many Indians. Anti-Americanism (Israel is rightly viewed as an American ally) is still entrenched in the intellectual elites, the Indian media and certain political circles. Pro-Palestinian feelings are also widespread at the expense of Israel. The May 2014 electoral victory of Narendra Modi and of his BJP party was welcomed in Israel.

He and his party have favoured better relations with the Jewish state. The meeting between Netanyahu and Modi in New York in September 2014 was warm and signalled the willingness of the two parties to forge ahead. Israel is waiting for his visit.

Conclusion

India and Israel represent two old civilisations. They share a British colonial past, and were the first to become independent (in 1947 and 1948 respectively) in the post-World War II decolonisation wave. Both were born out of messy partitions and have maintained democratic regimes under adverse conditions ever since. Despite the many similarities between the two states, it took over four decades to establish a warm relationship characterised by full diplomatic relations, a flourishing bilateral trade and a burgeoning strategic content. The rapprochement between India and Israel is an important component of a new strategic landscape evolving in the Greater Middle East that includes Central Asia and parts of the Indian Ocean littoral.

For Israel, good relations with India reflect the awareness of the structural changes in the international system—the centre of gravity is moving to Asia and the Pacific Rim. India is an extremely important protagonist that requires Israel's utmost attention. Moreover, Israel seems to be able to capitalise on its strengths particularly in technology, to advance its national interests. Meeting the Indian Air Force Chief on March 28, 2016, Prime Minister Netanyahu said: 'We're very excited by the prospects of greater and greater ties with India. We think the sky is the limit.'[44] Indeed, taking into consideration the interests of the two states, this optimistic evaluation is not a hyperbole.

Acknowledgements

The author thanks Zvi Gabay, former Deputy Director for Asian Affairs at Israel's Ministry of Foreign Affairs and Ambassador to India, for his comments, and gratefully acknowledges the research assistance rendered by Styliani Gerani.

Disclosure statement

No potential conflict of interest was reported by the author.

Notes

1. Moshe Yegar, *The Long Journey to Asia. A Chapter in the Diplomatic History of Israel*, Haifa University Press, Haifa, 2004 [Hebrew], pp. 24–31.
2. David Ben Gurion, *Memoirs*, Vol. 1, Am Oved, Tel Aviv, 1971 [Hebrew], p. 431.
3. For Gandhi's views, see Gideon Shimoni, *Gandhi, Satyagraha, and the Jews: A Formative Factor in India's Policy towards Israel*, Leonard Davis Institute for International Relations, Hebrew University, Jerusalem, 1977.
4. For the Indian attitudes and policies towards Zionism and the State of Israel, see P. R. Kumaraswamy, *India's Israel Policy*, Columbia University Press, New York, 2010.
5. For the Zionist diplomatic efforts towards India before the UN partition vote, see Moshe Yegar, No. 1, pp. 45–56.
6. Ibid., p. 142.
7. Ibid., p. 102.
8. Moshe Sharett, *Travelling in Asia*, Davar, Tel Aviv, 1964 [Hebrew], p. 125.
9. For Israel's aid programmes, see Shimon Amir, *Israel's Development Cooperation with Africa, Asia and Latin America*, Praeger, New York, 1974. The extensive Israeli involvement in aid

programmes did not prevent the beneficiary states from severing diplomatic relations follow-ing the 1973 war, indicating the limitations of such a diplomatic tool.

10. Moshe Yegar, No. 1, pp. 66–67.
11. The PLO committed to annul the articles in the Covenant calling for the destruction of the state of Israel at the 1993 Oslo Accords. Whether it did so, is still debated among various scholars.
12. P. R. Kumaraswamy, No. 4, pp. 217–21; Moshe Yegar, No. 1, p. 160.
13. P. R. Kumaraswamy, No. 4, pp. 222, 233.
14. Efraim Inbar, 'The Indian-Israeli Entente', *Orbis*, 48, Winter 2004.
15. H. V. Pant, 'India-Israel Partnership: Convergence and Constraints', *MERIA Middle East Review of International Affairs*, 8(4), 2004, p. 2.
16. For the upgrading of Indo-Israeli relations, see Moshe Yager, 'How Was Normalization Achieved in Indo-Israeli Relations?', *Nativ*, No. 90, January 2003 [Hebrew], pp. 1–11; Giora Bachar, 'The Normalization in Indian-Israel Relations', in Moshe Yegar, Yoseph Govrin and Aryeh Oded (eds), *The First Fifty Years*, Keter, Jerusalem, 2002 [Hebrew], pp. 543–49.
17. P. R. Kumaraswamy, No. 4, p. 240.
18. P. R. Kumaraswamy, 'India-Israel: Emerging Partnership', *Journal of Strategic Studies*, 25(4), December 2002, p. 198.
19. Interview with Isi Liebler, Jerusalem.
20. Moshe Yegar, No. 1, p. 165.
21. This part relies on Efraim Inbar, No. 14.
22. See Efraim Inbar, 'Israel's Strategic Environment in the 1990s', *Journal of Strategic Studies*, 25, March 2002; Efraim Inbar, 'Israel's National Security Amidst Unrest in the Arab World', *Washington Quarterly*, 35, Summer 2012.
23. For this dominant threat perception that has been shared by all Israeli governments since Yitzhak Rabin's (1992–95), see Efraim Inbar, *Rabin and Israel's National Security*, Wilson Center Press and Johns Hopkins University Press, Washington and Baltimore, 1999, p. 138.
24. Efraim Inbar, 'US Mideast Retreat a Boon for Moscow and Tehran', *Middle East Quarterly*, Summer 2016, at http://www.meforum.org/6042/us-mideast-retreat (Accessed February 10, 2017).
25. For the strategic engagement between the two states, see Efraim Inbar, No. 14; Efraim Inbar and Alvite Singh Ningthoujam, 'Indo-Israeli Defense Cooperation in the Twenty-First Century', *MERIA Journal*, 15, December 2011; S. Samuel C. Rajiv, *Indian Responses to Israel's Gaza Operations*, Mideast Security and Policy Studies No. 119, Begin-Sadat Center for Strategic Studies, Ramat Gan, May 2016, pp. 11–24.
26. *Defense News*, May 12, 2003, p. 10.
27. The latest deal for 10 Heron TP UAVs was in November 2016. See 'Israel Signs $1.4 Billion Contracts with India', *Israel Defense*, November 25, 2016, at http://www.israeldefense.co.il/en/node/27690 (Accessed February 10, 2017).
28. *Defense News*, May 12, 2003, p. 10.
29. 'Israel Signs $1.4 Billion Contracts with India', Note 27.
30. *Statesman* (New Delhi), February 28, 1992, quoted in P. R. Kumaraswamy, *Israel and India. Evolving Strategic Partnership*, Mideast Security and Policy Studies No. 40, Begin-Sadat Center for Strategic Studies, Ramat Gan, September 1998.
31. See the remarks of Maj. Gen. Uzi Dayan, National Security Advisor, in Amit Navon, 'The Indian Knot', *Maariv*, Weekend Magazine, September 20, 2002, p. 22.
32. 'India, Israel Defence Ties to Get a Boost', *Hindustan Times*, May 22, 2003.
33. For an exposition of Saudi mischief, see Dore Gold, *Hatred's Kingdom: How Saudi Arabia Supports the New Global Terrorism*, Regnery Publishing, New York, 2003; for concerns regarding the rise of Wahhabism in India, see Sunil Raman, 'The New Threat to Islam in India', February 4, 2016, at http://thediplomat.com/2016/02/the-new-threat-to-islam-in-india/ (Accessed April 26, 2017); see also Abhinandan Mishra, 'Saudi Cash Floods India to Promote Wahhabism', June 27, 2015, at http://www.sunday-guardian.com/news/saudi-cash-floods-india-to-promote-wahhabism (Accessed April 26, 2017).
34. *Defense News*, May 12, 2003, p. 25.
35. See *The Times of India* [online version], June 17, 2002.

36. Olga Oliker, 'Conflict in Central Asia and South Caucasus', in Olga Oliker and Thomas S. Szayna (eds), *Faultlines of Conflict in Central Asia and the South Caucacus: Implications for the US Army*, RAND, Santa Monica, 2003, pp. 225–6.

37. For a recent analysis of the relations between the two states, see C. Uday Bhaskar, 'India's perspective of US political leadership', in Efraim Inbar and Jonathan Rynhold (eds), *US Foreign Policy and Global Standing in the 21st Century: Realities and Perceptions*, Routledge, London, 2016, pp. 139–58.

38. See Larry Ramer, 'Pro-Israel Activists Seeking Allies Among Immigrants from India', *Forward*, October 11, 2002; Alan Cooperman, 'India, Israel Interests Team Up', *The Washington Post*, July 19, 2003, p. A5.

39. See P. R. Kumaraswamy, *Beyond the Veil: Israel-Pakistan Relations*, JCSS Memorandum, 55, Jaffee Center for Strategic Studies, Tel Aviv, 2000.

40. Talya Yariv and Shachar Zorani, 'Indian Air Force Commander Visited Israel', trans. Ofri Aharon, Events Log, Israeli Air Force, March 31, 2016, at http://www.iaf.org.il/4445-46314-en/IAF.aspx (Accessed February 10, 2017).

41. Amir Rapaport, 'The Israeli-Indian Alliance is Warming Up', *Israel Defense*, March 18, 2015, at http://www.israeldefense.co.il/en/content/"-israeli-indian-alliance-warming-up (Accessed February 15, 2017).

42. 'India and Israel Vow to Fight Terrorism', BBC, September 9, 2003, at http://news.bbc.co.uk/2/hi/south_asia/3089466.stm (Accessed February 15, 2017).

43. Ben Sales, 'With Israeli-EU Relations Strained, Netanyahu Looks toward India, China', *The Jerusalem Post*, December 2, 2015, at http://www.jpost.com/Israel-News/Politics-And-Diplomacy/With-Israeli-EU-relations-strained-Netanyahu-looks-toward-India-China-436029 (Accessed February 10, 2017).

44. 'Indian Air Force Chief Marshal in Israel for Official Visit', United with Israel, March 18, 2016, at https://unitedwithisrael.org/indian-air-force-chief-marshal-in-israel-for-official-visit/ (Accessed February 10, 2017).

Assessing US Influence over India–Israel Relations: A Difficult Equation to Balance?

Nicolas Blarel

Abstract: As India's Israel policy evolved over time, the US involvement in this bilateral relationship has been constant, albeit neither consistent nor direct. Breaking with traditional state-centric approaches, this article focuses on the key role played in shaping the nature of India–Israel ties by non-state and sub-state actors such as specific political personalities, for example Congressmen Emmanuel Celler in the 1940s and Stephen Solarz in the 1980s, as well as of pro-Israel interest groups based in the US, like the Anti-Defamation League (ADL) and the American Jewish Committee (AJC). The article shows that the US factor in India–Israel relations has evolved over time depending on the personalities, political constellations in power in India and regional developments in West Asia. Finally, while India, Israel and US interests seem to have converged at some crucial junctures, the article argues that their policies and strategies have rarely aligned over the long term.

In the summer of 1947, while many observers focused on the partition of the Subcontinent, one of India's first major forays into diplomatic and international politics was unfolding in the newly created United Nations (UN) in New York. On the initiative of Prime Minister Jawaharlal Nehru, India lobbied to become a member of the UN Special Committee on Palestine (UNSCOP). While this might have seemed like a logical step for a newly independent India which aimed at signalling its ambition to become a significant player in world politics, especially in the new global institutional architecture emerging out of the post-World War II order, it also embarked more or less knowingly into what would become one of its first major disputes with the US. This lesser known historical debate which took place between April and September 1947 at the UN structured a major bilateral disagreement between India and the US for decades to come.

As India's Israel policy evolved over time, moving from India's initial opposition to the partition of Palestine in September 1947 to the recognition of the state of Israel in September 1950, and then from the decision to defer the establishment of diplomatic relations for 42 years to the post-normalisation development of strong bilateral trade and military ties since 1992,[1] US involvement in this bilateral relationship has been constant, albeit neither consistent nor direct.

Various strands of scholarship have, for instance, insisted on the long-term influence of the US on India's policy of non-relationship with Israel. Some noted that leaders like Nehru had regarded Israel as a state that had been set up with the support of imperialist powers, and especially from the US.[2] These notably point to

Nicolas Blarel is Assistant Professor, at the Institute of Political Science, Leiden University, The Netherlands.

Prime Minister Nehru's criticism of the US government's involvement in the Palestine debate at the UN in 1947. Others argued that the prolonged estrangement between India and Israel until 1992 could be explained by Cold War divisions.[3] India and Israel were two countries considered to be more or less integrated in the two rival Cold War blocs, thus inhibiting any rapprochement.

However, both individual- and international-level arguments fail to understand how the US influence on India's Israel policy has varied over time, depending on the leadership in power in New Delhi and Washington, the regional developments in West Asia and the wax and wane of international factors such as the Cold War on both sub-continental and West Asian politics. In addition, this article breaks with traditional state-centric approaches which overlook much of the transnational activity that has happened between the Indian, Israeli and US policy systems and societies. For instance, it does not make the argument that the US directly and consistently pressured New Delhi to improve its ties with Israel. In fact, this issue was not a direct concern of US foreign policy towards South Asia and West Asia until the late 1980s. State-centric arguments have therefore neglected the indirect but decisive influence and transnational networks of particular historical characters, which were not in the executive branch or the foreign policy bureaucracy, such as US Congressmen Emmanuel Celler in the 1940s or Stephen Solarz in the 1980s, as well as of influential Jewish interest groups in the US political system, such as the Anti-Defamation League (ADL) and the American Jewish Committee (AJC).

For instance, while initially in disagreement with US policymakers over the conditions leading to the creation of the state of Israel, Nehru did maintain channels of communication with Israeli leadership which were facilitated through the mediation of American actors, albeit not part of government. This sustained dialogue can explain India's eventual recognition of Israel in 1950. In 1956, both India and the US criticised Israel's intervention alongside France and the UK during the Suez crisis. After 1991, while the end of the Cold War and US lobbying for a change in India's approach to Israel towards the establishment of diplomatic relations in January 1992 were important factors, the story of US influence is of a more indirect and incremental nature as it can be dated back and in the form of mediation of American Jewish organisations to the mid-1980s.[4] Finally, while the US has initially encouraged the development of defence ties between India and Israel, its defence industries find themselves today in direct competition with Israeli firms.

As a result, it is important to evaluate how interdependent were India–US and India–Israel ties since 1947, but also to assess when and how American influence, both direct and perceived, acted as a constraining or enabling influence over the development of India–Israeli relations. The remainder of the article is organised as follows: First, I discuss the initial exchanges between Indian and Jewish national-isms in the 1930s which were facilitated by the mediation of certain US actors. Second, I look at the US–India dispute over the creation of the state of Israel, leading all the way to the recognition of September 1950. In the third section, I explain the growing estrangement between the Indian and American positions over the various West Asian disputes from the 1950s to the 1980s. Fourth, I describe how US domestic politics, and especially certain US politicians and interest groups, encouraged the rapprochement between India and Israel and the normalisation of bilateral ties in January 1992. Subsequently, I evaluate in the fifth section the evolving role of US support for defence ties between India and Israel but also at possible hurdles as both American and Israeli defence industries increasingly compete for some markets. Finally, I conclude and suggest some possible future trends in the India–Israel–US equation.

Pre-1947: Dialogue between Indian and Jewish nationalism through American mediation

India's Israel policy was formed in the pre-independence period, and most especially when the Indian National Congress (INC) made its first statements on the Israel–Palestine issue in the 1920s and 1930s.[5] As a result, even before independence, there were regular interactions between members of the INC with advocates for the creation of the state of Israel, many of whom were US-based representatives of the Jewish agency.

Because of the mainly European and North American origins of the immigration movement to Palestine in the 1930s (mostly from Britain, Eastern Europe and the US), Indian nationalists initially identified Zionism with its countries of origin.[6] The fact that the Zionist movement drew most of its financial and political support from European and US sources initially led the INC leaders to consider Zionism as a movement that was directly under the influence of British and American interests. In parallel, since the major priorities for the Zionist movement were arms procurement, fund raising and facilitating Jewish immigration in Palestine, the INC was not considered a priority in its diplomatic efforts. The Zionist movement also avoided identifying itself with other nationalist movements in Asia and made a tactical choice to concentrate its diplomatic attention on British and American material and political support.[7]

However, US-based Zionists regularly engaged with Indian nationalist leaders. By the early 1930s, the Jewish agency attempted to establish contacts with Gandhi and Nehru whom they considered to be influential personalities both in India and internationally.[8] By the early 1930s, the Jewish Agency also realised that it needed to counter the anti-Zionist message circulated in India through the efforts of Mufti al-Hussayni. For instance, Hayim Greenberg, editor of the US-based *Jewish Frontier* newspaper, expressed his concerns about anti-Zionist sentiments spreading among Indian Muslim communities in a letter he sent to Gandhi in 1937.[9]

Repeated efforts from American Zionists to get Gandhi to publicly express himself about the Palestine issue paid off in 1938. However, his statements on Palestine belonging to the Arabs and his condemnation of Zionist collaboration with imperialist Britain in his famous 1938 *Harijan* article revealed the difficulties of the Jewish Agency's efforts in convincing the Indian nationalist leader of their cause. Americans like Hayim Greenberg directly accused Gandhi of being biased and unfair towards the Jews. He noted that Gandhi had overlooked the imperative existential need for a Jewish homeland. Gandhi responded to this accusation in another column in *Harijan* and even reproduced an abridgement of Greenberg's letter, pointing out that he saw no reason to change his opinion.[10]

According to Nehru, the problem of Palestine was primarily an Arab nationalist struggle against British imperial control. By contrast, the Jewish issue was a minority religious problem that had mainly been fostered by British policies. He notably suggested a federal arrangement which would guarantee Jewish religious rights in Palestine.[11] Like Gandhi, Nehru too was approached by Zionist emissaries before and after independence, who were looking for his support on the creation of a Jewish state.

After World War II, Gandhi's position seemed to have evolved. Although he condemned the persecution of the Jews in Europe in strong terms, he insisted that restoring Palestine to the Jews, partly or wholly, as their national home would be a crime against humanity, as well as against the Muslims.[12] In spite of this statement, Gandhi met the American Unitarian minister and pacifist John Haynes, who had been sent by New York Rabbi and noted Zionist Stephen Wise.[13] Gandhi also met in 1946 the American journalist Louis Fischer to whom he conceded that the Jews had a 'prior claim' to Palestine. However, in a later article in *Harijan* in July 1946, Gandhi clarified his position: he argued the Jews had been 'wronged by the world' but he also criticised their reliance on American and British help as well as on terrorist methods.[14]

These various statements demonstrate that Gandhi and Nehru did not have a static opinion of the Palestine issue but instead a nuanced and evolving perception of the situation, to some part informed by their meetings and discussions with American Zionists and members of the Jewish Agency. Gandhi died a few months before the creation of Israel, and did not therefore have any direct impact on India's Israel policy. By contrast, Nehru had a key foreign policy-making role after independence as he held both the positions of prime minister and minister of external affairs. His early contacts with American Zionists would prove important in the early post-independence years.

1947–1950: the creation of Israel as a first disagreement between India and the US

From April to September 1947, India and the US faced their first major diplomatic dispute as the Palestine question was presented by the British to the UN General Assembly (UNGA). Nehru supported the British proposal for the UN to deal with the Palestine question and nominated Asaf Ali, India's first ambassador to the US, as its first representative to the Special UNGA Session on Palestine. Ali was given very specific guidelines, notably to support a termination of the Mandate and ensure that India would be part of any fact-finding committee on Palestine. Ali was also warned not to commit the government to any position without any prior approval from New Delhi, and to avoid raising issues which might 'affect' India's relations with other countries.[15] The instructions showed that India's position was not fixed and remained open to debate. Furthermore, Nehru was conscious that India's decisions would be closely scrutinised by its international partners, especially the US.

At the UN, Ali actively argued against the interference and influence of great powers, such as the US and UK, on the Palestine issue. After an intense debate which lasted until May 15, 1947, it was decided that the five major powers (permanent members of the UN Security Council [UNSC]) would be excluded from membership of the specialised committee created to study the Palestine issue. Following Nehru's instructions, Ali lobbied for India to be a member of the UNSCOP. However, India had problems integrating the initial list of neutral members of the Committee as suggested by the US Ambassador to the UN, Warren Austin.

Nehru was disappointed with Ali's performance, which contradicted his instructions to avoid controversy.[16] Ali notably attempted to include in the Agenda of the Special Palestine Committee a proposal which demanded the immediate termination of the Mandate and the proclamation of the independence of Palestine. In addition, Ali invited the Arab Higher Committee, represented by Mufti Hussayni, to talk before the

Special Committee. However, he also supported inviting the Jewish Agency to testify. Ali's overt pro-Arab position led him to clash with other representatives on the Committee.[17] Nehru was therefore concerned that Ali's stance could affect relations with India's Western partners and cautioned him against raising divisive issues such as the Arab proposal for immediate independence. Nehru mentioned that he had heard 'adverse comments' following Ali's statements and he recommended making 'fewer commitments' on the issue.[18] While Nehru wanted India to maintain its sympathy for Arab grievances, he also preferred maintaining a cautious and open-ended policy to not upset ties with the US.

Finally, the UNGA decided to appoint a more representative UNSCOP. Membership was extended to two other members from the South Pacific and Asian regions, which were underrepresented in the initial nine-member committee. The expansion opened the door for India. After the initial reactions to Ali's statements, it became a priority for Nehru to reframe India's position as a more balanced observer of the dispute. One first move was to nominate Sir Abdur Rahman as India's representative to the UNSCOP. Nehru asked Rahman to support a federal solution which had to gain Arab approval. However, given the strong divisions on this issue and the uncertain outcome of the deliberations, Nehru also suggested to keep a 'vague' position and to remain 'friendly' to both parties.[19] Nehru did not want Rahman to make the same mistakes as Ali and to rhetorically commit India in one direction.

However, significant disagreements emerged between Rahman and Nehru. Rahman, for instance, expressed doubts about the continuing legal status of India in the UN structure following the partition of the Subcontinent. Consequently, Rahman defended India's federal solution at the UNSCOP, but also offered a dissenting note on August 14, 1947. Rahman agreed with Nehru's position that partition was not a viable solution as it would not lead to a lasting peace plan between Arabs and Jews.[20] However, in his personal note, he rejected the federal solution which he judged equally impractical as it was opposed by all parties.[21] Ultimately, Rahman personally supported a unitary state where a clear Muslim Arab majority (three-fourths) had a right to self-determination. A partition scheme would, in the view of Rahman, be opposed to the principle of self-determination.[22] However, Rahman also argued that religious, cultural, linguistic and educational rights should be defended by the constitution of a new Palestinian state, and that there should be proportional quotas for Jewish participation in government and other public offices.

The Jewish Agency closely monitored these disputes between New Delhi and its representative given its apprehensions that Rahman would support the Arab case within the UNSCOP. There were various efforts to inform Nehru of Rahman's perceived bias. American Congressman and Zionist Emmanuel Celler notably played an important role by directly expressing his concerns about Rahman in a cable he sent to Nehru. Celler was popular in India because of his support to the Indian struggle for independence in the American Congress. In the 1940s, Celler also became an advocate of more flexible US immigration laws to help Jewish refugees fleeing the Holocaust. Celler had also been instrumental in facilitating the invitation of a Jewish delegation to the New Delhi Conference of the Asian Relations Organisation which took place in March–April 1947. India had initially invited 32 delegations, including a delegation from Palestine. There was a strong opposition within the INC against inviting a Jewish delegation.[23] However, pressure from both Sarojini Naidu and especially Nehru's sister and India's representative to the UN, Vijaya Lakshmi

Pandit, who had discussed the issue with Celler in Washington, proved decisive.[24] Following the conference, the Jewish delegation highlighted the importance of seeking the assistance of US politicians who had supported both Indian nationalism and Zionism, such as Congressman Celler. Consequently, in his response to Celler, Nehru explained he had given instructions to Rahman that highlighted the quasi-judicial character of the inquiry and confirmed India's impartial stance.[25]

In October 1947, as the UNGA vote on the Palestine issue was nearing, Celler attempted to influence the Indian voting by directly appealing to Pandit, who was the Indian representative to the UNGA. The US supported partition, while India supported a federal plan. Pandit had her personal reservations with Nehru's position.[26] She notably had warned the Ministry of External Affairs (MEA) through a letter on October 8, 1947 that India's federal plan had little support as both contending parties, including the Arabs, rejected it.[27] In addition, a report was reportedly sent to Ben-Gurion stressing the fact there had been a debate within the Indian delegation on the voting and that Pandit had suggested to Nehru to abstain on the partition plan.[28]

However, Celler's efforts to sway India towards a support of the partition plan proved unfruitful, as Pandit did not directly defy Nehru's instructions from New Delhi and the Indian delegation stood by its support for the federal plan on November 29, 1947. India and the US disagreed on the partition plan but also on the recognition of the state of Israel following its proclamation of independence on May 14, 1948. Although there was a debate in the Harry Truman administration, the US recognised Israel within hours of the proclamation.[29] On May 17, 1948, Moshe Sharret, the minister of foreign affairs of the provisional government of Israel, sent a cable to Nehru to seek India's formal recognition of the new state of Israel.[30] Eliahu Eilat (Epstein), the representative of Israel's provisional government of Israel in the US, sent another cable to the Indian *chargé d'affaires* in Washington.[31]

Since there was no official reaction from New Delhi, Israel actively used the channels of communication between Eilat and Indian diplomats in Washington and New York to push for recognition. Israeli diplomats also tried to use India's close links with the US to pressure Delhi into changing its policy. Since the US financial support at the time was considered by Indian decision-makers as necessary for the success of India's first five-year plan, diplomatic pressure (or at least a perception of such) was considered important.[32] Congressman Celler was regularly invited to meetings between Israeli and Indian diplomats to help persuade the latter.[33]

In September 1948, after the second Arab-Israeli ceasefire was signed, India's Ambassador to the US, B. N. Rau, mentioned the possibility of recognition to his Israeli counterpart Eliahu Eilat in Washington. In a later discussion in May 1949, Pandit, now Indian Ambassador to the US, reportedly acknowledged to Eilat in Washington that the situation in Kashmir had postponed the recognition.[34] In September 1949, following the acceptance of Israel as an official member of the UN, Pandit assured Eilat that India was moving towards recognition.[35] In October 1949, during a visit to Washington, Nehru met with Ambassador Eilat and Congressman Celler. Nehru explained that the recognition of Israel had been delayed because of internal opposition which had to be treated carefully. Nehru did, however, concede that recognition of Israel could not be indefinitely postponed.[36] In a letter to Sharett, Eilat also said that Nehru had directly discussed the impact of the 'painful' partition on the '30 million Indian Muslims' and that the Palestine question was a 'constant source of agitation' for this community.[37] Nehru reportedly also indicated to

Celler that it would be 'unwise' for him to recognise Israel during his stay in the US as it could be interpreted as 'American pressure'.[38]

In spite of these regular meetings, India deferred the recognition of the state of Israel until September 1950 and decided to indefinitely postpone the establishment of diplomatic relations. As a result, barring a few exceptions, India and the US stood at odds when it came to the Israel–Palestine dispute for the next four decades.

1950s–1980s: India and the US on different sides of the West Asian divides

During three decades, India and the US stood on different sides of the sectarian and/or geopolitical disputes which divided West Asia. For some time, their interests also directly conflicted. This had an important effect on India's policy towards Israel. In the early 1950s, for instance, the US initiated an alliance, institutionalised through the Baghdad Pact of 1955, which was officially conceived to contain Soviet Expansion in West Asia and which included Pakistan.[39] This alliance was perceived as directly affecting India's security interests as it permitted Pakistan to boost its military arsenal and to thereby reject any diplomatic settlement of the Kashmir dispute. In order to counter this new military alliance project, and the introduction of Cold War politics in West Asia, Nehru decided to reinforce India's relations with other Arab states such as Egypt and Syria.

As a result, at that time, Nehru was reluctant to establish diplomatic relations with Israel. India felt it was necessary to emphasise a shared outlook with Arab states on most West Asian issues, including the Israel–Palestine dispute. Beyond Egypt, other Arab states lauded India for its opposition to the Baghdad Pact and criticised Pakistan's membership. Saudi Arabia's King Saud, two years after he had visited and supported Pakistan on the Kashmir issue, expressed his disappointment that the 'Islamic State of Pakistan should accede to those who have joined hands with the Zionist Jews' by joining a 'Western Military Pact'.[40] The rapprochement between India and key Arab states helped to check Pakistan's diplomatic attempts to create a coalition of Muslim Arab states and to dispel the notion that the Government of India was pro-Zionist following the recognition of Israel.

In spite of these contrasting diplomatic alignments in West Asia, India and the US agreed to jointly condemn Israeli policies during the Suez crisis. In July 1956, the Egyptian President Gamal Abdel Nasser decided to nationalise the Suez Canal. This sudden and drastic move was the result of a protracted political dispute which had developed over a proposal between Egypt, the US and UK for the funding for the construction of the Aswan High Dam. As the Suez Canal was a strategic trade link which had remained under British control after Egyptian independence, the decision to nationalise was considered a move that directly defied European powers which had important stakes in the Canal.

India's initial reaction was to support Nasser's decision. Nehru argued in August that the Egyptian decision complied with the terms of sovereign Egypt's laws.[41] However, looking to also support international legal principles, Nehru referred to the 'international character' of the Suez waterway according to the Anglo-Egyptian Agreement of 1954. Nehru equally regretted the 'suddenness' of the decision and of its implementation, which directly affected European economic interests. The Indian argument was that Egypt was competent to nationalise the Suez Canal but should have done so in 'the normal way of international expropriation'.[42] Nehru therefore deplored the lack of consultation through UN-led mechanisms between the UK and Egypt on this matter.

India's position during the Suez crisis was not only shaped by moral and legal consideration but also by its own national self-interest. Nehru was concerned by the long-term consequences linked to the closing of the Canal to international circulation. India was not a 'disinterested party' but a 'principal user of this waterway' whose 'economic life and development' was directly affected.[43] Consequently, India advised all the involved countries to abandon threats, violence and unilateral acts in order to avert an escalation to a crippling conflict in the region.[44] In spite of these specific national interests, Nehru directly corresponded with US President Dwight Eisenhower and British Prime Minister Anthony Eden concerning a conference of the canal users to be held in London. Nehru notably supported Eisenhower's decision to include as many participants as possible to the conference. Nehru also convinced Nasser to not boycott the conference and to send one representative along with Krishna Menon, the Indian representative to the London Conference.[45]

In spite of mediating efforts during the London conference, India did not manage to broker an agreement between the various parties. Nehru was concerned by the risk of escalation following the refusal of European countries to further negotiate after the American proposal was rejected by Egypt. Nehru sent out a message to the Secretary of State John Foster Dulles asking the US to exercise influence to stop British troops from landing in Egypt. Dulles replied stating that 'while the US would not support any disregard of Egypt's rights, it was not clear what precisely these rights were'.[46] Because the Suez Canal was deemed to be of 'vital importance' to India, Nehru continued to push for a 'peaceful negotiated settlement'.[47]

Nehru therefore continued to urge Eisenhower and Eden to consider the Egyptian proposals. The Foreign Ministers of Britain, France and Egypt initiated private talks in New York, at which Krishna Menon was present in a mediatory role.[48] India was optimistic about a peaceful settlement until Israel launched a sudden military attack on Egypt on October 29, 1956. Two days later, British and French troops took control of the Suez Canal. Along with the US and USSR, India sternly criticised the Anglo-French-Israeli operation. Nehru encouraged the US to intervene. India denounced the Anglo-French ultimatum on the cession of the Suez Canal as a 'flagrant violation of the UN Charter'.[49] In a letter sent to Dulles, Nehru called the Israeli military operation as a 'clear, naked aggression' and argued that 'the whole future of the relations between Europe and Asia hangs in the balance'.[50] Arthur Lall, India's ambassador to the UN, also urged the American Ambassador to the UN Henry Cabot Lodge to stop the British-French-Israeli action against Egypt.[51]

India's priority was to put an end to a conflict which closed the access to the Suez Canal. India backed the UNGA's efforts in a Special Emergency Session to obtain an immediate ceasefire by all parties and the withdrawal of troops behind the armistice line. On November 2, 1956, India supported a US-sponsored resolution at the UNGA that urged immediate ceasefire and asked all sides to withdraw behind the armistice lines. This proposal came to be referred to as 'the Eisenhower–Nehru formula', and Eisenhower was keen to quickly meet Nehru, 'just the two of them because he thought they came closer to commanding the respect of the world'.[52] India also agreed to contribute along with 10 other countries to the UN Emergency Force (UNEF) on the condition that Egypt would agree to have such forces based on the 1949 demarcation line separating Egypt from Israel.

India's involvement in the Suez crisis and the subsequent deployment of the UNEF was driven by an ambition to play an active mediating role between the European powers (France and the UK), the great powers (the US and USSR) and Egypt. Nehru and Eisenhower exchanged sustained correspondence during the crisis, leading to a convergence of interests and a joint condemnation of the Israeli military attack against Egypt.[53]

However, the Suez events and the condemnation of the use of military force were one of the rare instances where Arab, US, Soviet and Indian positions aligned. While the US gradually moved closer to Israel in the following years, Nehru and India broke with the earlier position which had always left open the possibility of diplomatic exchanges. After 1956, the establishment of diplomatic ties was explicitly discarded as it was perceived as potentially hurting India's relations with Arab states and complicated India's potential role as a mediator in the region. As a result, India and the US would stand on opposite sides during the 1967 and 1973 conflicts, with New Delhi unconditionally supporting Egypt and Syria and Washington standing behind Israel.

However, in spite of this decision to defer the development of diplomatic relations, Nehru still met with Israeli diplomats such as Abba Eban, Israel's ambassador to the US, in Washington in December 1956. In a meeting organised by the American diplomat Chester Bowles, Nehru also met with Nahum Goldmann, the president of the Jewish World Congress in 1957. Goldmann did not succeed in convincing Nehru of the necessity of having diplomatic relations with Israel. He reportedly judged Nehru's attitude towards Israel to be 'ambivalent'.[54] The US back channel of communication between Indian and Israeli officials was discontinued both because of the personal decisions and dispositions of Nehru's successors, Lal Bahadur Shastri and Indira Gandhi, but also because of international alignment policies as India was drawn closer to the USSR following the signing of the Indo-Soviet Treaty of Peace, Friendship and Cooperation in 1971. The US would not play an indirect influence on India–Israel relations until the 1980s.

1984–1992: US efforts in facilitating the India–Israel rapprochement

As the Cold War was waning in the 1980s, Rajiv Gandhi revived the US-based diplomatic channels that his grandfather had previously built on to discuss with Israeli authorities. The Rajiv Gandhi government was also trying to find solutions to improve India's relations with the US, and especially economic ties. Bilateral relations had deteriorated since the Soviet invasion of Afghanistan and the subsequent US military aid given to Pakistan. Another negative development was the increasing criticism of India's 'discriminatory' treatment of Israel coming from the Jewish community in the US, and particularly from the influential ADL.[55] In May 1987, the ADL published a report condemning India's discriminatory behaviour *vis-à-vis* Israel. The report highlighted the fact that India had refused to grant visas to Israeli citizens since the mid-1960s and quoted numerous statements hostile to Israel. The report explicitly recommended the imposition of US sanctions on India.

Consequently, the Indian Government became conscious that efforts should be made to prevent pro-Israel American organisations from being obstacles to renewed diplomatic efforts to engage the US. Certain steps were taken by Rajiv Gandhi's government to amend ties with Israel, even before the publication of the ADL report. A few days before the 1985 UNGA annual session, Israel bombarded the Palestine

Liberation Organisation (PLO) headquarters in Tunis. Rajiv Gandhi condemned the attack and expressed his concern for the safety of Yasser Arafat.[56] At the UN, India's Minister of External Affairs Bali Ram Bhagat also criticised Israel's 'aggressive and expansionist policies' and called the air raid a 'threat to peace and security'.[57] At first glance, this position seemed in line with India's traditional support of the Arabs and Palestinians against Israel. However, the response in October 1985 was different. In reaction to the raid, 18 Arab states sponsored a UNGA resolution calling for the expulsion of Israel from the UN. Breaking with its traditional support for Arab-backed resolutions, this time India decided to abstain.[58] In fact, Rajiv Gandhi even met with Israel's Prime Minister Shimon Peres during the 40th UNGA session. This was the first public meeting between two sitting prime ministers of the two countries. As another indication of change, India also decided to relax the visa restrictions for Israeli citizens. For instance, the Rajiv Gandhi government allowed an Israeli tennis team to play against the Indian team in New Delhi for the Davis Cup Tournament in July 1987.[59]

Rajiv Gandhi had also seemingly realised the influence of pro-Israel organisations and of specific personalities in Congress like Stephen J. Solarz on US policy in that region.[60] Solarz was a US Congressional Representative from New York. In the 1980s, he chaired the Asian and Pacific Affairs Subcommittee of the House Foreign Affairs Committee. In the House, Solarz represented a district that had one of the country's largest Jewish populations, and he had been a long-time supporter of Israel. He also had an interest in India, and was instrumental in setting up the South Asia Bureau in the US Department of State.[61] Rajiv Gandhi therefore organised a meeting with Solarz and representatives of various American Jewish organisations in June 1988 in New York.[62] At the meeting in Rajiv Gandhi's hotel suite, in addition to Solarz the Chairman of the Conference of Presidents of Major Jewish Organisations (and former President of the American Jewish Committee), Morris Abram, the Conference's Executive Vice Chairman Malcolm Hoenlein, the President of the American Jewish Congress Robert Lifton, the Executive Director of the ADL Abe Foxman, and the Executive Director of the American Jewish Committee Ira Silverman, were present.[63] Gandhi reportedly stated that he wanted to improve economic and political ties with the US. The Jewish organisations encouraged the Indian Prime Minister to change India's policy towards Israel and its citizens, notably on the question of visa restrictions.[64] They also asked India to pressure the Palestinians to renounce their call for the destruction of Israel and to follow the Egyptian example.[65] Some Israeli media later suggested that Prime Minister Rajiv Gandhi had pledged during the meeting to upgrade official ties with Israel.[66]

Soon after these discussions, India allowed an Israeli diplomat to be stationed in Bombay (now Mumbai) as vice-consul. This was an important diplomatic move: since the expulsion of the Israeli consul in Bombay by Indira Gandhi in 1982, India had regularly refused requests to replace the position.[67] In addition, a delegation of the ADL and Congressman Solarz visited New Delhi in 1989. Two of the members of this delegation had been signatories of the 1987 ADL report. The delegation met the Minister of External Affairs Narasimha Rao, Foreign Secretary Alfred Gonsalves and the MEA's Joint Secretary to the Prime Minister P. K. Singh.[68] One report stated that the delegation of the ADL lobbied in favour of improved Indo-Israeli relations but was notified that change would not be imminent.[69] Following the meeting, there was another diplomatic gesture towards Israel with the formal extension of the Israeli consulate's jurisdiction by the Government of India to the southern state of Kerala which had had a historical and relatively significant Jewish population.[70]

However, in spite of these discussions with pro-Israel organisations and a number of important steps in the direction of change, the Rajiv Gandhi government was unable to bring about a complete reversal of India's foreign policy towards Israel. Instead, in November 1988, India became one of the first non-Arab countries to recognise the newly proclaimed state of Palestine. Domestic political and electoral constraints and regional developments, like the Palestinian Intifada of 1987, restricted any further rapprochement with Israel. US influence on India's Israel policy further increased in the early 1990s, especially in the aftermath of the Gulf War. India's shift of position regarding Iraq and its acceptance to let US military planes refuel at Indian airports was a first important signal that India had to come to terms with the increased American presence in the West Asian region.

The domestic economic crisis in India in 1991 and the disappearance of India's traditional Soviet partner also made New Delhi more dependent on US economic support. In June 1991, Prime Minister Rao inherited an important economic crisis from his predecessor. The crisis was an opportunity for a traditionally self-reliant India to liberalise and to open its economy to the world. With his Finance Minister Manmohan Singh, Rao fundamentally changed India's economic policies. Rao notably sought investments and loans from international institutions such as the International Monetary Fund (IMF) and the World Bank, as well as from the US.[71] The objective for Rao and Singh was to neutralise all obstacles in Washington to the urgent loans India needed. As Minister of External Affairs in 1988, Narasimha Rao had also been involved in discussions with Solarz and American Jewish organisations and was therefore conscious that the lack of relations with Israel precluded a better understanding with the US whose financial support was essential for India's economic recovery.

Consequently, India first joined the US-backed move to revoke the UNGA Resolution 3379 equating Zionism with racism in December 1991. In the second week of January 1992, the Director General of the Israeli Ministry of Foreign Affairs Joseph Hadass met with the Deputy Chief of the Mission of the Indian Embassy in Washington Lalit Mansingh. Reportedly, Hadass made it clear to Mansingh that it was up for India to take the initiative of establishing diplomatic relations if it wanted to be invited to participate in the nascent West Asian peace process.[72] Narasimha Rao then announced the establishment of diplomatic relations with Israel on the eve of a visit to the UN in New York where he would meet with US President George H. W. Bush. Following the announcement, Congressman Stephen Solarz also issued a press release welcoming the new diplomatic development.[73]

1992–2016: the defence equation

Following the establishment of diplomatic relations between India and Israel in January 1992, defence ties, and especially arms sales from Israel to India, became a major component of this emerging partnership. The US role in the development of defence relations has, however, been neither direct nor systematic. In fact, the Bill Clinton administration initially opposed Israeli defence sales to India because of technology transfer regimes and the embargo linked to the Indian nuclear tests of 1998. This situation evolved under the George W. Bush administration which then openly encouraged defence cooperation between two partners it was openly trying to enrol in its global War on Terror. The contemporary situation is uncertain as both American and Israeli defence industries are now openly competing for access to the growing Indian market.

There were international obstacles to defence technology transfer in the 1990s. Some of the Israeli technology which had been co-produced with the US could not be shared without a prior approval from Washington. The US had, for instance, previously blocked the Israeli transfer of Lavi, patriot missile and Phalcon technologies to China.[74] Nevertheless, the US first indirectly helped Israeli defence industries gain a foothold on the Indian market following the Indian and Pakistani nuclear tests of May 1998. In the immediate days following the tests, the US placed both India and Pakistan under economic sanctions.[75] The sanctions included banning US economic assistance and the export of defence material and technologies.

Unlike the US, and even Russia, Israel did not condemn the nuclear tests and did not join the weapons embargo against New Delhi. Instead, just a few days after the tests, a delegation from Israeli Aerospace Industries (IAI) visited India to accelerate the sale of Israeli-made Unmanned Aerial Vehicles (UAVs).[76] A few weeks later, the IAI also finalised a large-scale deal to sell India advanced electronic equipment for warplanes. The fact that this equipment was solely developed and manufactured in Israel and contained no American technology helped circumvent the existing sanctions, but the US nevertheless opposed the deal by arguing that it violated international arms control treaties. In spite of this criticism, Israel honoured the deal that had been signed in 1996.[77] In fact, Israel also assured India that all contracts and joint ventures which had been negotiated prior to the tests would be respected.[78]

The initial American apprehensions were, however, put aside in the early 2000s. At the time, the Bharatiya Janata Party (BJP) government was negotiating with Israel the $1.1 billion purchase of the Phalcon Airborne Warning and Control System (AWACS). This deal was a game-changer for two main reasons. First, the Phalcon system brought a new qualitative edge to Indo-Israeli defence operations. Second, the deal marked the evolution of the US position on technology transfer between Israel and India. In 2000, under intense pressure from the Clinton administration, Israel had been forced to cancel the sale of the Phalcon radar system to China despite the loss of a billion-dollar contract.[79] Weary of the Chinese precedent, India and Israel coordinated their efforts with high-ranking US officials during the negotiations. After four years, Washington finally authorised the Phalcon sale in 2003.[80]

The success of the Phalcon deal was also the result of a new strategy of political lobbying from the BJP in Washington. Since Rajiv Gandhi's tenure, Indian policymakers, including in the BJP government, had realised that the engagement of Jewish organisations based in the US was necessary to mobilise American support for defence relations with Israel. Since 1992, India and Israel had been regularly discussing defence exchanges but India could only purchase weapons and technologies which were exclusively Israeli-made. There were institutional and legal obstacles to the purchase of the Phalcon AWACS, and of ballistic missile defence systems, as some of the technology originated from the US. India was still targeted by US technological embargoes and sanctions which had been imposed after the nuclear tests of 1974 and 1998. Consequently, India actively engaged American Jewish organisations to gain the approval of the US administration. Indian–American organisations like the US–India Political Action Committee have also both emulated and established institutional links with the American–Israel Political Action Committee (AIPAC), and the AJC to push for a rapprochement between India and the US.[81]

India's National Security Adviser Brajesh Mishra's visit to the US and speech to the AJC in May 2003 must be seen within this objective of improving relations with both Israel and the US. In his speech, Mishra formulated the idea of a tripartite axis between the US, Israel and India. Noting that all these countries were democracies which shared a 'common vision of pluralism tolerance and equal opportunities', he argued that stronger relations between the three countries had a 'natural logic'.[82] He added that the three democracies shared similar security threats and should form a 'viable alliance' to combat the common threat of 'global terrorism'.[83] While there has been no attempt to follow up with concrete initiatives on these statements, this appearance of an ideological rapprochement enabled further Indo-Israeli defence cooperation without any explicit US opposition.

For instance, in other high-technology niche areas such as missile defence where India had failed to build robust indigenous capabilities, Israel offered key equipment and expertise, such as the Barak-I point-defence systems that India bought in 2001.[84] Israel also proved to be an indirect access to US defence technology (such as sub-elements of the Arrow system like Green Pine Radar).[85] However, the burgeoning defence partnership between India and Israel has also now created problems for some US defence industries which are increasingly targeting Indian defence contracts in niche markets. While Israel stands only in fourth position as arms supplier to India behind Russia, the US and France, and that Israel and the US will not be directly contesting major platforms like combat aircrafts, US and Israeli firms have competed over specific tenders.

A recent example is symptomatic of the possible tensions related to the growing competition between India and Israel in specific sectors. India originally considered buying the US-made 'Javelin' Anti-Tank Guided Missiles (ATGM). Negotiations were 'nearly completed' for the two countries to jointly develop the ATGM by late 2016.[86] However, the negotiations ultimately stalled because of Washington's reluctance to share technology with India and to not allow India to then indigenously manufacture the 'tank killer' missiles. In parallel, India also discussed with Israel the supply of the 'Spike' third-generation ATGMs. India is reportedly in the final stages of inking a deal with Israel's Rafael Advanced Defence Systems for the purchase of the ATGMs.[87] This development has confirmed Israel's flexibility in technology transfer and its imposition of very minimal conditions in its dealings with India compared to the US.

Over the last two decades, Israeli defence industries have proven to be appealing partners for India because of their willingness to transfer technology and to engage in joint ventures, production and research and development in high-technology military equipment.[88] By contrast, India–US defence ties have historically been hindered by suspicion in developing jointly defence platforms.[89] In spite of the signing of the Defence Trade and Technology Initiative (DTTI), and discussions of collaboration on developing India's next generation aircraft carrier, India remains wary of the reliability of the US as a defence partner given past embargoes. American defence industries on the other hand are still working on how to comply with India's defence offset policy.

Conclusion

This article's main objective was to demonstrate that, contrary to popular and even academic belief in India, the US factor in India–Israel relations has never been consistent and has evolved over time depending on the personalities, political constellations in power in India and the regional developments in West Asia. While most observers of India–US relations note that one of the foundational disagreements between these powers was American support for Pakistan, few bring up the early disputes over the creation of the state of Israel. Rarely is it also evoked that India and the US coordinated their condemnation of Israeli actions during the Suez crisis of 1956.

Often overlooked by state-centric approaches, another important finding is that non-state and sub-state actors such as specific political personalities like Congressmen Celler and Solarz, as well as pro-Israel interest groups based in the US, have played an important role in shaping the nature of India–Israel ties. The US government has never consistently or directly attempted to pressure India to change its policy towards Israel. In fact, it was the opening of an indirect channel of communication of Rajiv Gandhi with US-based Jewish organisations through the mediation and support of Congressman Solarz in the 1980s which paved the way for the ultimate establishment of diplomatic relations in 1992.

Furthermore, while India, Israel and US interests seem to have converged at some junctures in history like in 2003, their policies and strategies rarely align. As mentioned previously, India and the US stood together against Israeli actions and interests in 1956. As detailed in the last section, the US has promoted but also directly opposed Israeli arms sales to India because of concerns of technology transfer but also due to increasing competition concerns. Another important development to monitor is whether Israel's 'clear and purposeful' engagement of Asian partners like China and India is not also a response to a more lukewarm or uncertain US support to its policies over the last decade.[90] Whether it has been driven by President Barack Obama's explicit criticism of Israel's settlement policies or President Donald Trump's varying rhetoric on the two-state solution, it seems clear that Prime Minister Benyamin Netanyahu's government has been hedging towards consolidating alternative partnerships in Asia,[91] and especially with India, which remains its main market for defence exports. It remains to be seen, however, if closer Israel–India ties develop at the expense of the third party in this difficult strategic equation.

Disclosure statement

No potential conflict of interest was reported by the author.

Notes

1. For more on the historical background of the relationship, see Nicolas Blarel, *The Evolution of India's Israel Policy: Continuity, Change, and Compromise since 1922*, Oxford University Press, New Delhi, 2015; P. R. Kumaraswamy, *India's Israel Policy*, Columbia University Press, New York, 2010.
2. Michael Brecher, 'Israel and Afro-Asia', *International Journal*, 16, 1961, pp. 107–137; Michael Brecher, *The New States of Asia; A Political Analysis*, Oxford University Press, London, 1963, pp. 129–130; Michael Brecher, *India and World Politics: Krishna Menon's View of the World*, Oxford University Press, Oxford, 1968; P. R. Kumaraswamy, no. 1; B. R. Nanda (ed.), *Indian Foreign Policy: The Nehru Years*, University Press of Hawaii, Honolulu,1976; Gideon Shimoni, *Gandhi, Satyagraha and the Jews: A formative Factor in India's Policy towards Israel*, Leonard Davis Institute for International Relations, Hebrew University of Jerusalem, Jerusalem, 1977.

3. Stephen P. Cohen, *India: Emerging Power*, Oxford University Press, New Delhi, 2001; P. R. Kumaraswamy, 'Israel-India Relations: Seeking Balance and Realism', in Efraim Karsh (ed.), *Israel: The First Hundred Years: Israel in the International Arena*, Frank Cass, London, 2004; C. Raja Mohan, *Crossing the Rubicon: The Shaping of India's Foreign Policy*, Penguin, London, 2005.

4. Nicolas Blarel, 'Indo-Israeli Relations: Emergence of a Strategic Partnership', in Sumit Ganguly (ed.), *India's Foreign Policy: Retrospect and Prospect*, Oxford University Press, New Delhi, 2009, pp. 143–161.

5. Nicolas Blarel, no. 1, Chapter 1.

6. Ariel Glucklich, 'Brahmins and Pharisees: The Roots of India's Anti-Zionism', *Midstream*, 34, 1988, pp. 12–15.

7. Michael Brecher, 'Israel and China: An Historic "Missed Opportunity"', in Michael Curtis and Susan Aurelia Gitelson (eds), *Israel in the Third World*, Transaction Books, New Brunswick, 1976.

8. P. R. Kumaraswamy, no. 1, pp. 31–35; Gideon Shimoni, no. 2.

9. Joseph Schechtman, 'India and Israel', *Midstream*, 12, 1966, pp. 48–71.

10. Gideon Shimoni, no. 2, p. 49.

11. Jawaharlal Nehru, *Glimpses of World History*, Penguin, New Delhi, 2004 [1934], p. 891.

12. Shimoni, no. 2, pp. 39, 51.

13. Ibid., pp. 58–59.

14. Mohandas Karamchand Gandhi, *The Collected Works of Mahatma Gandhi*, vol. 84, Publications Division, New Delhi, 2000, pp. 440–441.

15. Cited in P. R. Kumaraswamy, no. 1, p. 87.

16. Sarvepalli Gopal (ed.), *Selected Works of Jawaharlal Nehru*, Series II, vol. 2, Orient Longman, New Delhi, 1988, p. 494.

17. Itzhak Gerberg, *The Changing Nature of Israeli-Indian Relations: 1948–2005*, University of South Africa, Pretoria, 2008, p. 193.

18. Sarvepalli Gopal, no. 16, p. 497.

19. Ibid., pp. 474–475.

20. United Nations Special Committee on Palestine (UNSCOP), *Report to the General Assembly*, vol. 1, ch. IV, United Nations, New York, 1947, p. 44.

21. Gopal Krishan and Sarabjit Sharma, *India and Israel: Towards Strategic Partnership*, Authors Press, New Delhi, 2007, pp. 122–123.

22. UNSCOP, *Report to the General Assembly*, Vol. 2, A/364, Add. 1, United Nations, New York, 1947, p. 44.

23. P. R. Kumaraswamy, no. 1, p. 64; Gideon Shimoni, no. 2, p. 57.

24. Nicolas Blarel, no. 1, p. 88.

25. Ibid., p. 94.

26. Benny Morris, *1948: A History of the First Arab-Israeli War*, Yale University Press, New Haven, 2008, p. 56.

27. P. R. Kumaraswamy, no. 1, p. 104.

28. Itzhak Gerberg, no. 17, pp. 194–195; Prithvi Ram Mudiam, *India and the Middle East*, British Academic Press, London, 1994, pp. 144–147.

29. Michael J. Devine (ed.) *Harry S. Truman, The State of Israel, and the Quest for Peace in the Middle East*, Truman State University Press, Kirksville, 2009; Evan M. Wilson, *Decision on Palestine: How the United States Came to Recognize Israel*, Hoover Press, Stanford, 1979.

30. G. Parthasarathi (ed.), Jawaharlal Nehru, Letters to Chief Ministers, vol. 1: 1947–1949, Oxford University Press, Delhi, 1987, pp. 127–128.

31. P. R. Kumaraswamy, no. 1, p. 109.

32. Paul McGarr, *The Cold War in South Asia: Britain, the United States and the Indian Subcontinent, 1945–1965*, Cambridge University Press, New York, 2013, ch. 1.

33. Itzhak Gerberg, no. 17, pp. 77, 209–210, 215.

34. Shimon Avimor (ed.), *Relations between Israel and Asian and African States: A Guide to Selected Documentation*, Maor-Wallach Press Ltd, Jerusalem, 1991, p. 172.

35. P. R. Kumaraswamy, no. 1, p. 112.

36. Shimon Avimor (ed.), no. 33, p. 172; Itzhak Gerberg, no. 17, pp. 230–231.

37. Itzhak Gerberg, no. 17, pp. 230–231.

38. Cited in P. R. Kumaraswamy, no. 1, p. 119.

39. Paul McGarr, no. 31, pp. 16–25.

40. Donald Eugene Smith, *South Asian Politics and Religion*, Princeton University Press, Princeton, 1966, p. 440.

41. The Canal Corporation was an Egyptian company subject to Egyptian law, and the nationalisation was therefore considered to be within the competence of Egyptian law. See Lok Sabha Debates, vol. 7, pt 2, Lok Sabha Secretariat, New Delhi, August 8, 1956, pp. 2536–2544.

42. Quote by Krishna Menon at London Conference, in *Foreign Relations of the United States, 1955–1957, Suez Crisis, July 26–December 31, 1956*, vol. 16, US Government Printing Office, Washington,1956, pp. 159–178.

43. Lok Sabha Debates, no. 40.

44. Ibid.

45. Swapna Kona Nayudu, *The Nehru Years: Indian Non-Alignment as the Critique, Discourse and Practice of Security (1947–1964)*, Doctoral Thesis, King's College London, 2015, pp. 135–136.

46. Quoted in ibid., p. 141.

47. Lok Sabha Debates, vol. 8, pt 2, September 13, 1956, pp. 6963–6968.

48. Swapna Kona Nayudu, no. 44, p. 143.

49. *Foreign Affairs Record*, vol. 2, no. 10, Ministry of External Affairs, October 10, 1956.

50. M. S. Rajan, *India in World Affairs, 1954–1956*, Asia Publishing House, London, 1964, p. 151.

51. Ibid., p. 144.

52. Ibid., p. 145.

53. Dwight D. Eisenhower, *The White House Years: Mandate for Change 1953–56*, Doubleday, Garden City, 1963, p. 83.

54. Nahum Goldmann, *Sixty Years of Jewish Life*, Holt, Rinehart and Winston, New York, 1969, p. 310.

55. *India's Campaign against Israel*, Anti-Defamation League of BnaiBrith, New York, 1987.

56. *Annual Report*, External Publicity Division of the Ministry of External Affairs, New Delhi, 1985–1986, p. 20.

57. *The Times of India*, October 3, 1985.

58. Richard E. Ward, *India's Pro-Arab Policy: A Study in Continuity*, Praeger, New York, 1992, p. 124.

59. P. R. Kumaraswamy, 'India, Israel and the Davis Cup Tie 1987', *Journal of Indo-Judaic Studies*, 5, 2002, pp. 29–39.

60. It is important to note here that I am referring to perceptions of the Indian Government of the influence of Jewish-American organisations in the US context on US foreign policy which led to the engagement of these organisations. The US political system is widely regarded as very favourable to interest groups, and particularly ethnic interest groups' influence, as argued by Allan J. Cigler and Burdett A. Loomis, *Interest Group Politics*, CQ Press, Washington, 2007; Patrick Haney, 'The Role of Ethnic Interest Groups in US Foreign Policy: The Case of the Cuban American National Foundation', *International Studies Quarterly*, 43(2), 1999, pp. 341–361; Henriette M. Rytz, *Ethnic Interest Groups in US Foreign Policy-Making: A Cuban-American Story of Success and Failure*, Palgrave Macmillan, New York, 2013; Tony Smith, *Foreign Attachments: The Power of Ethnic Groups in the Making of American Foreign Policy*, Harvard University Press, Cambridge, 2000; and John J. Mearsheimer and Stephen M. Walt, *The Israel Lobby and US Foreign Policy*, Farrar, Straus and Giroux, New York, 2007. However, this scholarship has generally found that ethnic interest groups' influence over US foreign policy has not been consistent over time. Even the most influential coalition of pro-Israel organisations, loosely referred to as the 'Jewish Lobby' by Mearsheimer and Walt, has not always been successful at shaping US policy towards the Middle East. The sale of AWACS aircraft to Saudi Arabia in the 1980s or the Iran nuclear deal of 2015 were pushed through by two different US administrations, against the will of the American Israel Public Affairs Committee (AIPAC).

61. Itzhak Gerberg, no. 17, p. 246.

62. P. R. Kumaraswamy, no. 57.

63. Robert Lifton, *An Entrepreneur's Journey: Stories from a Life in Business and Personal Diplomacy*, Author House, Bloomington, 2012, pp. 255–256.

64. *Los Angeles Times*, June 10, 1988.

65. Robert Lifton, no. 61, p. 256.

66. *Los Angeles Times*, June 10, 1988.
67. P. R. Kumaraswamy, no. 1, p. 227.
68. *The Hindu*, January 6, 1988.
69. Richard E. Ward, *India's Pro-Arab Policy: A Study in Continuity*, Praeger, New York, 1992, pp. 128–129.
70. Itzhak Gerberg, no. 17, pp. 113–114.
71. 'Economic Crisis Forcing Once Self-Reliant India to Seek Aid', *New York Times*, June 29, 1991.
72. Interview with Ambassador Lalit Mansingh, October 12, 2011, New Delhi.
73. Itzhak Gerberg, no. 17, p. 336.
74. Yitzhak Shichor, 'Israel's Military Transfers to China and Taiwan', *Survival*, 40, 1998, pp. 68–91.
75. 'Clinton Imposes Full Sanctions on India', *Business Standard*, May 14, 1998.
76. *International Herald Tribune*, June 10, 1998.
77. Farah Naaz, 'Indo-Israel Military Cooperation', *Strategic Analysis*, 24, 2000, pp. 969–985.
78. *The Statesman*, August 20, 1998.
79. P. R. Kumaraswamy, 'Israel-China Relations and the Phalcon Controversy', *Middle East Policy*, 12, 2005, pp. 93–103.
80. 'US Approves Israeli Phalcon Sale to India', *Indian Express*, May 23, 2003.
81. For more on the Indian lobby, see Jason A. Kirk, 'Indian-Americans and the US–India Nuclear Agreement: Consolidation of an Ethnic Lobby?', *Foreign Policy Analysis*, 4 (3), 2008, pp. 275–300.
82. NSA Brajesh Mishra's speech at the American Jewish Committee dinner, May 5, 2003, at http://www.mea.gov.in/Speeches-Statements.htm?dtl/4526/Address+by+Shri+Brajesh+Mishra +National+Security+Advisor+at+the+American+Jewish+Committee+Annual+Dinner (Accessed April 10, 2017).
83. Ibid.
84. Shishir Gupta, 'India to Buy Missile Defense Systems from Israel', *Hindustan Times*, February 11, 2001.
85. Ninan Koshy, 'US plays Matchmaker to India, Israel', *The Asia Times*, June 10, 2003.
86. Vivek Raghuvanshi, 'US, India Said to be Nearing Javelin Co-Production Agreement', DefenseNews.com, September 21, 2016, at http://www.defensenews.com/articles/us-india-said-to-be-nearing-javelin-co-production-agreement (Accessed April 10, 2017).
87. Rahul Singh, 'India, Israel seal $2 billion missile deals: What it means for New Delhi?', *Hindustan Times*, April 7, 2017.
88. Elizabeth Roche, 'India Calls for Broadening of Defence Ties with Israel', *Livemint*, November 16, 2016.
89. Seema Sirohi, 'The US Defence Secretary's Visit to India Is about One Thing—Technology', *Quartz India*, June 3, 2015, at https://qz.com/418514/the-us-defence-secretarys-visit-to-india-is-about-one-thing-technology/ (Accessed April 10, 2017).
90. Herb Keinon, 'Israel Is Clearly Pivoting to Asia, Netanyahu Announces in Singapore', *Jerusalem Post*, February 21, 2017.
91. Leslie Shaffer, 'Israeli Prime Minister Netanyahu: We Are Pivoting toward Asia', CNBC, February 20, 2017, at http://www.cnbc.com/2017/02/20/israel-prime-minister-netanyahu-we-are-pivoting-toward-asia.html (Accessed April 10, 2017).

Redefining 'Strategic' Cooperation

P. R. Kumaraswamy

Abstract: A quarter century after normalisation of relations, India and Israel have shown considerable maturity in handling bilateral relations and dexterity in managing their occasional differing worldviews. Relations have weathered political changes within India as well as periodic upheavals in West Asia and the stalemate in the Israeli-Palestinian negotiations. Military-security cooperation played a pivotal role in carrying forward relations even when political contacts were minimal, as was the case during the decade-long United Progressive Alliance (UPA) rule. A crucial aspect of bilateral relations has been Israel's ability to utilise the federal system in India to its advantage by actively engaging with various state governments. As a result, cooperation in the fields of agriculture and water management, among others, has emerged as the principal tool in the promotion of Indo-Israeli relations. Besides boosting economic ties, this strategy is also aimed at providing and consolidating the support base in India beyond the urban elites.

The term 'strategic' has assumed an interesting meaning within the Indian foreign policy establishment. It has been frequently used to refer to high-level exchanges with many foreign countries. Of late, even think tanks have 'strategic' dialogue with their foreign counterparts. India has regular 'strategic dialogues' with several countries; these include countries which have serious geostrategic differences with one another, namely the US and Russia; China and Japan; and Iran and Saudi Arabia. In pursuing such dialogues with geopolitical rivals, the foreign policy establishment appears to skirt possible pitfalls. Can India's strategic dialogues with China and Vietnam, for example, ignore the Sino-Vietnamese rivalry and tension over the South China Sea? Can India expect a strategic partnership with Japan without accommodating the latter's concerns vis-à-vis an increasingly assertive China? The same holds true for other groups of rivals when India seeks a 'strategic' partnership with both. Without an adequate understanding and nuanced approach, 'strategic' dialogue becomes a euphemism for high-level meetings and consultations.

To be meaningful, 'strategic' dialogue or partnership presupposes certain common traits.[1] First, and foremost, 'strategic' relations presuppose a degree of geopolitical and/or ideological convergence. The post-Second World War trans-Atlantic alliance was the result of the US and countries of Western Europe sharing a common geostrategic and ideological threat from the USSR and communism, respectively. Before long, the countries of Europe found themselves as members of the rival blocs. As a result of this alliance politics, much of the international community was divided during the Cold War and reeled under the bipolar political order. Some of the countries of the Non-Aligned Movement (NAM) gradually came to recognise the

---

Professor P.R. Kumaraswamy teaches contemporary Middle East at the Jawaharlal Nehru University (JNU), New Delhi.

USSR as their 'natural ally'—a theory propounded by Fidel Castro during the 1979 Havana NAM summit—and in the process raised doubts over their stated objective of not joining either of the Euro-centric Cold War political groups.

The formation of military blocs, such as the North Atlantic Treaty Organization (NATO), Warsaw Pact, Central Treaty Organization (CENTO; formerly Baghdad Pact) and Southeast Asia Treaty Organization (SEATO), among others, can be cited as an example of this alliance system. Though they were primarily geostrategic in nature, these blocs were established by the US and USSR with the explicit intention of containing the influence of their rivals; NATO, for example, is not an alliance of democracies even though most of its members have embraced and adopted liberal democracies as their political model. Shared interests as well as fears resulted in Turkey joining the US-led military bloc against the USSR. During the Cold War, Pakistan used the same 'containment' argument to be a part of CENTO. Until 1960, ideological convergence brought the USSR and communist China closer.

The end of the Cold War weakened if not destroyed communism/socialism as the binding force in international relations for the countries of the erstwhile Soviet bloc. Despite local variations and differences, most communist parties, groups and indivi- duals looked up to and became dependent upon Moscow for their political relevance. The demise of the USSR was sudden and complete and the new Russian state not only took time to resurface as a political force, it also ceased to be an ideological counter- weight to the West. The geostrategic relevance of the other communist giant, China, rests less on communism and more on its economic domination and emergence as the major player in the international economy. Under its 'communism with a Chinese character',[2] ideology became subservient to economic progress and integration with the global economy; and the communist ideology has been used to ensure party discipline towards achieving internal wealth and external influence.

Thus, when the Cold War ended, so did the four decades of ideological division, and after an initial period of American hegemony, the situation moved to a more defused and often chaotic international order with multiple power aspirants if not centres. A series of economic crises in the West challenged and destroyed the notion of market-driven liberal democracy, or the End of History as depicted by Francis Fukuyama, as the ultimate model of human progress and development.[3] The same holds true for the other ideological option, namely Islam, which seemed a viable basis for alliance in the wake of the Islamic Revolution in Iran.

In the initial years, the Islamic Republic of Iran sought to project Islam as an ideology that could unite various countries. Regional upheavals, political resurrection of Shia-Sunni rivalry, fears of an Iranian hegemony, prolonged sanctions over the nuclear controversy, and diversity of Islamic societies gradually resulted in Islamic ideology taking a secondary role in Iranian foreign policy.[4] In other words, since the end of the Cold War, national interest and economic calculations have trumped the ideological component in shaping inter-state strategic partnerships.

Second, 'strategic' relations largely involve a high degree of military-security cooperation, accompanied by a steady and sustained supply of sophisticated military hardware, especially during national emergencies. They involve the transfer of front- line weapons and systems, often at subsidised or 'friendly' prices. After the end of the Second World War, the US and USSR supplied large quantities of arms to their client states.[5] During the Cold War, the Soviet Union forged closer ties with countries such as Cuba, Syria, Egypt (until the 1970s) and to a lesser extent India, primarily through arms trade.[6] Indeed, Egypt-Soviet relations were consecrated through the Czech arms deal of 1955.[7] The same holds true for the US, which had emerged as the principal supplier of weapons to Israel, Iran (until the Islamic Revolution), Pakistan and a host of oil-rich Arab countries. The willingness to supply frontline MiGs by the USSR and F-16s by the US was the hallmark of strategic relations between them and their clients. This pattern has not changed since the 1990s and the strategic component of relations with major powers is dominated by the quantum of the arms trade; countries such as the US, Russia, Britain and France define and pursue their 'strategic' partners primarily through arms trade.

Third, political convergence is yet another aspect of 'strategic' partnership. This was manifested clearly during the Cold War. NATO and the Warsaw Pact highlighted the shared worldview of the member states. At times, even nominally non-military arrangements, such as the Association of Southeast Asian Nations (ASEAN), also reflected a common view towards the outside world. The emergence of NAM, which included countries with diverse social, cultural and historic backgrounds, is another example. Their shared political agenda following decolonisation and independence brought them under a common umbrella of Third World solidarity and in some cases resulted in closer bilateral relations, as was the case between India and Egypt under Jawaharlal Nehru and Gamal Abdel Nasser, respectively. The post-Cold War world order has also disrupted this relatively neat arrangement of interest convergence and the international order has become more defused, thereby enabling countries to adopt issue-based understandings even with their rivals and competitors, as happens between India and China and China and Japan.

Fourth, at times, closer economic relations, especially the dependency of a smaller country upon another, can also be described as strategic. Nepal-India, New Zealand-Australia, North Korea-China or Lebanon-Syria relations can be viewed as strategic, especially from the vantage point of the weaker party. For long, many countries attributed their relations with the US as 'strategic' due to the latter being their principal trading partner, but gradually this position has been taken over by China. As a result of its economic growth since the late 1970s, China has not only become the second largest economy in the world but also the largest trading partner of most countries of the world. With notable exceptions like Taiwan, South Korea, Australia and Germany, it enjoys a surplus with all its trading partners. Hence, greater economic engagement can also be defined as strategic.

And fifth, countries seek and establish closer ties due to shared strategic interests and these are tactical in nature and are short-term arrangements. The interest convergence is the result of concerns or fears vis-à-vis a third party which both parties seek to mitigate or reduce. Fears over the territorial ambitions of the USSR partly induced Turkey and Iran to join the US-led military alliances during the Cold War. Sino-Pakistani relations are primarily driven by the India factor; if the former seeks to contain India, the latter wants to overcome its politico-strategic vulnerability.[8] Iranian-Syrian relations after the Islamic Revolution were guided by their mutual security concerns and isolation in the region and their shared animosity towards Ba'athist Iraq under Saddam Hussein. If Damascus refused to join the Arab consensus over the Iranian nuclear controversy, Tehran eschewed the Arab chorus against the Assad regime following the outburst of popular protests and civil war. Both countries also share an interest in the emergence and growth of Hezbollah and its resistance and confrontation with Israel.[9]

Shared interests between Israel and Saudi Arabia vis-à-vis the militant Palestinian group Hamas could be noticed in the subdued response from Riyadh to the Gaza crisis of 2014. Likewise, apprehensions over Iranian hegemony, especially in the wake of the nuclear agreement, led to low-level contacts and understanding between Saudi Arabia and Israel. For long, Israel and Jordan have maintained close but clandestine ties due to their shared concerns over the emergence of an independent Palestinian state. Thus, narrow or long-term interest convergence often results in countries evolving closer partnerships, which at times transform into strategic ties.

In a similar vein, Israel has also been seeking strategic partnership with a number of countries, but the patterns are different and unique. As will be shown, this is true for Indo-Israeli relations.

Patterns of Israel's strategic ties

Israel has sought to forge closer ties with a number of countries since its founding. This search has been compounded by a number of unique factors and challenges: the unilateral character of Israel's declaration of independence; regional hostility towards Israel's existence; and a prolonged Arab campaign for political and economic boycott and the resultant regional and international isolation. Furthermore, Israel has fought five full-fledged wars, has engaged in more than two dozen military operations, and has had to confront prolonged terror campaigns. More than six decades after its formation, its international acceptance remains contested and diplomatic recognition by others continues to be its prime foreign policy objective.

Egypt and Jordan remain the only Arab countries with whom Israel has formal, but cold relations, and most countries of West Asia have not formally recognised the Jewish state. Even outside the region, a number of countries belonging to the Organisation of Islamic Cooperation (OIC), such as Bangladesh, Malaysia and Pakistan, remain hostile towards Israel. Likewise, until January 1992 both China and India refused to have formal ties with Israel.[10] In recent years, European countries like Britain and France, which were once friendly towards Israel, have also turned against it. As the two United Nations Educational, Scientific and Cultural Organization (UNESCO) resolutions adopted in 2016 underscored, even Jewish claims to the city of Jerusalem have been challenged.[11]

The instruments available for Israel to further its foreign policy interests are also limited. It is not a member of any regional organisations and forums; its natural resources and economic strengths are limited; and it heavily depends upon the US for political patronage, economic largesse and military-strategic support. In other words, Israel's political, diplomatic and economic leverages to further its interests abroad are limited. Despite the role played by France until 1967, Israel's strategic relations are dominated by and confined to the US.

As a result, military-security cooperation has become the most effective foreign policy instrument available to Israel. This has a number of subcomponents which make security cooperation a robust enterprise. The first component involves the sale of weapons, systems and technology to the outside world. In the initial years, Israel was exporting obsolete weapons or those it had captured from its Arab adversaries to a number of countries in the Third World, especially in Sub-Saharan Africa and Latin America. Gradually it began to upgrade Soviet weapons it had captured, and this innovation paid dividends when a number of countries lacked the resources for a wholesale modernisation of their military inventories.[12] Through such technological upgrading, Israel was able to prolong the lifespan of these weapons and in the process reduce the cost of modernisation.

The second component of relations was the training of personnel whereby Israel facilitated the establishment of a professional military in a number of African countries.[13] This involved both the training of military personnel as well as helping establish related basic infrastructure.

The third and most important component is intelligence cooperation. Over the years, Israel has established its primacy in obtaining, processing and acting on live intelligence. Even the strategic surprise of the October War of 1973 was the result of inaccurate reading of available information and the failure to gather actionable intelligence.[14] Despite the political controversies and outcomes, a number of counter-terrorism operations undertaken by Israel have been the result of accurate intelligence gathering and swift operations. Hence, at one time or another, a number of countries, including those who are formally at war with the Jewish state, have sought and benefited from their intelligence cooperation with Israel. In some cases, such coopera-tion existed when there were no formal diplomatic relations between the two countries —a case in point was the intelligence cooperation between Israel and Sri Lanka during the late 1980s.[15] Intelligence and counterterrorism cooperation with Israel also involve effective border management techniques, which have been scouted by other countries.

Driven by regional hostilities and political isolation, Israel has been using arms trade and other forms of security assistance as an effective foreign policy instrument since the early 1950s. In some cases, it employed arms sales to open new avenues and in others to consolidate existing ones. Occasionally, pronounced public unfriendliness did not inhibit Israel from forging military-security cooperation. Indeed, the vigour and intensity of its relations with countries such as South Africa (during the apartheid era)[16] and China (until normalisation in 1992)[17] have been dominated by military-security ties. Even when political ties were not possible or were difficult, many countries did not hesitate to seek Israeli help, Sri Lanka being a prime example. Given the centrality of the military component in its domestic and foreign policy arena, the depth of Israel's relations with a country is often measured by the presence or absence of arms trade. Its willingness to trade technology, along with weapons, indicates the proximity and *bonhomie*. The desire for weapons technology and intelligence sharing enabled a number of countries to overcome political hurdles such as Arab boycott calls to forge closer ties with Israel.

In the light of the above discussions, is there a strategic dimension in Israel's policy towards India? If so, how is it manifested?

Non-relations phase

In the closing stages of the First World War, India began to figure in Jewish political aspirations and their demand for a homeland in Palestine. Delays in the Balfour Declaration were partly attributed to the British concerns over the response of the Indian Muslims, the largest population in the world at that time. The Khilafat struggle signalled an Indian interest and involvement in the post-Ottoman political order in West Asia and raised concerns among the Zionist leadership. Through personal meetings with Congress and Muslim League leaders and through the dispatch of special emissaries to India, the Yishuv (the Jewish community in Mandate Palestine) sought to quarantine India from the Palestine issue. This was especially visible when the Grand Mufti of Jerusalem, Hajj Amin al-Husseini, was seeking the support of the Muslim communities in British India for his fight against Zionism.

At the same time, the realisation of the Jewish homeland project depended heavily upon the British, at least until 1939 when the Mandate power disassociated itself from the Balfour Declaration. This situation precluded the Zionist leadership from actively supporting India's nationalist struggle. This became a problem in later years. Without appreciating the unique circumstances and historical necessity, under the influence of Jawaharlal Nehru, the Indian nationalists viewed the Jewish aspirations for a home-land in Palestine through the prism of anti-colonialism. This resulted in a naïve but powerful conclusion—while the Arabs were fighting the British, the Zionists were collaborating with them. The Zionist strategy was not different from the one pursued by a section of the Indian nationalists led by Netaji Subhas Chandra Bose who sought the support of imperial Japan and Nazi Germany to end British colonialism in India. This understanding of Jewish nationalism was also compounded by the prolonged Zionist neglect of India and its leaders; the first known formal communication with Nehru by a senior leader had to wait until Chaim Weizmann wrote to Prime Minister Nehru on December 16, 1947.[18]

As a result, long before the Palestine question came before the United Nations (UN) and the formation of the 11-member UN Special Committee on Palestine (UNSCOP) in May 1947, the Indian nationalists firmly identified themselves with the Arabs of Palestine. While not prepared to endorse the unitary demand of the Arabs, supported by Iran and the then Yugoslavia, India proposed a federal solution to Palestine. The Indian plan, however, fell short of the expectations of both the contending parties; it promised civil and religious rights when the Jews were demand-ing political rights and sovereignty. The Arabs were equally disappointed with the plan as it promised autonomy to the Jews who immigrated to Palestine. Hence, both Arabs and Jews agreed, the only time in 1947, to reject the Indian plan and the Federal Plan was never discussed in the UN and was largely ignored by the interna-tional academia. Thus, when the partition plan came before the UN on November 29, 1947, India joined the Arab and Islamic countries and voted against it.

On May 17, 1948—the second working day after the Declaration of Independence —Moshe Sharett, Foreign Minister of the interim Israeli government, wrote to Prime Minister-cum-Foreign Minister Nehru and sought India's recognition. Because of the obvious diplomatic implications, India chose not to acknowledge this communication and in May 1949 it opposed Israel's entry into the UN. Political realism eventually compelled India to re-examine its previous position. Religion-centric minority nation-alism—India's stated opposition towards Israel—was also the basis for the creation of Pakistan, and the latter was also forging closer ties with the Muslim countries of West Asia. Despite the past support of the Congress party, many West Asian leaders, including the Grand Mufti of Jerusalem, were getting closer to Pakistan, and Nehru also came under pressure from the US over non-recognition of Israel. All this compelled India to formally recognise Israel on September 17, 1950.[19]

Normalisation was not followed up with the establishment of diplomatic relations. There is sufficient historical evidence that indicates Nehru's desire to have formal relations with Israel, including reciprocal resident missions in both countries. He made a promise to this effect when the Director General of the Israeli Foreign Ministry, Walter Eytan, met him in New Delhi on March 4, 1952. Nehru even asked the Foreign Ministry to work out the budget details.

The exchange of diplomatic relations, however, did not happen then—it only materialised four decades later. According to Indian and international accounts, Education Minister and former Congress President Maulana Abul Kalam Azad opposed the move on the grounds that normalisation would face opposition from the Indian Muslims and could be used by Pakistan for anti-India propaganda in the Arab world. Nehru acceded to the counsel and deferred normalisation. The Suez crisis and Israel launching war against Egypt in collaboration with former colonial powers provided an opportunity for Nehru to declare that the time was not conducive for the establishment of diplomatic relations with Israel. Subsequently, a host of other reasons and justifications were added for maintaining the status quo of non-relations. India continued its support for the Arabs and endorsed various political measures aimed at Israel's exclusion from a number of regional and international forums such as the Bandung Conference, NAM, the Group of 77 and even the Asian Games.

Prolonged non-relations and political exclusion of Israel enabled India to endorse and sponsor various resolutions in the UN and other international bodies that were critical of Israel and its policies. At times, India used these as an opportunity to exhibit its pro-Arab and pro-Palestinian credentials. The erstwhile Congress-Muslim League rivalry mutated into Indo-Pakistani competition in West Asia and India sought to further its interests in the Arab-Islamic world by flagging its pro-Palestinian positions. Its unfriendly position continued until the end of the Cold War when structural changes in the international political order and the marginalisation of the Palestinian issue in inter-Arab relations following the Kuwait crisis enabled India to establish formal diplomatic relations with Israel in January 1992.

Post-1992 strategic trajectory

Since January 1992, political, economic and above all military-security relations between the two have been flourishing.[20] In the initial years, the military ties were confined to upgrading of ageing MiG aircraft and supply of fast patrol boats. Gradually, they expanded into avionics, border management, small arms, missiles, anti-missile systems and counterterrorism. Both entered into joint research in missile defence and India launched an Israeli satellite in 2008. Until February 2015 there have been no visits by defence ministers from either side, service chiefs and heads of various intelligence and security institutions have been periodically visiting one another. The US, which in the past encouraged India to normalise relations with Israel, has been accommodative and was supportive of Indo-Israeli military cooperation. This was different from Washington's pressure tactics vis-à-vis the Israeli supply of the Phalcon Airborne Warning and Control System (AWACS) to China.[21] By the early 2000s, Israel had emerged as a major arms supplier to India and the latter as Israel's principal market.

However, depicting the Indo-Israeli ties as 'strategic' merely because of arms trade and other forms of security cooperation would be inaccurate on two counts. One, there is considerable political opposition within India to closer ties with Israel, especially in the military-security arena; and two, to circumvent the ideology-driven opposition which frequently crops up during periodic tension and violence in West Asia, Israel has to focus on and prioritise non-political areas.

Moreover, quarter of a century after normalisation, the two countries do not have a shared worldview, especially vis-à-vis West Asia. Diplomatic relations have not modified or diluted New Delhi's position on some of the key issues of the Arab-Israeli conflict, namely Palestinian statehood, borders, settlements or the Jerusalem question. With the notable exception of the vote in July 2015 in the UN Human Rights Council (UNHRC) over the Gaza crisis of 2014, India's voting pattern in the UN and other multilateral agencies has not changed.[22] As highlighted by the UNESCO vote in April 2016, India continues to support the traditional Arab-Islamic position regarding Jewish religious claims to the old city of Jerusalem. India however abstained during the second vote in October. In early 2017, however, one could notice a subtle change in India's policy and during the visit of President Mahmous Abbas it avoided any direct reference to East Jerusalem being the capital of the future Palestinian state.

More over, one cannot ignore the not too insignificant changes in India's position favourable to Israel. Unlike the pre-1992 phase, India has been urging both parties to the Arab-Israeli conflict to seek a political solution through negotiations and has been opposed to any unilateral moves by either side. It no longer blames Israel for all the problems but has been adopting a more nuanced position towards violence in the region. The bilateral differences are more pronounced over the Iranian nuclear controversy. India did not share the position and strategies of Israel and was opposed to any military solution to the problem. Despite the negative impact upon its relations with the US, India recognised Iran's right to peaceful use of nuclear energy as guaranteed under the Nuclear Non-Proliferation Treaty, which incidentally India did not sign. It further urged Tehran to seek a negotiated settlement in line with the latter's commitments to non-proliferation and undertakings to the International Atomic Energy Agency. Hence, it quickly embraced the P5 + 1 [China, France, Russia, the UK and US, plus Germany] Vienna agreement signed in July 2015.[23]

Above all, there is no ideological convergence between India and Israel. When Atal Bihari Vajpayee was heading the National Democratic Alliance (NDA)-I government (1998–2004), the Left parties depicted the bilateral relations as an ideological convergence between the Bharatiya Janata Party (BJP) in India and Likud in Israel. They also argued that closer ties with Israel had harmed India's relations with Arab and Islamic countries of West Asia and hence demanded a 'course correction' when Manmohan Singh became Prime Minister of the United Progressive Alliance (UPA) government in May 2004.[24] Despite his dependence upon the support of the Left parties, especially during his first term in office (2004–2009), Singh did not alter the basic trajectory of relations with Israel. At the same time, public display of warmth and friendship was absent and high-level visits rare. This posture continued even after Left parties walked out of the UPA in 2008 over the Indo-US nuclear deal. The periodic upsurge of violence between the Israelis and the Palestinians rekindled anti-Israeli sentiments and protests, and there were occasional calls to 'recall' the Indian ambassador from Israel or for the cancellation of defence deals.[25] In other words, differences on foreign policy issues and domestic opposition from a vocal section of the population would preclude the formation of a strategic partnership between the two.

The economic component of the bilateral relations is significant but not overwhelming. The normalisation of relations witnessed a substantial increase in bilateral trade; it grew from under $100 million in 1992 to nearly $5 billion in 2016. The growth trajectory is faster and better than that of many countries with whom India has had formal ties for over half a century. Yet, Israel is not among the top 10 trading partners of India and, because of the energy component, oil-rich countries along the Persian Gulf are its principal trading partners. During 2015–2016, five out of the 15 top trading partners of India were from the Persian Gulf region.[26] If Israel emerges as a possible gas supplier, that might change the situation in the future, but until then, the trade component in itself would be insufficient to make bilateral relations strategic.

The military dimension, though receiving considerable attention inside and outside the country, is unlikely to be the driving force behind bilateral relations. Currently, Israel is a principal arms supplier to India, and the latter the major export market for Israel. There are a number of structural issues that would impede an Indo-Israeli strategic partnership based solely on military-security ties. First, Israel does not produce and hence does not export platforms such as aircraft or large ships. Even though it indigenously produces Markava main battle tanks, security concerns over possible third party transfers would preclude their export to India. While Davar fast patrol boats are vital for naval surveillance, such export items are limited. Platforms are not only costlier but they also lead to long-term partnership in the form of spare parts, maintenance and upgrading. Much of Israeli export inventories are avionics, radar or surveillance systems that are force multipliers but do not generate significant revenues in the same way as large platforms.

Second, some of Israel's principal export inventories are mounted on foreign platforms. For example, the Phalcon AWACS is the outcome of Israeli technology mounted on a Russian Il-76 and a certain degree of trilateral cooperation becomes inevitable. Moreover, a significant portion of Israel's export items have American connections; either they contain American parts or technology or have been funded by the US and hence are subject to a potential US veto. Even when there are no direct connections, the US has been pressuring Israel when geopolitical calculations demanded. For example, the lucrative Chinese market is denied to Israel due to the post-Cold War shifts in Washington's calculations vis-à-vis Beijing.

Third, Israel is facing stiff competition from other major arms exporters such as the US, Russia, France and South Africa, and these countries are eager to meet India's growing demands for advanced weapons. Some of these countries can offer not only favourable financial terms but can partake in the Make in India campaign of indigenisation of production. Israel's ability to compete with them in financial terms, especially long-term payment arrangements, is extremely limited.

Political controversies, lack of ideological convergence, the small size of trade, and limitations on the military-security front seriously prevent Israel from forging a strategic partnership with India in the conventional sense of the term. At the same time, regional isolation, prolonged hostilities, declining interests and influence of the US in West Asia and the weakening of its traditional ties with the West compel Israel to seek an alternative partner if not an ally. This is where India comes into the picture. Israel pursues this approach to India by redefining the traditional understanding of the notion of 'strategic'.

Redefining strategic

The unconventional Israeli approach towards India has three basic and interrelated components, namely recognition of India's federal political structure; India's economic agenda; and the need to develop grassroots support by focusing on non-political issues.

Federal structure

While the establishment of diplomatic relations in 1992 marked a dramatic shift, it did not result in India adopting an overtly pro-Israeli position internationally. During the 1990s, P. V. Narasimha Rao and his successors were circumspect vis-à-vis Israel and each move was carefully calibrated to minimise a possible backlash from the wider West

Asian region. High-level contacts and statements were invariably accompanied by meetings with the Palestinian leadership. In May 1993, India hosted Foreign Minister Shimon Peres but was lukewarm to suggestions of a visit by Prime Minister Yitzhak Rabin. Visits by ministers and officials to Israel were accompanied by similar ones to Gaza City and later on to Ramallah when Yasser Arafat shifted his headquarters following Hamas-led violence in the Gaza Strip. Even the NDA-1 government was an exception; both Home Minister L. K. Advani and External Affairs Minister Jaswant Singh paid a visit to Ramallah while visiting Israel. This 'balancing' was maintained by Manmohan Singh and later on by Modi; both S. M. Krishna (January 2012) and Sushma Swaraj (January 2016) visited Israel and Palestine, and this was the case when President Pranab Mukherjee visited the region in October 2016.

The chilliness in New Delhi resulted in Israel diverting its attention to state governments. Over the years, due to prolonged non-relations, Israel had cultivated various non-Congress leaders and figures such as N. G. Ranga, George Fernandes, M. L. Sondhi and others, and this pattern was more vigorously pursued after 1992. In June 1994, for instance, Bhairon Singh Shekhawat of Rajasthan became the first non-Congress Chief Minister to visit Israel following normalisation. Israel gradually hosted chief ministers belonging to the Congress party (Chimanbhai Patel of Gujarat in 1993, and Digvijay Singh of Madhya Pradesh in 1995), Janata Dal-Secular (Deva Gowda of Karnataka in 1995) and eventually the Marxist Communist Party (Jyoti Basu of West Bengal in 2000).

Economic agenda

While the central government is preoccupied with delicate foreign policy issues, the priorities of the state governments are different; they are concerned with immediate economic issues such as agriculture, farming, water management, health care and other developmental issues. Despite ideological differences at the Centre, for example, communist-ruled West Bengal was soliciting investments from Israel.[27] This approach meant that the state and regional leaders could visit and engage with Israel without making any political statements on the vagaries of the peace process, thus avoding controversies.

As a result, since the early 1990s, a host of chief ministers, their cabinet colleagues and officials belonging to different political parties and states have been visiting Israel. Indeed, former Congress Chief Minister Y. S. Rajasekara Reddy of the unified Andhra Pradesh initiated the offer of financial subsidy to Christian pilgrims visiting Jerusalem and Bethlehem, on par with the subsidy offered to Muslim Hajj pilgrims. This policy has been continued by Andhra Pradesh as well as the newly-formed state of Telangana.[28]

Currently, states ruled by the BJP, Congress and various other political parties including Trinamool Congress, All India Anna Dravida Munnetra Kazhagam (AIADMK), Janata Dal (Secular), Biju Janata Dal, Samajwadi Party, and Akali Dal, among others, are actively engaged with Israel on various issues. There is a general consensus in many states on the opportunities available in Israel and the need to benefit through cooperation. In short, the prime discourse is politics in New Delhi but economics in state capitals.

Grassroots non-political issues

Israel has been cooperating with various state governments on a host of non-political and non-controversial issues such as agriculture, floriculture, horticulture, farming techniques, water management, water harvesting, dairy, rural health, sanitation, and skill development. Since the early 1990s, various state governments and their agencies have entered into memorandums of understanding (MoUs) with a host of Israeli ministries, agencies and companies. The Union government has largely been a facilitator of these endeavours. Interestingly, despite their long presence in India, most other diplomatic missions, including those representing Western countries with greater resources at their command, have not been able to penetrate the Indian states. Even though some Western countries, especially the US and Germany, have been active with larger budgets, Israel has been more successful with more active grass-roots engagement. Israeli missions reach different parts of the country where international politics is not the dominant discourse.

The state-centric focus of the Israeli efforts in India includes the following:

- India has been taking part in agriculture exhibitions in Israel since 2008. Besides ministers and senior officials from the Union Ministry of Agriculture, these attract agriculture ministers from various states as well as hundreds of ordinary farmers who are exposed to modern technologies.[29]
- Beginning in 2012, Israel has established 10 agricultural farms in seven states that showcase Israeli expertise and innovations in agriculture, horticulture and related issues. These farms also act as training centres.[30]
- Israel has established a niche in cultivation in arid and semi-arid areas and these techniques are put to use in the deserts of Rajasthan through the bilateral Action Plan 2012–2015.[31]
- States such as Gujarat, Haryana, Karnataka, Punjab, Rajasthan and Tamil Nadu are cooperating with Israel on water management techniques.[32]
- Negotiations are going on to establish desalination plants in Tamil Nadu.[33]
- Israel has been pursuing efforts to partake in the massive Clean Ganga Mission announced in July 2014.[34] In sheer financial terms, cleaning the Ganges is larger and more attractive for Israel than any lucrative military contract.
- Floriculture techniques are the principal area of cooperation between Israel and the states of Haryana and Himachal Pradesh.[35]
- Some of the major joint ventures and takeovers are happening in agriculture and allied sectors. Jain Irrigation, India's largest private company in the agriculture sector, has bought the Israeli company Naandan and similar ventures exist with Sun Pharma, Triveni Engineers, TCS, etc.[36]

Indeed, since the 1990s, states such as Gujarat, Haryana, Punjab and Rajasthan have been in the forefront of cooperation with Israel irrespective of which political party was in power. An interesting aspect of the non-political dimension of cooperation of state governments with Israel is that it cannot be quantified only in monetary terms. In financial terms, its value is much smaller than a military deal but it has the effect of a force multiplier and contributes to the socio-economic welfare of rural India.

Israel's focus away from New Delhi has partly benefited from another trend. Some of the crucial issues concerning bilateral relations are dominated by ministries which can be defined as professional (Defence) and non-political (Agriculture) as opposed to the Ministry of External Affairs (MEA), which has to 'balance' Israel with other countries of the region. Unlike the MEA, they are less concerned about the Arab-Israeli conflict or the Middle East peace process.

Though not completely free from the influence of the MEA, these ministries have greater leeway in pursuing issues within their domain.

Israel since the mid-1990s has been cognisant of the political challenges facing bilateral relations. Normalisation did not alter some of the basic premises of India's Israel policy. Having recognised the political hurdles in New Delhi, Israel began to invest significantly in state governments by focusing on non-political issues and concerns such as economic growth, development and prosperity. These efforts continued during the decade-long UPA rule when political winds in New Delhi were chilly towards Israel. The arrival of Narendra Modi on the national scene and his development agenda are more conducive for this Israeli focus on economic rather than political issues, and hence greater cooperation with state governments will continue to be the fulcrum of Israel's engagements with India.

Conclusion

Recognising the political hurdles within India for greater expansion of bilateral relations, Israel consciously adopted a policy of moving away from New Delhi and engaging with various state governments. This is a long-term strategy and is likely to significantly transform the anti-Israeli sentiments currently prevalent among sections of the Indian elite and in urban centres. The farmers of rural India are more concerned with higher yields and greater harvest per hectare than the boycott, divestment and sanctions (BDS) movement. A wheat farmer is preoccupied with higher per hectare yield with less water rather than political controversies over Israel. For the farmers in water-deficient regions, drip irrigation technology from Israel is more critical than demands for a cultural boycott. Thus, by bringing in tangible economic gains to rural India, Israel is trying to dent the ideologically driven urban bias. While shunning Israeli movies, cosmetics or artists might be appealing for some, the boycott of drip irrigation technology would be suicidal for the Indian farmer. Therein lies the logic and foundations for Israel's evolving strategic partnership with India.

Acknowledgements

The author wishes to acknowledge two anonymous referees for their critical comments in improving this article.

Disclosure statement

No potential conflict of interest was reported by the author.

Notes

1. Lucyna Czechowska, 'The Concept of Strategic Partnership as an Input in Modern Alliance Theory', *The Copernicus Journal of Political Studies*, 2(4), 2013, pp. 36–51.
2. 'Socialism with Chinese Characteristics', The 17th Congress of the Communist Party of China, September 30, 2007, at http://en.people.cn/90002/92169/92211/6275043.html (Accessed November 30, 2016).
3. Francis Fukuyama, *The End of History and the Last Man*, Simon & Schuster, New York, 1992; Robert Kagan, 'The End of End of History', *New Republic*, April 23, 2008, at https://newrepublic.com/article/60801/the-end-the-end-history (Accessed November 30, 2016); Timothy Stanley and Alexander Lee, 'It's Still Not the End of History', *The Atlantic*,

September 1, 2014, at http://www.theatlantic.com/politics/archive/2014/09/its-still-not-the-end-of-history-francis-fukuyama/379394/ (Accessed November 30, 2016).

4. Barbara Ann Rieffer-Flanagan, 'Islamic Realpolitik: Two-Level Iranian Foreign Policy', *International Journal on World Peace*, 26(4), 2009, pp. 7–35; Daniel Byman, Shahram Chubin, Anoushiravan Ehteshami and Jerrold D. Green, *Iran's Security Policy in the Post-Revolutionary Era*, Santa Monica, Rand Corporation, 2001.

5. Joe Stork and James Paul, 'Arms Sale and the Militarization of the Middle East', *MERIP Reports*, 13(112), January/February 1983, pp. 5–15.

6. Bruce D. Porter, *The USSR in Third World Conflicts: Soviet Arms and Diplomacy in Local Wars 1945–1980*, Cambridge University Press, New York, 1984.

7. Motti Golani, 'The Historical Place of the Czech-Egyptian Arms Deal, Fall 1955', *Middle East Studies*, 31(4), October 1955, pp. 803–827.

8. Andrew Small, *The China-Pakistan Axis: Asia's New Geopolitics*, Hurst Publishers, London, 2015.

9. Abbas William Samii, 'A Stable Structure on Shifting Sands: Assessing the Hizbullah-Iran-Syria Relationship', *Middle East Journal*, 62(1), 2008, pp. 32–53.

10. P.R. Kumaraswamy, *India's Israel Policy*, Columbia University Press, New York, 2010.

11. 'Unesco Passes Contentious Jerusalem Resolution', BBC, October 18, 2016, at http://www.bbc.com/news/world-middle-east-37697108 (Accessed February 25, 2017).

12. Aaron S. Klieman, *Israel's Global Reach: Arms Sales as Diplomacy*, Brassey's, Oxford, 1985.

13. Bernard Reich, 'Israel's Policy in Africa', *Middle East Journal*, 18(1), 1964, pp. 14–26.

14. Uri Bar-Joseph, *The Watchman Fell Asleep*, SUNY Press, New York, 2005.

15. P. Venkateshwar Rao, 'Foreign Involvement in Sri Lanka', *The Round Table*, 78(309), 1989, pp. 88–100.

16. Sasha Polakow-Suransky, *The Unspoken Alliance: Israel's Secret Relationship with Apartheid South Africa*, Pantheon Books, New York, 2011.

17. P.R. Kumaraswamy, 'The Star and the Dragon: An Overview of Israeli-PRC Military Relations', *Issues and Studies* (Taipei), April 1994, pp. 36–55; and P.R. Kumaraswamy, 'The Military Dimension of Israel-China Relations', *China Report*, April–June 1995, pp. 235–249.

18. P.R. Kumaraswamy, 'India's Recognition of Israel, September 1950', *Middle Eastern Studies*, 31(1), 1995, pp. 124–138.

19. Ibid. The current Prime Minister Narendra Modi was incidentally born on this very day.

20. P.R. Kumaraswamy, *India and Israel: Evolving Strategic Partnership*, Mideast Security and Policy Studies No. 40, Begin-Sadat Center for Strategic Studies (BESA Center), Ramat Gan, September 1, 1998; Efraim Inbar and Alvite Singh Ningthoujam, *Indo-Israeli Defense Cooperation in the Twenty-First Century*, Mideast Security and Policy Studies No. 93, BESA Center, Ramat Gan, 2012.

21. Yoram Evron, 'Between Beijing and Washington: Israel's Technology Transfer to China', *Journal of East Asian Studies*, 13(3), 2013, pp. 503–528.

22. Suhasini Haidar, 'India Abstains from UNHRC Vote against Israel', *The Hindu*, July 3, 2015, at http://www.thehindu.com/news/india-abstains-from-unhrc-vote-against-israel/article7383796.ece (Accessed February 25, 2017).

23. Suhasini Haidar, 'India Welcomes Iran Deal, Wary of Implications', *The Hindu*, July 15, 2015, at http://www.thehindu.com/news/national/india-welcomes-iran-deal-wary-of-implications/article7422406.ece (Accessed February 25, 2017).

24. P.R. Kumaraswamy, 'Israel: A Maturing Relationship', in David M. Malone, C. Raja Mohan and Srinath Raghavan (eds.), *The Oxford Handbook of Indian Foreign Policy*, Oxford University Press, New Delhi, 2015, pp. 539–551.

25. 'Left Wants Missile Deal with Israeli Firm Cancelled', *The Times of India*, February 11, 2009, at http://timesofindia.indiatimes.com/india/Left-wants-missile-deal-with-Israeli-firm-cancelled/articleshow/4108163.cms (Accessed February 15, 2017).

26. 'Export-Import Database', Director General of Foreign Trade, Ministry of Commerce and Industry, Government of India.

27. Subodh Ghildiya, 'Jyoti, Somnath Visited Israel', *The Pioneer*, New Delhi edition, June 9, 2004.

28. 'Subsidy for Christians Visiting Jerusalem', *The New Indian Express*, November 25, 2008, at http://www.newindianexpress.com/states/andhra-pradesh/2008/nov/25/subsidy-for-christians-visiting-jerusalem-2295.html (Accessed December 10, 2016).

29. 'India-Israel Relations', Ministry of External Affairs, Government of India, January 2016, at https://www.mea.gov.in/Portal/ForeignRelation/Israel_13_01_2016.pdf (Accessed February 25, 2017).

30. 'Indo-Israel Agriculture Project', Embassy of Israel, New Delhi, at http://embassies.gov.il/delhi/Relations/Indo-Israel-AP/Pages/default.aspx (Accessed February 25, 2017).

31. 'India-Israel Relations', No. 29.

32. Ibid.

33. 'India, Israel Sign MoU on Water Management, Desalination: Govt', *The New Indian Express*, November 24, 2016, at http://www.newindianexpress.com/nation/2016/nov/24/india-israel-sign-mou-on-water-management-desalination-govt-1542226.html (Accessed March 5, 2017).

34. Smriti Kak Ramachandran, 'Israel Offers Help to Clean up Ganga', *The Hindu*, July 19, 2015, at http://www.thehindu.com/news/national/israel-offers-to-help-clean-ganga/article7440855.ece (Accessed March 5, 2017).

35. 'India-Israel Relations', No. 29.

36. Ibid.

India–Israel Defence Engagement: Land Forces' Cooperation

Alok Deb

Military tradition and practice

The Israeli military has been tested through the entire range of conflict from the conventional to the asymmetric since its inception in May 1948 to the present day. In the process, it has become one of the most powerful military forces in West Asia, with a reputation to match. Not many are aware that Indian Jews, notably the Bene Israelis, have served with distinction under Indian chieftains as well as the East India Company a few hundred years ago.[1] This military tradition ensured that despite rapidly dwindling numbers post-independence, some Indian Jews continued to serve the Indian Army and contribute towards its higher military leadership.[2]

Similarly, the sacrifices of Indian soldiers in the battlefields of Palestine in both world wars are immortalised in the cemeteries at Haifa, Jerusalem, Ramleh and Khayat in modern-day Israel.[3] On a visit to that country, one is likely to come across Israeli soldiers of Indian origin, indistinguishable from their comrades in arms. Being cognisant of these historical and contemporary linkages pertaining to military tradition and practice is essential as we trace the trajectory of cooperation between the land forces of India and Israel over the past quarter century.

Diplomatic non-engagement and military cooperation prior to 1992

India's lack of engagement with Israel for over four decades after recognising it has been commented upon extensively and does not warrant repetition. Despite this, research throws up instances of Israel providing military aid to India in all the wars that have been fought after the First Kashmir War of 1947–1948. Israel is reported to have acceded to Prime Minister Jawaharlal Nehru's request for aid in 1962 and supplied mortars for the Indian Army (delivered by ships flying the Israeli flag, overruling Indian requests for anonymity).[4] A similar request during the 1965 War for mortars and ammunition was again accepted by Israel.[5]

Despite a frosty patch during the 1967 Six-Day War when some Indian soldiers of the United Nations Emergency Force were killed in Gaza by Israeli air and artillery strikes, resulting in a resounding condemnation by India,[6] a covert relationship between the Research and Analysis Wing (RAW) and Mossad commenced soon after RAW's inception in 1968.[7] This was followed by Israeli assistance of mortars and ammunition to India during the 1971 War.[8]

Maj. Gen. Alok Deb (Retd) is Deputy Director General, Institute for Defence Studies and Analyses, New Delhi.

As an aside, it would be interesting to conjecture just how much India's decision to establish full diplomatic relations with Israel in 1992 was driven by the Indian need for dependable, alternative arms suppliers following the breakup of the Soviet Union in 1991 and the consequent fragmentation of its arms industry. Be that as it may, establishing formal relations was a long overdue display of realpolitik and paved the way for enhanced military-to-military cooperation between both nations.

Equipment purchases and joint development

While balanced India–Israel military cooperation in the fullest sense is unlikely to fructify (at least in the near term) for well-understood reasons, the commercial aspect of the relationship has begun to boom, with the Indian land forces, like the sister services, becoming major customers of the Israeli defence industry. In terms of relative importance, the foremost contribution of Israel to the Indian Army occurred immediately in the aftermath of the Kargil War, in the domain of surveillance and target acquisition, with the purchase of the Long-Range Reconnaissance and Observation System for the Artillery. These systems, deployed along with hand-held thermal imagers (again mostly of Israeli origin) have added greater teeth to the Army's anti-infiltration measures, proving their worth along the Line of Control and also when deployed along the International Border/Line of Actual Control. During the Kargil War, Israeli supply of laser-guided bombs for modified Indian Air Force Mirages[9] and artillery shells for the Indian Army is well documented.[10]

Heron Unmanned Aerial Vehicles (and Searchers) manufactured by Israel Aerospace Industries (IAI) are now the mainstay of the Indian Army's aerial surveillance operations, with larger numbers being inducted progressively. Despite a number of teething problems pertaining to spares and serviceability issues, these aircraft have proved to be true force multipliers, operating in a multiplicity of terrain and weather conditions along our northern and western borders.[11]

Other branches of the Army are also benefitting through induction of new equipment with state-of-the-art technology. After a long hiatus, the Army Air Defence has received a shot in the arm with the decision to equip five missile regiments with the Barak Medium Range Surface-to-Air Missile systems, to be developed jointly by the Defence Research and Development Organisation (DRDO) and the IAI.[12] The Army's anti-tank capability will enhance manifold once the Spike Anti-Tank Guided Missile (ATGM), produced by Rafael Advanced Defence Systems, begins to be inducted.[13]

Specialised equipment such as Tavor lightweight assault rifles and Galil sniper rifles,[14] inducted a few years earlier, continue to equip some of our forces. Punj Lloyd from India and Israel Weapon Industries (IWI) are to set up a factory in central India to make these weapons.[15] And moving to the other end of the spectrum, the Long-Range Tracking Radar, which forms an integral part of India's efforts at evolving an Anti-Ballistic Missile system, has been developed by the DRDO in collaboration with ELTA Systems Limited of Israel.[16] It may be noted that items mentioned above are in my view just the relatively more important of several ongoing or recently concluded ventures, including those pertaining to supply of new-generation radio sets, specialised ammunition for guns and tanks, up-gunning of artillery pieces and the like.

Military training

That sensitivities towards the Arab cause and its impact on India's domestic politics still remain of consequence can be gauged from the fact that the Indian and Israeli militaries have never carried out institutionalised joint training or exercises, which is the norm with countries with a significant strategic component in their bilateral relationship.

This is despite worldwide acknowledgement (including in India) of the sheer professionalism of the Israeli Army. The 1967 Six-Day War and the 1973 Yom Kippur War have been prescribed campaign studies in Indian Army promotion exams for years, and the Indian military has studied the leadership styles of legendary commanders like Gen. Moshe Dayan.[17] Most noteworthy has been the mastery that the Israeli military has displayed in the prosecution of mechanised warfare, through a combination of innovation, boldness and pro-active decision making, enabling it to emerge victorious at the end of each campaign, invariably against an array of numerically superior enemy forces.

The particular Israeli emphasis on non-traditional military thinking, necessitated by the peculiarities of their unique strategic environment, was brought home in stark fashion to me in a personal interaction with a senior Israeli general during his visit to India recently. After his visit to some of our training institutions, the General in a lighter vein remarked that an Israeli cadet sent to train at an Indian military academy would be sent back to Israel within a few days! So great was the difference in approach he had observed between his military's training methods and those of the Indian Army. Notwithstanding the above, efforts towards learning from each other have commenced since the late 2000s, whereby selected officers have been attending courses at each other's National Defence College every year.

Allied matters

Another important arena where India–Israel cooperation has been gradually increasing is that of combating terrorism and assorted hybrid threats. For different reasons, both countries face similar threats from terrorist groups in their neighbourhoods. The Israeli experience in this regard has been keenly observed by India. Initial overtures were made during the visit of then Home Minister L. K. Advani in June 2000, who was accompanied by senior officers from the Intelligence Bureau, Border Security Force and Central Bureau of Investigation.[18] This was followed by the visit of then External Affairs Minister Jaswant Singh in July 2000. Cooperation between both countries on terrorism-related matters has become institutionalised, more so after 26/11.[19]

The scope of this cooperation has since enhanced, and now encompasses sharing of best practices and as well as crucial intelligence.[20] The website of the Indian Embassy in Tel Aviv lists a large number of agreements relevant to the arena. These include agreements on Cooperation in Homeland and Public Security, Protection of Classified Material, Treaty on Mutual Legal Assistance in Criminal Matters (all of the above in February 2014), Extradition Treaty (January 2012) and Cooperation in Combating Illicit Trafficking and Abuse of Narcotic Drugs and Psychotropic Substances (September 2003).

Ideas and innovation

Apart from the pertinent details of the military dimensions of the India–Israel relationship described above, the most important takeaway for India's military would in the long term, and pertains to the domain of ideas and innovations, of which Israel has proved to be a repository. An example is the Israeli military's Unit 8200, where the best and brightest of Israeli youth (who have been identified through national screening as they near graduation from high school) are posted as soon as they enter military service. These recruits are 'mandated to deploy the latest technology, often in life-or-death situations, with surprisingly little guidance'.[21] Analysts describe it as 'a boot camp of the mind', where small teams 'study, brainstorm, train, analyse, solve problems, from early in the morning to very late at night'. Some of the Unit's alumni have gained national and international recognition.[22] Many of the unit's former soldiers now run some of the most successful start-ups in Israel.

To summarise, the India–Israel military relationship has the potential for developing in a truly multi-dimensional manner. While certain elements might not fructify, it is through exploitation of new ideas and technologies, and development of supporting ecosystems that India's land forces would gain the most, enabling them to harness Israel's vast potential for meeting our national security requirements. It is therefore likely that the trajectory of this relationship will continue to move upwards for some time to come.

Disclosure statement

No potential conflict of interest was reported by the author.

Notes

1. Kaustav Chakrabarti, *Glory in Arms: Bene Israel Soldiers in the Indian Army*, Lambert Academic Publishing, December 1, 2016.
2. Lt.Gen. J.F.R. Jacob from the Artillery, one of the prime architects of the Bangladesh victory, and Lt.Gen. Reuben Mordecai of the Corps of Engineers are two examples.
3. Embassy of India, Tel Aviv, Israel, at https://www.indembassy.co.il/ (Accessed February 15, 2017).
4. Prithvi Ram Mudiam, *India and the Middle East*, British Academic Press, London, 1994, pp. 161–162.
5. Nicolas Blarel, *The Evolution of India's Israel Policy*, Oxford University Press, New Delhi, 2015, p. 158.
6. Ibid., p. 166.
7. Ibid., p. 177.
8. Ibid., p. 186.
9. K.P. Nayar, 'Why India Chose Rafale', *The Telegraph*, February 6, 2012.
10. Suhasini Haider, 'Paradigm Shift after Israel's Aid during Kargil', *The Hindu*, July 21, 2014.
11. Formalities for induction into the Indian Army of the latest batch of Heron UAVs are currently underway in Israel at the time of writing.
12. Rahul Bedi, 'India Approves MR SAM Acquisition', *IHS Jane's Missiles and Rockets*, February 28, 2017.
13. Bharat Shakti, 'India Completes Price Negotiations for Israeli Spike ATGMs', May 27, 2016, at http://bharatshakti.in/india-completes-price-negotiation-for-israeli-spike-atgms/ (Accessed February 15, 2017).
14. Press Information Bureau, 'Import of Defence Products', August 12, 2013.
15. Nayanima Basu, 'Punj Lloyd ties up with Israeli co to manufacture assault rifles in India', May 4, 2017, at http://www.thehindubusinessline.com/companies/punj-lloyd-iwi-to-jointly-manufacture-tavor-galil-assault-rifles-in-india/article9680111.ece (Accessed May 29, 2017).
16. Ajai Shukla, 'An Untold Story: How India Got its Missile Defence', *Business Standard*, January 29, 2008, at http://www.business-standard.com/article/economy-policy/an-untold-story-how-india-got-its-missile-defence-108013001071_1.html (Accessed February 25, 2017).
17. Moshe Dayan, *Story of My Life*, William Morrow and Company, New York, 1976.

18. 'Advani Meets Israeli President', *The Hindu*, June 15, 2000.

19. Ashok Sharma and Dov Bing, 'India Israel Relations: The Evolving Partnership', *Israel Affairs*, 21 (4), 2015, p. 623.

20. This author recently attended a presentation by an Israeli police official on handling terror attacks, at the 17th International Seminar on Counter Terrorism at the NSG Centre in New Delhi in February 2017.

21. Richard Behar, 'Inside Israel's Secret Start-up Machine', *Forbes*, May 31, 2016.

22. Ibid. Unit alumna Kira Radinsky received the Israel Defence Prize, the nation's highest honour for security. She also gained global recognition for her work at Microsoft, where she developed algorithms that identified early warning signs of globally impactful events, such as political riots and epidemics.

India–Israel Defence Engagement: A Naval Perspective

Prakash Gopal

Introduction

P. V. Narasimha Rao took over as the ninth Prime Minister of India on June 21, 1991. Rao, a reluctant prime minister, presided over a period that witnessed the most defining events in modern history, both within India and across the world.[1] He charted an unprecedented course for the Indian economy, bringing the country back from the edge of bankruptcy to a period of sustained economic growth that continues even today.[2] The Soviet flag was lowered forever on Christmas day of 1991, bringing the Cold War to an anti-climactic end.

Over a month later, on January 29, 1992, as Rao prepared to board his flight to New York for the United Nations General Assembly meetings, India's then Foreign Secretary J. N. Dixit announced the government's decision to establish full diplomatic relations with Israel, nearly 44 years after the formation of the Jewish state in 1948.[3] Events over the rest of his term would somewhat eclipse this significant achievement of Prime Minister Rao's government. The decision to establish full diplomatic ties with Israel required astute statecraft, to overcome deep-rooted prejudices and apprehensions within the political establishment in India.

This Essay places in perspective the significant strides in the India–Israel bilateral relations, specifically in the maritime-military domain. In doing so, it will briefly examine significant historical developments in the period from 1948 to 1992, events that occurred in a vastly different geo-political environment, but nevertheless laid the foundation for India–Israel relations to flourish in the current century. The Essay also flags potential areas for greater naval collaboration and cooperation between India and Israel, which could contribute significantly to maritime security in West Asia and the larger Indian Ocean Region.

The covert years (1948–1992)

Few countries have come into being under such similar circumstances as have India and Israel. The British withdrew from India in 1947 and from Palestine in 1948. Both states had to grapple with contentious partitions, and both chose democratic forms of governance that sustain to this day. And yet, relations between India and Israel were characterised by hesitation, especially on the Indian side. A belated and somewhat reluctant Indian recognition of the state of Israel materialised only in September 1950, and that too without a mention of establishing diplomatic missions.[4] It took more than four decades for this to change, a period in which the geo-political landscape of the

Commander Prakash Gopal is Research Fellow, National Maritime Foundation (NMF), New Delhi.

world transformed beyond recognition. Diplomatic relations were finally established when it became evident that its absence was constraining the potential for cooperation on multiple fronts.

The primary factor for India's reticence in recognising and engaging with Israel was its traditional pro-Arab position, consolidated over the previous three decades of the freedom struggle. The Muslim League, which positioned itself as the representative of Indian Muslims, took up the cause of preservation of the Caliphate against European threats. Even after the collapse of the Ottoman Empire, the Muslim League continued to oppose British efforts towards partitioning Palestine, a cause which found resonance across India.[5] The Indian National Congress, keen to find support among Indian Muslims, also supported the Arab cause and opposed the partition of Palestine. The Indian position on this issue was probably driven by both a genuine concern for the Arab people and also by the fact that it entailed opposition to the British Empire. But undoubtedly, the Indian view of West Asia that evolved in this period deeply influenced India's foreign policy long after independence in 1947.

During the Cold War, India's foreign policy outlook was shaped by non-alignment, and an anti-West outlook. Israel's proximity to the US, therefore, did not find favour with the Indian political establishment, and relations between the two countries remained 'cool' at best. Nehru's friendship with the Egyptian leader Gamal Abdel Nasser reinforced the ideological schism between India and Israel.[6] All this, and the fact that India had the largest Muslim minority population in the world, made the prospect of close India–Israel ties highly improbable.

The irony, however, was that even in this state of visible frigidity, India received covert military assistance from Israel during the wars of 1962, 1965 and 1971.[7] Even earlier, in the 1950s, India received technical assistance in agriculture and insights into the working of cooperative mechanisms from Israel. India's Research and Analysis Wing received assistance from Mossad, its Israeli counterpart. India too covertly helped Israel with military equipment during the 'Six-Day War' of 1967.[8] While at that time it served little to thaw the diplomatic iciness, operational exchanges beneath the surface, especially between the defence establishments on both sides, set the tone for bilateral engagement in the years to come.

Establishment of full diplomatic relations between India and Israel was undoubtedly more a question of time and not one of possibility. The interplay of a number of factors finally brought it about in January 1992. The end of the Cold War and the beginning of the unipolar world was probably the most important factor that encouraged India to reorient its foreign policy outlook towards West Asia.[9] The erstwhile Soviet Union had thus far demonstrated its capacity and will to provide military equipment on favourable terms to India. Russia's ability to sustain that cooperation was doubtful at the very least, and it became important for India to seek alternate sources of advanced weaponry.

In the face of repeated resolutions passed by the Organisation of Islamic Countries against India's Kashmir position, India found support on the issue from Israel.[10] The Middle East peace process had also softened the position held by Muslim countries, allowing India the space for overt diplomatic engagement with Israel.[11] It was a combination of all these influences, together with the inevitability of developing closer ties with the US, that led to the otherwise unremarkable press conference where Dixit announced the establishment of diplomatic ties between India and Israel.

The naval dimension of India–Israel relations

While India–Israel relations have flourished since 1992 on multiple fronts, the defence technology aspect has undoubtedly dominated the bilateral engagement over the last 25 years. This was primarily driven by the demonstrated capability of Israeli weapons systems in multiple conflicts, which won the admiration of the Indian military establishment. Moreover, as India sought greater self-reliance in defence equipment, it had the competent Israeli military-industrial complex as a model to emulate. Defence ties were quick to take off as both countries signed the first deal in December 1992 for the supply of Searcher and Ranger Unmanned Aerial Vehicles (UAVs) to the Indian Air Force (IAF).[12]

There was also a willingness on the part of Israel to transfer technology, as also the capacity to upgrade old Soviet equipment that India had in ample quantities. The significant potential that this aspect offered was evident as early as 1993, when two Israel-based companies, Elbit systems and Israel Aerospace Industries (IAI), bid for the contract to upgrade IAF's ageing MiG-21 fighter aircraft.[13] While the contract was finally awarded to a Russian firm, it showcased the willingness of Israel's military-industrial complex to supply to, and collaborate with, the Indian Armed Forces.

On the naval front, a deal was signed in 1996 for the supply of two Super Dvora Mk-2 fast patrol boats from the IAI.[14] The willingness of Israel to transfer technology was also demonstrated by the award of licences by the IAI for India to manufacture these boats in Goa Shipyard. While two of these boats were purchased from the IAI, an additional six were manufactured in India in subsequent years. The Indian Navy (IN) also went on to acquire advanced electronic equipment for use onboard ships and aircraft from Israeli firms such as Elta (a subsidiary of the IAI) and Tadiran.

The 1999 Kargil War and its aftermath reinforced the reputation of Israel as a reliable defence technology partner, as it provided critical equipment to all three Services. While a forward posture by the IN deterred any Pakistani naval operation, one of the most critical vulnerabilities of India's maritime forces was in the defence against US-supplied Harpoon missiles that the Pakistan Navy had in its inventory. This shortcoming was made good in 2001 with the signing of the contract with the IAI and Rafael for the supply of nine Barak-I Anti-Missile Defence (AMD) systems.

At $270 million, it was the largest single defence deal between India and Israel until then. But more importantly, it equipped the IN with an unparalleled, state-of-the-art weapon system, which opened more avenues for cooperation and collaboration in future years.[15] The opportunity that the Kargil War and its aftermath presented were effectively utilised by Israel to demonstrate its commitment and capacity to deliver on its promises. This period was therefore important for removing or diluting potential obstacles to greater political, economic and military ties between India and Israel.

The years since have seen the induction of a significant number of assets with Israeli origins in the IN. A fairly long list of these include the entire Indian naval UAV fleet, Electronic Warfare suites for surface and aerial platforms, avionics systems, radars to be installed on aerostats for coastal security, ship-borne and airborne surveillance radars, communication equipment and weapons for the naval special forces—the Marine Commandos.[16]

In March 2010, the two countries signed a major deal involving the Defence Research and Development Organisation (DRDO) of India and the IAI to jointly develop the Long-Range Surface to Air Missile (LRSAM) system for the IN. Similar systems were also to be developed for the Army and the IAF.[17] Besides the fact that the deal was worth a whopping $1.4 billion, it was also an unprecedented opportunity for the Indian defence industry to be exposed to design, manufacturing and testing of high-end weapon systems. The collaborative effort attained fruition on December 29 and 30, 2015, when Indian Naval Ship (INS) Kolkata successfully fired the LRSAM missiles into the Arabian Sea.[18]

While the Indian military establishment had long desired an active engagement with its Israeli counterpart in the years preceding 1992, the same did not materialise due to political constraints. In fact, it took five years after the establishment of diplomatic relations, for India to send its first Military Attaché to its Embassy in Tel Aviv.[19] Since then, however, it has been a highly visible relationship that appears to be unfettered by political factors that still exist in some measure. For instance, in economic and social terms, India's engagement with the Arab countries and Iran is very significant. This has brought to bear diplomatic exertions on India to restrain its ties with Israel.[20]

However, in the defence domain, especially with the navy, the bilateral exchange has deepened significantly over the years. This is also evident in the large number of high-level visits from both sides, with the Israeli Commander-in-Chief of Navy visiting India as recently as August 2015.[21] Indian naval ships have regularly been making port calls in Israel, with the latest being the visit of INS Trikand to Haifa in August 2015.[22] With renewed diplomatic effort in the larger West Asia region, it is likely that defence, especially naval relations with Israel, will increase in the coming years.

There are many reasons for the military-strategic component dominating the bilateral relations between India and Israel. The Indian military establishment has long exposed its officers to the successful military campaigns of Israel since 1948. Most Indian soldiers, sailors and airmen have held Israeli military tactics, equipment and doctrines in awe. Since the break-up of the Soviet Union, Israel has also demonstrated its capability and intent as a reliable weapon and technology supplier, leading also to the much-needed diversification in the sources of Indian military equipment.[23] In addition, in recent years, the scourge of Islamist terrorism has affected both countries. As both India and Israel try to mitigate the threats posed by fundamentalist groups, this could also possibly be an aspect of cooperation between both countries, especially in the naval domain.

Potential areas for Indo-Israeli naval cooperation

While the military equipment and technology facet of naval relations with Israel progresses satisfactorily, there is significant potential for collaboration in the operational realm that remains yet untapped. While it is true that Israel's immediate area of maritime interest is generally restricted to the Mediterranean Sea, the Indian Ocean promises to play an increasing role in Israel's maritime security concerns. With greater economic integration between the Indian and Pacific Ocean littorals, a number of Sea Lines of Communication (SLOCs) in the Indian Ocean would be of interest to both Israel and India.

There is also the increasing threat of maritime terrorism, proliferation of arms and weapons of mass destruction and human trafficking in the Indian Ocean, Gulf of Aden and Red Sea regions. This would again be of immediate concern to both India and Israel. So while it may be easy to believe that Israel's primary area of maritime interest lies west of where India's area of maritime interest ends, the body of water between the Indian subcontinent and West Asia will play a progressively important role in the maritime security of both India and Israel. It would therefore become increasingly important for both India and Israel to expand the scope of their naval cooperation in this maritime space.

Maritime Domain Awareness (MDA) is critical to combating traditional and non-traditional maritime threats. It also offers significant scope for calibrated cooperation between countries. This could play an important role, especially in cooperation with Israel, as it could allow the bilateral arrangements to reflect India's larger political and diplomatic considerations. For instance, a beginning could be made with an agreement for exchanging 'white-shipping' information, akin to the agreements India has signed with countries such as Australia, Singapore, the US and France, among others.[24]

Since 'white-shipping' or non-military shipping information is generally benign, it is unlikely to raise diplomatic red flags for India, especially from other regional states. This could subsequently be scaled up for sharing 'non-white-shipping' information and intelligence exchange, when the situation so demands and permits. A shared maritime picture could also be useful for humanitarian and law enforcement operations such as Search and Rescue (SAR) and anti-piracy operations. The considerable assets and experience that India has in these maritime domains could add significant value to the Israeli Navy's operational capabilities.

Another area where India could augment the Israeli Navy's operational prowess is in logistic support. With a fleet that consists predominantly of 'brown-water' assets, the Israeli Navy is somewhat constrained in its ability to sustain operations at long distance from its bases. The IN, on the other hand, has been maintaining a permanent presence off the Horn of Africa for anti-piracy operations. The IN could allow Israeli naval vessels access to logistics supplies, both at sea and ashore. India's experience in providing and availing of such facilities with other countries and the specific mutual logistic support agreement signed with the US could facilitate such an arrangement with Israel. While enabling Israeli naval units to operate more frequently in the Indian Ocean Region, this would also allow for greater navy-to-navy exchanges and promote interoperability among the two maritime forces.

Since the 26/11 terrorist attacks on Mumbai, in which Israeli citizens were also killed, the IN has committed significant resources and time to mitigate threats to coastal security.[25] Together with the Indian Coast Guard (ICG), and other stakeholders, the IN has undertaken a large-scale revamp of its surveillance and monitoring wherewithal, as well as the national coastal security doctrine. India and Israel could actively collaborate in this domain, as both navies face similar seaborne threats of the non-traditional kind. A periodic bilateral exchange, focused on best practices for coastal security, could yield significant benefits to both sides. This could be initiated at a working-level exchange to begin with, and with increasing understanding could move on to bilateral coastal security exercises. The ICG could also find suitable representation in such an exchange.

While India and Israel have witnessed high-level naval exchanges and visits, much more may now be necessary at the operational level, to graduate from a supplier–buyer relationship, to one with greater functional synergy. Despite 25 years of diplomatic engagement, and shared military-strategic interests, joint exercises between the two countries are yet to take off.[26] Due to some relatively benign roles, navies are arguably the best armed forces the world over to 'test the waters', so as to say, with their counterparts in other countries, especially when there may political and diplomatic inhibitions.

Thus far, the shared operational exposure for Indian and Israeli navies has been limited to basic exercises of opportunity, when Indian naval ships make port calls in Israel. This may now be escalated to structured exercises, focusing initially on non-contentious issues such as SAR, Humanitarian Assistance and Disaster Relief (HADR), Non-combatant Evacuation Operations (NEO) and SLOC protection. With time, as has been the experience of the IN with other partners, the scale and complexity of bilateral exercises may be progressively enhanced. Augmenting the operational relationship between the two navies is especially important in the current context, when uncertainty looms on the future role of the US in the region. It is therefore vital for a start to be made.

Conclusion

It is evident that the bilateral relationship between these countries in entering an exciting new phase, 25 years after India and Israel established diplomatic ties. This is evident in the flurry of political, diplomatic and military engagement activities between the two countries in recent months. While the span of engagement includes agriculture, commerce, science and technology, space and trade, defence technology has undoubtedly been the mainstay of Indo-Israeli ties.

Recent years have also seen the shedding of political apprehension, especially on India's part, with the realisation that improving ties with Israel is not a zero-sum proposition *vis-à-vis* India's relationship with regional countries. While President Reuven Rivlin of Israel visited India in November 2016, Prime Minister Modi will create history by being the first Indian Prime Minister to visit Israel in July 2017, since the establishment of diplomatic ties between the two countries.[27] The political atmosphere in both countries seems ripe to take this bilateral relationship to a new level.

Israel has proven to be a dependable supplier of state-of-the-art weapons and technology to India over the last two decades. In 2015 and 2016, Israel supplied $874 million worth of defence equipment to India, second only to Russia.[28] Besides the advantage of greater diversity of sources, what has stood out is the willingness of Israel to share technology and its keenness for joint development. On the naval front, this has been highlighted firstly by the capabilities of the Barak-1 AMD system procured in the wake of the Kargil War, and secondly by the recent fruition of the LRSAM project jointly developed by the DRDO and IAI.

In the context of India–Israel bilateral relations, analysts draw attention to the distinction between 'common perceptions of interest' versus 'perception of common interest', and note that focus on the former, rather than the latter, will likely push closer ties between two countries.[29] With the right political environment in both countries and a realisation that India and Israel can develop stronger relations independent of other considerations, the time is ripe for seeking greater operational synergy, especially in the maritime domain.

With a number of shared security interests in the Indian Ocean Region, Indian and Israeli maritime forces have significant potential for evolving a larger functional relationship. This could initially encompass relatively benign aspects such as MDA, intelligence sharing, SAR, HADR, NEO and SLOC protection, and graduate to those with greater complexity and scope. Both the navies have a lot to benefit from such an engagement that not only promises to add value to their individual capacities, but will also promote maritime security in this vital part of the world.

Disclosure statement

No potential conflict of interest was reported by the author.

Notes

1. See Vinay Sitapati, *Half-Lion: How PV Narasimha Rao Transformed India*, Penguin Books, Delhi, 2016, pp. 70–82.
2. Ibid., p. 174.

3. P.R. Kumaraswamy, *India's Israel Policy*, Columbia University Press, New York, 2010, p. 238.
4. Ibid., p. 114.
5. Harsh V. Pant, 'India-Israel Partnership: Convergence and Constraints', *Middle East Review of International Affairs*, 8(4), 2004, p. 1.
6. P.R. Kumaraswamy, No. 3, p. 171.
7. Joshua Falk, 'India's Israel Policy: The Merits of a Pragmatic Approach', *Stanford Journal of International Relations*, 10(2), 2009, p. 3.
8. Prithvi Ram Mudiam, 'Indian Power Projection in Greater Middle East', in M. Parvizi Amineh (ed.), *Global Politics*, Koninklijke Brill NV, Leiden, 2007, p. 420.
9. Harsh V. Pant, No. 5, p. 2.
10. Rajendra Abhyankar, 'The Evolution and Future of India-Israel Relation', Research Paper No. 6, S. Daniel Abraham Center for International and Regional Studies, Tel Aviv University, 2012, p. 14.
11. Avielle Kandel, 'The Significant Warming of Indo-Israeli Relations in the Post-Cold War Period', *Middle East Review of International Affairs*, 13 (4), 2009, p. 1.
12. Nicolas Blarel, *The Evolution of India's Israel Policy: Continuity, Change, and Compromise since 1922*, Oxford University Press, New Delhi, 2015, p. 281.
13. 'The Indian Defence Industry Looks Abroad', *Whitehall Papers*, 31 (1), 1995, p. 51.
14. Efraim Inbar and Alvite Singh Ningthoujam, 'Indo-Israeli Defense Cooperation in the Twenty-First Century', Begin-Sadat Center for Strategic Studies, Ramat Gan, 2012, p. 4.
15. Nicolas Blarel, No. 12, p. 300.
16. Ibid., pp. 324–325.
17. These systems for the Army and the IAF were called Medium Range Surface to Air Missiles (MRSAM) systems. These have also been referred to in various documents as the 'Barak 8' or 'Barak NG' missile systems.
18. Dinaker Peri, 'Navy Successfully Launches Long-Range Air Defence Missile Barak-NG', *The Hindu*, December 30, 2015.
19. Interestingly, the first Indian Military Attaché to the Indian Embassy in Tel Aviv was the then Group Captain N.A.K. Browne, who served from 1997 to 2000. The next time he visited Israel was as the Chief of Air Staff, IAF, and Chairman, Chiefs of Staff Committee, in January 2013. See 'Chief of the Indian Air Staff Visits Israel', Embassy of India, Tel Aviv, Israel, at https://www.indembassy.co.il/events.php?event_id=5 (Accessed February 14, 2017).
20. Nicolas Blarel, No. 12, p. 314.
21. 'Commander-in-Chief of Israeli Navy Calls-on Chief of the Naval Staff at New Delhi', Press Release, Indian Navy, at https://www.indiannavy.nic.in/content/commander-chief-israeli-navy-calls-chief-naval-staff-new-delhi (Accessed February 14, 2017).
22. 'INS Trikand Enters Haifa, Israel', Ministry of Defence, Government of India, at http://pib.nic.in/newsite/PrintRelease.aspx?relid=126175 (Accessed February 17, 2017).
23. Avielle Kandel, No. 11, p. 2.
24. Dipanjan Roy Chaudhury, 'India, France Sign Pact on Maritime Information Sharing in Indian Ocean Region', *The Economic Times*, January 24, 2017.
25. The terrorists involved in the 26/11 attacks attacked the Chabad House, a Jewish cultural centre in Mumbai. Six Israelis lost their lives in the attack. For an analysis, See S. Samuel C Rajiv, '26/11, the "Israeli Way" and Relevance for India', November 26, 2009, at http://www.idsa.in/idsacomments/26-11TheIsraeliWayandRelevanceforIndia_sscrajiv_261109 (Accessed February 10, 2017).
26. Rahul Datta, 'India, Israel to Lift Defence Ties Veil', *The Pioneer*, October 7, 2015.
27. Kalol Bhattacharjee, 'Israel President to Tour India', *The Hindu*, December 2, 2016. See also Editorial, 'Modi in Israel?', *The Times of India*, March 6, 2017.
28. Arms Transfer Database, Stockholm International Peace Research Institute (SIPRI), at http://armstrade.sipri.org/armstrade/page/values.php (Accessed February 18, 2017).
29. See Martin Sherman, 'Indo-Israeli Strategic Cooperation as a US National Interest', Policy Paper No. 89, Ariel Center for Policy Research, at http://www.acpr.org.il/pp/pp089-shermane.pdf (Accessed February 14, 2017).

India–Israel Defence Trade: Issues and Challenges

Amit Cowshish

Abstract: To achieve strategically critical self-reliance in defence production, there needs to be a greater focus on co-development, co-production projects with important partners like Israel, with an essential emphasis on exports to third countries. For the full realisation of the potential of the India–Israel defence partnership, India on its part needs to strengthen elements of its procurement processes—including the proper implementation of laid down policies. Further, it needs to put forward a procurement 'policy' as distinct from a procurement 'procedure', ensure greater clarity and transparency about the future procurement needs of the armed forces and align defence plans with realistic assessments of the financial resources likely to be made available for executing those plans.

Introduction

The visit of Prime Minister Narendra Modi to Israel in July 2017, the first ever by an Indian head of government, is a befitting gesture to celebrate 25 years of diplomatic relations between the two countries. A process that started on a cautious note, and against some heavy odds, comes of age with this visit, signifying two things. First, this could possibly herald an era of greater 'openness' in political interactions between the two sides. Second, the visit sends the message that now, perhaps more than ever before, India is keen on a closer engagement with Israel, de-hyphenating it from its relations with Palestine. The prime minister's visit caps a string of other high-level visits since mid-2014 when the present National Democratic Alliance (NDA)-led government came to power.

While India–Israel defence ties have not been affected by the vagaries of the Israel-Palestine conflict, during 2014–2015, just one defence contract worth Rs 875.49 crore[1] was signed with an Israeli firm. During the same period, the total Foreign Direct Investment (FDI) was less than Rs 62 crore, whereas during the preceding financial year, it was approximately Rs 128 crore.[2] It is pertinent to note that the time period corresponded with the July–August 2014 Israeli military intervention in the Gaza Strip. These indicators may be tenuous but cannot be shrugged off.

There is no point in second guessing Prime Minister Modi's agenda during his July 2017 visit to Israel. It would, however, be surprising if it encompasses anything substantially different from the grounds covered by President Pranab Mukherjee in October 2015 and other cabinet ministers during their visits to Israel since the NDA came to power. Needless to say, cooperation on matters related to defence and security would figure prominently in the talks as these areas have tremendous potential for

Amit Cowshish is Distinguished Fellow, Institute for Defence Studies and Analyses (IDSA), New Delhi.

sustained and mutually beneficial cooperation. More specifically, India could be looking for acquisition of technology and high-tech military equipment from Israel, which has done exceedingly well in this field.

The article examines pertinent aspects of defence trade between India and Israel and the nature of the equipment bought so far. While highlighting the Trend Indicator Value (TIV) of defence exports from Israel, the article argues that the future of defence cooperation and trade between India and Israel, as indeed between India and other countries, lies in projects relating to co-development and co-production of defence equipment in India. This would ensure strategically critical self-reliance in defence production. Such an approach further fits into the 'Make in India' policy of the Modi government. For the full realisation of the potential of the India–Israel defence partnership, India needs to strengthen elements of its procurement processes—including the proper implementation of laid down policies. Further, the article argues that India needs to put forward a procurement 'policy' as distinct from a procurement 'procedure', ensure greater clarity and transparency about the future procurement needs of the armed forces and align defence plans with realistic assessments of the financial resources likely to be made available for executing those plans.

Defence trade between India and Israel

It was not just in 1999 that Israel provided much needed ammunition for 155 mm guns to India during the Kargil conflict with Pakistan. Even before diplomatic relations were established in 1992, India is believed to have received 'less publicly acknowledged' help from Israel during earlier wars with Pakistan in 1965 and 1971.[3] In 1997, President Ezer Weizman, who was the first Israeli head of state to visit India, sealed a deal for supply of Barak-I vertically launched Surface-to-Air Missiles (SAMs) to India. These missiles can intercept anti-ship missiles, and India needed them badly to counter the threat posed by Lockheed P-3 Orion maritime surveillance aircraft and Harpoon sea-skimming anti-ship missiles Pakistan had acquired from the US. In 1998, Israel was one of the few countries, apart from notably Russia and France, which did not join the international chorus in condemning India for the Pokharan II nuclear tests.[4]

This is just a small glimpse of the early history of defence cooperation between India and Israel during the period when the latter 'did not really figure on India's list of defence suppliers'.[5] Since then, there has been a steady increase in supply of military equipment and other hardware. Between 2002 and 2005, India had concluded contracts with Israel worth $2.76 billion, according to the information provided by the then Defence Minister Pranab Mukherjee to the Indian parliament in August 2005.[6] These included three Phalcon Airborne Warning and Control Systems (AWACS), fitted with Israel Aircraft Industry (IAI) radars mounted on Russian IL-76 aircraft in 2003 at a cost of $1 billion. Given that the two countries had established diplomatic relations just a decade earlier, this was a significant deal indeed.

The collaboration between India and Israel is not limited to aerospace and defence, and within that sector, to procurement of military equipment. The mutual engagement extends to areas such as intelligence, science and technology, tourism, agriculture and other forms of trade. However, aerospace and defence have emerged as an extremely important segment of the mutual engagement, with India procuring a wide variety of equipment from Israel since the turn of the century.

Table 1.   Contracts signed between 2013–2014 and 2015–2016. Rs in crore.

Country	2013–2014		2014–2015		2015–2016	
Russia	2	1,341.72	7	6,084.72	3	947.19
Israel	5	3,751.00	1	875.49	4	2,979.26
US	7	6,787.02	2	57.64	4	22,049.97
France	2	298.96	3	1,537.05	0	0.00
Others	6	1,072.15	5	2,706.82	6	3,195.33
Total	**21**	**13,250.85**	**18**	**11,261.72**	**17**	**29,171.75**
Indian Vendors	21	10,676.36	29	53,597.80	44	18,705.54
Grand Total	**42**	**23,927.21**	**47**	**64,859.52**	**61**	**47,877.29**

The list includes various types of missiles, aerostat balloons, Unmanned Aerial Vehicles (UAVs), assault rifles, electronic suites and avionics, Thermal Imaging Stand Alone Systems (TISAS), fast attack craft fitted with modern surveillance systems, Long Range Observation Systems (LOROS), Hand Held Thermal Imaging Systems (HHTI), hi-tech sensors, Portable Laser Designating Systems (PLDS) and Thermal Imaging Fire Control Systems (TIFCS). Israeli companies have also been engaged in upgrades and other developmental projects with India's Defence Research and Development Organisation (DRDO).[7]

Given the range of defence equipment being procured from Israel, it is no wonder that the latter has emerged as one of the top three suppliers of arms to India. According to the data furnished by the Indian Ministry of Defence (MoD) to the Standing Committee on Defence (SCoD), in terms of the number of contracts signed, Israel was ahead of Russia both in 2013–2014 and 2015–2016 (see Table 1).[8]

The figures for 2016–2017 are presently not available, but it will be surprising if Israel does not figure among the top five, if not the top three, suppliers of arms to India. With the Government of India clearing—some would say as a prelude to Prime Minister Modi's visit to Israel in July 2017—the multi-billion-dollar contract for procurement of SAMs for the Indian Army in April 2017, Israel could consolidate its position further in the current fiscal year (2017–2018), especially if the much-talked about deal for Spike Anti-Tank Guided Missiles (ATGMs) also goes through. Considering the likelihood of repeat orders for missiles and several other co-development projects that are on the discussion table, Israel has the potential of emerging as a formidable player in India's defence market which is expected to be worth $150–250 billion over the next 10–15 years.

Potential areas for trade and cooperation

Data from the Stockholm International Peace Research Institute (SIPRI) shows that defence exports from Israel are related to aircraft, air defence systems, armoured vehicles, artillery, missiles, naval weapons, sensors, ships and other defence products and technologies. As Table 2 shows, Israel has done very well in respect of exports related to aircraft, air defence systems, missiles and sensors.[9] These are the potential areas for greater collaboration in future, but India could also tap into Israeli expertise in some other areas, such as naval weapons, where indigenous production requires an immediate leg up to bring India closer to self-sufficiency in shipbuilding.

Table 2. Trend indicator value (TIV) of arms exports from Israel, 2010–2016.

Category	2010	2011	2012	2013	2014	2015	2016	Total
Aircraft	156	27	69	104	30	76	71	533
Air defence systems		16	16			70	362	464
Armoured vehicles	60	22	9	10	22	27	16	166
Artillery	13	2		5	3	5	2	29
Missiles	140	123	116	115	99	151	408	1151
Naval weapons	20	21	20		15	15	15	106
Other	19	6	6	5	9	8	6	58
Sensors	248	270	215	180	205	247	297	1661
Ships		87		12	16	95	84	293
Total	**655**	**572**	**449**	**432**	**399**	**694**	**1260**	**4461**

Note: Figures are expressed in US$ in million at constant (1990) prices.

The current engagement between India and Israel is in the field of co-development and co-production as well as outright procurement of equipment. While outright purchase of equipment, as well as licensed manufacturing, may continue for some time, it is more than evident that the future of defence cooperation and trade between the two countries, as indeed between India and other countries, lies in projects relating to co-development and co-production of defence equipment in India. This fits into the 'Make in India' policy of the Modi government, apart from helping India reduce its embarrassing dependence on imports of defence equipment. According to the SIPRI figures, between 2010 and 2014, India topped the list of importers of arms, accounting for 15 per cent of total global trade. During the same period, its exports totalled up to a paltry $57 million,[10] which does not account for even two per cent of global exports. On the other hand, Israel, accounting for just two per cent of the global exports, was the 10th largest exporter of arms.

One of the objectives of the 'Make in India' policy of the government is to boost exports. This objective cannot be met in the defence sector unless this is tied up with co-development and co-production of equipment in India in collaboration with the foreign companies which have had a longer history of investment in defence research and development (R&D), and consequently, enjoy an edge over the Indian domestic industry. This is where Israel fits into the scheme of things very well. Development of the medium-range Barak SAM interceptor, which goes by the nomenclature of Long Range SAM (LRSAM) for the Indian Navy and Medium Range SAM (MRSAM) for the other two services, is a fine example of what can be achieved through a co-development, co-production project. The design of this interceptor missile is the result of the joint efforts by Israel's Rafael Advanced Defence Systems, India's DRDO and several local manufacturers, including Larsen & Toubro (L&T) and Tata Power Strategic Engineering Division (Tata SED). The missile system will be integrated by the state-owned Bharat Dynamics Limited (BDL), while the radar will probably be supplied by Israel's Elta Systems. It is this kind of synergy which is much more rewarding than a seller-buyer relationship, which India is becoming increasingly weary of.

What is holding up further progression?

There is recognition in India—perhaps now more than ever before—that the domestic defence industrial base will have to be strengthened to achieve strategically critical self-reliance in defence production. Not that the domestic industry is not capable of meeting this challenge on its own, but India cannot afford the luxury of waiting for long periods for equipment to be designed and developed by the Indian industry from scratch. Even commercially, it does not make sense to reinvent the wheel, as it were. Indian industry can make rapid strides in acquiring the capability in defence manu-facturing by tying up with the foreign companies willing to transfer already developed technologies. Arguably, the foreign companies are also willing to do that, except when it comes to transfer of state-of-the-art technologies, which is understandable. In the given circumstances, transfer of matured technologies should also be of immense help. What then is the reason why very few co-development, co-production projects have materialised on ground?

The fundamental problem seems to be the absence of a well-articulated defence procurement policy. The churning in the defence establishment following the traumatic Kargil conflict of 1999 resulted in many new initiatives being undertaken by the government which included creation of a fragmented procurement structure in 2001 and promulgation of a Defence Procurement Procedure (DPP) in 2002. But in the absence of an overarching procurement policy—distinct from the procurement procedure—these initiatives have not had the desired result. One of the consequences of this is the ambiguity that surrounds what could be described as 'Make in India' projects. It is never very clear to foreign companies as to what it is it that India wants them to do under this policy and how. It is not clear to them, as well as to Indian industry, as to what the MoD wants to buy off-the-shelf, and what it is it that it wants to be manufactured in India through indigenous design and development by the Indian industry or through transfer of technology from foreign companies.

The dilemma that foreign companies probably face is whether to make *suo moto* offers for outright sale of, or transfer of technology for manufacturing, defence equipment in India or to wait for the Request for Information (RFI) to be issued by the MoD. All defence plans, starting from the 15-year Long Term Integrated Perspective Plan (LTIPP), down to the five-year plans (including the corresponding Services Capital Acquisition Plan [SCAP]) and the Annual Acquisition Plans (AAPs), are classified. Consequently, there is an element of suspense surrounding the timing of RFIs for various procurement programmes. All that the companies can do is to wait for the RFI to be issued or to make *suo moto* offers. Marketing of products is a legitimate business activity but in the Indian context it could be risky as this could be seen as an effort at lobbying with, or influencing decision making in, MoD. Absence of an institutional mechanism for interaction with MoD and the impervious-ness of ministry officials have added to the problem not only for foreign companies but also for Indian industry.

The 'Make in India' call given by Prime Minister Modi from the ramparts of the historic Red Fort in Delhi on August 15, 2014, was well intended but it seems to have created some confusion in the context of defence production. It is not clear whether this is a call to foreign companies to come to India to make defence equipment, or a call to Indian private sector companies to take the lead, or a mix of both? Notwithstanding the fact that a number of big-ticket contracts have been bagged by foreign companies in the last two years, the general perception that has emerged in the last two years is that 'Make in India' is primarily focused on the Indian private sector industry. The foreign companies, therefore, seem to be veer-ing around to the view that they must tie up with Indian industry as a prelude to participating in future procurement programmes. What, however, seems to be obstructing such tie-ups is the uncertainty surrounding the 'strategic partnership model'.

It may be recalled that the MoD had set up a Committee of Experts in 2015 to help it evolve a policy framework for 'Make in India' and to make concomitant changes in the procurement procedure to align it with the underlying objectives of 'Make in India'. One of the recommendations of the committee related to adoption of a 'strategic partnership model' for creating additional capacities in the private sector in major segments of defence production. Conceptually, this model entails selection of 'Strategic Partners' (SP) by the MoD, who could then be nominated as the Indian Production Agency (PA) in procurement programmes that entail transfer of technology from the foreign vendor. The primary focus of the partners 'would be to support sustainability and the incremental improvements in capability of platforms through technology insertions over their life-times'. To facilitate this process, the MoD would enter into long-term covenants with them spanning not just the first contract (after determination of the segment and SP) but also the ones to follow, so that resources are utilised optimally over long periods of time.[11]

The segments recommended by the committee were: (i) Aircraft, including fighter and transport aircraft, helicopters and their major systems; (ii) Warships of stated displace-ments and submarines and their major systems; (iii) Armoured Fighting Vehicles and their major systems/weapons; (iv) Complex weapons which rely on guidance systems, to achieve precision hits, which may include anti-ship, air defence, air to air, air-to-surface, anti-submarine, land attack; (v) Command, Control, Communication and Computers, Intelligence, Surveillance, Target acquisition and Reconnaissance (C4ISTR); and (vi) Critical materials (Titanium alloys, Aluminium alloys, Carbon composites, Nickel/Cobalt alloys, etc.).[12] This pretty much encompasses the entire range of defence production.

As can be seen from the brief description of the model given above, it has far-reaching implications. At one stage, the MoD seemed very eager to adopt it, going to the extent of reserving a chapter on 'Strategic Partners and Partnerships' in DPP 2016 with the promise to notify the contents of the chapter separately. Almost a year down the line, the scheme is yet to be notified. This endless wait has taken its toll in two ways. One, it has prevented the MoD from nominating private sector entities as PAs in procurement programmes involving transfer of technology; and two, it has come in the way of tie-ups between foreign and Indian companies as the former would obviously prefer to enter into partnerships with the SPs who would be assured of long-term relationships with the MoD under the 'strategic partnership model'.

While the MoD takes its time in deciding on the 'strategic partnership model', it is business as usual in so far as defence procurement is concerned. The DPP 2016,[13] which regulates capital procurements, requires preference to be given to procurement from Indian sources. Each procurement programme has to be placed under one of the categories mentioned in the DPP, which are arranged in hierarchical order of descend-ing preference. This implies that a procurement programme can be placed in one of the categories lower down in the hierarchy only if it can be demonstrated while seeking approval-in-principle to commence the procurement process that it is not feasible to place it under any other category that ranks higher in the hierarchy.

The hierarchy consists of the following categories:

– Buy (Indian—Indian Designed, Developed and Manufactured[IDDM])
– Buy (Indian)
– Buy and Make (Indian)
– Buy and Make
– Buy (Global)

Apart from these five categories, there is another category of 'Make' projects which involves indigenous design, development and manufacture of prototypes of equipment and other systems identified by the MoD.

Foreign companies can receive Request for Proposals (RFPs) only under the 'Buy and Make' and 'Buy (Global)' categories. In all other categories, they can only play a complementary role by tying up with Indian companies. The primary reason why tie-ups between foreign and Indian companies are not materialising has been discussed earlier, along with the reason why private sector entities are not getting nominated as PAs in procurement 'Buy and Make' programmes that involves transfer of technology. This leaves scope for foreign companies to be the prime contractors only in respect of procurement programmes under the 'Buy (Global)' category, which only entails outright purchase of equipment.

Contrary to the general perception, the problem that vendors face does not arise primarily from the procurement procedure *per se* but with the unpredictable manner in which it is followed. According to the timeline for processing a procurement proposal through various stages laid down in the DPP, it should ideally take not more than 14 weeks from the time vendors submit their response to the RFPs to complete the scrutiny of the technical proposals and call those bidders whose offers are found to be technically compliant for field trials which, in turn, should not take more than 16 to 24 weeks (an additional 12 weeks where winter trials are required).

The contract negotiation should ideally be completed within four to 26 weeks, depending on whether it is a multi-vendor or a resultant single vendor case, and it should not take more than four to 16 weeks to obtain the final financial approval, depending on who the competent financial authority is. These timelines are, however, seldom adhered to, and the reasons why the case is held up at a particular stage are never communicated to the bidders. To make matters worse, there is a perpetual fear of the RFP being retracted at any stage of the procurement process without any reasons being given for it.

A special mention must be made of offsets. All capital acquisition contracts worth Rs 2,000 crore or more entail offset obligations. Despite several changes made in the offset policy, it continues to be quite complex. The biggest problem vendors faced earlier was on account of the requirement of submitting the details of the Indian Offset Partners (IOPs) as a part of the offset proposal. Considering the time gap between submissions of the offer and signing of the contract, which could often stretch to several years, the vendors found it difficult to adhere to the details given by them while responding to the RFP. This created various problems in execution of the offset contract. Although the vendors now have the option of submitting these details at the time of seeking the offset credits or one year prior to discharge of offset obligation through a particular IOP, it has not eased the situation for vendors as these details are subject to acceptance by the MoD. This entails a great risk as rejection of an IOP proposed by the vendor at such a belated stage could result in default of the contractual obligation.

Lastly, much confusion has been created by contradictory narratives about the financial viability of MoD's procurement plans. The common refrain is that adequate funds are not available for signing new procurement contracts. According to a SCoD report, after providing for all payments against committed liabilities, a total sum of only Rs 8,590.37 crore was available for new schemes in 2016–2017.[14] The situation was not very different in the preceding years. This fact cannot be challenged but the inferences drawn from it are not appropriate. For one thing, the amount earmarked for meeting the

Table 3.   Number and value of contracts for procurement of defence equipment (2012–2013 to 2015–2016).

Year	Number of contracts	Value (Rs in crore)
2012–2013	73	44,306.56
2013–2014	42	23,927.21
2014–2015	47	64,859.52
2015–2016	61	47,877.29

committed liabilities, which is often as high as 85–90 per cent of the total allocation for capital acquisitions, does not always get utilised as planned.

This is due to the inability of suppliers to reach contractual milestones, which is a pre-condition for making the payment related to that milestone. The amount thus saved can always be spent on signing new contracts. But more importantly, only an advance payment of 15 per cent of the contract value is made at the time of signing of new contracts with the rest of the payment getting staggered over the entire delivery period. Thus, the sum of Rs 8,590.37 crore was sufficient to sign new contracts worth approximately Rs 57,000 crore in 2016–2017. This is more than the value of contracts signed in 2012–2013, 2013–2014 and 2015–2016 but slightly less than the value of contracts signed in 2014–2015 (see Table 3).[15]

It is equally important to note that India has never defaulted on any contractual payment, and there is no empirical evidence of signing of a new procurement contract being held up because of paucity of funds. Even then, the perception persists that the MoD's ambitious defence procurement plans may be financially unsustainable. This is not to suggest that the allocation for signing new capital acquisition contracts need not be increased. The point being made here is that the current level of funding is not out of sync with the pace at which new contracts are being signed. More funds will indeed be required as and when this pace picks up or when very high value contracts are to be signed.

What next?

The problems highlighted here are not specific to defence trade with Israel, but it is important to address them as a prelude to country-specific engagement with Israel. Some recommendations are made here to address these problems.

First, the mystique surrounding the procurement policy will need to be dispelled by actually laying down a *policy* distinct from the *procedure*. It bears recalling that the DPP is a *procedure* and not a statement of *policy*. It does contain a few policy precepts but mixing the policy with the procedure is problematic for any procedural deviation tends to be viewed as a departure from policy. This affects decision making as deviation from policy has unpleasant consequences for bureaucracy (both civilian and military) and also the political class. It bears recalling that the MoD laid down a Defence Production Policy in 2011,[16] defining the objectives of defence production in India. It is important to lay down a procurement policy that shows the way for achieving these objectives.

One of the questions the procurement policy will need to answer is the role that the MoD expects foreign companies to play in future in the context of 'Make in India' in defence, which itself could do with a little bit of conceptual clarity. If preference is to be given to procurement under 'Buy (IDDM)', 'Buy (Indian)' and 'Buy and Make (Indian)' categories, or even the 'Make' category, to Indian companies, where does it leave foreign companies? For projects under the 'Buy and Make' category, the MoD requires nominating a PA, but there are no guidelines in place as yet to facilitate nomination of private sector companies.

It is not clear whether this problem is going to be addressed through the strategic partnership scheme and, if so, when this scheme is likely to be notified. All this could be simplified if, in respect of those cases where the MoD does not want to nominate a Defence Public Sector Undertaking (DPSU), it is left to the foreign companies to select the Indian PA, for which a provision exists in DPP 2016.[17] Alternatively, the circumstances in which the MoD would nominate a PA and those in which it will permit foreign companies to select the PA will need to be addressed at the level of the policy.

In so far as the 'Buy (Global)' category is concerned, in recent years, the MoD has shown its preference for government-to-government (G2G) deals rather than competitive bidding. There is nothing inherently wrong with that, but there has to be clarity as to when the MoD would resort to G2G deals and when would it would resort to competitive bidding. This would help foreign companies in deciding when to rope in their governments to strike defence deals with the Indian MoD under the provision in the DPP which permits acquisition of defence equipment on strategic considerations.[18]

Second, one of the objectives of 'Make in India' in defence is to boost exports. The then Defence Minister Manohar Parrikar had set an export target of $2 billion for 2016.[19] This was several times more than the value of export by the DPSUs and the Ordnance Factories in the years 2013–2014 and 2014–2015, which was Rs 867.35 crore and Rs 1,898.47 crore, respectively. During the year 2015–2016, the MoD could manage to export defence equipment worth Rs 1,282.94 crore (about $200 million) only against the target of $2 billion set by the defence minister.[20]

Apart from various other reasons,[21] one of the important factors why exports are not picking up is the MoD's reluctance to buy equipment made in India by foreign companies through wholly-owned subsidiaries. This is inexplicable, considering that the MoD has no problem with buying the same equipment made abroad by the same company. Consequently, contracts for the manufacturing of equipment in India are confined to licensed production, targeted at meeting contractual obligations, and not necessarily for exports. Permitting companies to set up base in India, without this being linked to specific MoD contracts, would boost the manufacturing sector in general and promote exports. In any case, exports should constitute an essential part of co-development, co-production projects.

Third, there has to be clarity about what India needs to buy, when it would buy and under which category the equipment would be procured. As of now, the earliest a vendor gets to know about the MoD's intention to procure a particular piece of equipment, weapon system or platform is when the RFI is issued by the MoD. This requires prospective suppliers to remain in a reactive mode in that they can only respond when the RFI is issued. The current corporate culture, however, is not comfortable with such passivity. The defence companies are ever eager to follow a proactive policy to enter the Indian defence market. It will help if there is clarity about what the armed forces require. It will help companies to build up a business case for meeting the requirement. It will also minimise, if not prevent, the role of unscrupulous agents who thrive on getting the 'inside' information or on claims of being able to influence decision making within the services and the MoD. All this boils down to transparency about the needs of the armed forces.

It may be recalled that the MoD had released a Technology Perspective and Capability Roadmap (TPCR) in 2013.[22] This was the public version of the LTIPP intended to sensitise the industry about the future requirements of the Indian armed forces so that the industry could prepare itself to meet the challenge. This document contained the list of only those capabilities and technologies that the MoD intended to acquire though the 'Make' procedure. One would have expected the industry to seize this opportunity with both hands, but this document failed to enthuse the industry for a variety of reasons.

For one thing, the TPCR did not contain information on even the provisional Services Qualitative Requirements (SQRs) of the equipment that the armed forces would need in future. Two, there was no indication of the quantity to be procured. This is crucial for making a business case for investment. Three, there was no indication of the timeframe within which the industry could expect the MoD to come out with an RFI or RFP. Considering that the TPCR covered a 15-year period, it was necessary for the industry to be aware of the timing of RFI/RFP for making out a business case for investment. No wonder then that more than a decade after the 'Make' procedure was adopted by the MoD and more than four years after the TPCR was released, not a single contract has been signed for any 'Make' project.

While the TPCR provided a broad overview of the requirements, based on the 15-year LTIPP, the information that is critical from a business point of view is contained in the five-year SCAP and the AAPs. If a public version of the LTIPP could be released, there is no reason why public versions of these two documents cannot be released. Of course, while doing so, the MoD needs to make sure that the information contained therein is of use to the industry. Needless to say, the public version of SCAP and AAPs should not be confined to only the 'Make' projects.

Fourth, rather than investing its time and energy in amending the procurement procedure every two or three years, the MoD needs to concentrate on ensuring ease of doing business in defence. Among other things, this will require the MoD to be more transparent and willing to interact with industry representatives even in their individual capacity, and not as a part of some industry association delegation. It is equally important to ensure greater transparency in dealings between the MoD and the industry and setting up of an effective grievance redressal mechanism that actually delivers.

It may surprise many in the establishment that the vendors, both foreign and Indian, do not have so much of a problem with the procurement procedure as they have with the way it is implemented. Every acquisition programme throws up its own peculiar challenges for which answers cannot be found in the DPP. Therefore, the MoD will need to create institutional mechanisms to deal with these challenges as and when they surface in an equitable manner. A case in point is execution of the offset contracts. The general perception is that the primary focus of the MoD is on penalising vendors for contractual defaults rather than going into the reasons for such defaults and making it possible for vendors to discharge offset obligations.

What constitutes ease of doing business in defence is different from how it is perceived in general. Clarity about procedural requirements, information about the status of the bidders' response to RFIs/RFPs as the case moves through the bureaucratic labyrinth, and quick response to the issues raised by the prospective vendors/ bidders are at the heart of ease of doing business in defence. There are some other issues, such as industrial licensing and FDI, which are beyond the MoD's purview. Even so, a single-window handling of all these issues is of paramount importance. There is tremendous scope for providing such single-window service by the MoD through interactive web portals. There is also a room for improvement in the policy and procedures that have a bearing on defence production and procurement. All this is a continuous process, and the MoD cannot afford to lose sight of it or take inordinately long to address the issues as and when they crop up. The policy and procedures must keep evolving and adapting themselves based on feedback from stakeholders.

Lastly, the entire production and procurement policy has to be financially viable. It is essential to clear the air about sustainability of the acquisition programme of the MoD, but it is equally important to align defence plans with a realistic assessment of the financial resources likely to be made available for executing those plans. The AAPs need to be completely in sync with the allocation made for the given year, and these must be made public at least in regard to the details essential for the companies to gear up for meeting the MoD's requirements. Considering that the budgetary allocations are always less than the money asked for by the MoD in the run up to formulation of the union budget, it is ironic that the allocated funds do not get fully utilised.

This is as much on account of the absence of outcome-oriented monitoring of budgetary outlays as on account of quality and pace of decision making within the government in general and the MoD in particular. There is no reason why more than one year after the price negotiations were completed, Israel's Rafael Advanced Defence Systems should still be waiting for the contract for Spike ATGM systems to be signed.[23] More to the point, there is no reason why the deal should have been reactivated only on the eve of the Prime Minister's visit to Israel.[24] This fits-and-starts approach, which epitomises all that ails the system, must give way to pragmatism in fixing priorities and a dogged result-oriented pursuit of those goals.

Disclosure statement

No potential conflict of interest was reported by the author.

Notes

1. Standing Committee on Defence (2015–2016), 16[th]Lok Sabha, Lok Sabha Secretariat, Ministry of Defence, 'Twenty-Second Report, Demands for Grants (2016–2017), Capital Outlay on Defence Services, Procurement Policy and Defence Planning (Demand No. 23)', New Delhi, May 2016, p. 31, at http://164.100.47.134/lsscommittee/Defence/16_Defence_22.pdf (Accessed April 13, 2017).
2. Department of Industrial Policy and Promotion (DIPP), 'FDI Statistics', at http://dipp.nic.in/English/Publications/FDI_Statistics/FDI_Statistics.aspx (Accessed April 13, 2017).
3. Tanvi Madan, 'Why India and Israel Are Bringing Their Relationship Out from "under the Carpet"', Brookings, February 11, 2016, at https://www.brookings.edu/blog/order-from-chaos/2016/02/11/why-india-and-israel-are-bringing-their-relationship-out-from-under-the-carpet/ (Accessed April 13, 2017).
4. These details have been compiled from various media reports and other sources.
5. Tanvi Madan, No. 3.
6. Ibid.
7. These details have been provided by Rahul Bedi, Correspondent, IHS Jane's.
8. Standing Committee on Defence (2016–2017), 16[th]Lok Sabha, Lok Sabha Secretariat, 'Thirty First Report, Demands for Grants (2017–2018), Capital Outlay on Defence Services, Procurement Policy and Defence Planning (Demand No. 21)', New Delhi, March 2017, p. 29, at http://164.100.47.193/lsscommittee/Defence/16_Defence_31.pdf (Accessed April 14, 2017).
9. Stockholm International Peace Research Institute (SIPRI), 'SIPRI Arms Transfers Database—Methodology', at http://www.sipri.org/databases/armstransfers/background (Accessed April 12, 2017).
10. These figures have been derived from '10. International Arms Transfers and Arms Production', *SIPRI Yearbook 2015: Armaments, Disarmament and International Security,*

Oxford University Press (on behalf of SIPRI), Oxford, 2015, at https://www.sipri.org/year book/2015/10 and 'Trade Registers', SIPRI, at http://armstrade.sipri.org/armstrade/page/trade_register.php (Accessed April 12, 2017).

11. Ministry of Defence, 'Report of the Experts Committee, Committee of Experts for Amendments to DPP 2013 Including Formulation of Policy Framework', July 2015, at http://mod.nic.in/writereaddata/Reportddp.pdf (Accessed April 15, 2017).

12. Ibid., para. 7.8.02.

13. Ministry of Defence, 'Defence Procurement Procedure 2016', at http://mod.nic.in/writeread data/dppm.pdf.pdf (Accessed April 15, 2017).

14. Standing Committee on Defence (2015–2016), 'Twenty Second Report', No. 1, para. 1.20.

15. The figures for 2012–2013 to 2014–2015 have been taken from the reply furnished by the Defence Minister to a Lok Sabha unstarred question No. 593 on February 26, 2016, and the figure for 2015–2016 has been taken from para. 3.10 of the 31st report of the Standing Committee on Defence (16th Lok Sabha). These are accessible respectively at http://164.100.47.194/Loksabha/Questions/QResult15.aspx?qref=29378&lsno=16 (Accessed April 15, 2017), and http://164.100.47.193/lsscommittee/Defence/16_Defence_31.pdf (Accessed May 9, 2017).

16. Ministry of Defence, 'Defence Production Policy, Department of Defence Production', January 1, 2011, at http://mod.nic.in/writereaddata/DPP-POL.pdf (Accessed April 16, 2017).

17. Ministry of Defence, 'Defence Procurement Procedure 2016', No. 13, Chapter II, para. 20.

18. Ibid., Chapter II, para. 107.

19. 'Target to Raise India's Defence Exports to $2 Billion: Manohar Parrikar', The Hindu, May 14, 2016, at http://www.thehindu.com/news/national/target-to-raise-indias-defence-exports-to-2-billion-defence-minister-manohar-parrikar/article8600611.ece(Accessed April 15, 2017).

20. Standing Committee on Defence (2016–2017), 'Thirty First Report', No. 8, para.2.20.

21. See Sushant Singh, 'In fact: Why Parrikar's $2 Billion Defence Exports Target Faces Hurdles', The Indian Express, January 13, 2017, at http://indianexpress.com/article/explained/in-fact-why-parrikars-2-billion-defence-exports-target-faces-hurdles-4471455/ (Accessed April 15, 2017).

22. 'Technology Perspective and Capability Roadmap', January 2013, at http://mod.gov.in/writer eaddata/TPCR13.pdf (Accessed April 15, 2017).

23. Rahul Bedi, 'India Completes Price Negotiation for Israeli Spike ATGMs', IHS Jane's Defence Weekly, May 25, 2016, at http://www.janes.com/article/60741/india-completes-price-negotia tion-for-israeli-spike-atgms (Accessed April 15, 2017).

24. Vivek Raghuvanshi, 'India to Buy Anti-tank Missiles from Rafael', Defense News, March 27, 2017, at http://www.defensenews.com/articles/india-to-buy-spike-anti-tank-missiles-from-rafael (Accessed April 16, 2017).

India–Israel: The View from West Asia

Sanjay Singh

The view from West Asia of India–Israel ties has been interlinked not only with the region's negative perception of Israel but also with Israel's evolving position in the West Asian geo-political framework. The growing economic and political power of India in the last two decades and its deepening economic ties with countries in West Asia, however, have brought new factors into play. This perspective, along with the promise of the positive role India can play in West Asian affairs, now colours the Arab appreciation of India–Israel ties as well. The Israeli opposition to the activities of the Islamic Republic of Iran and its allies and proxies in the region is adding another dimension to the Arab perspective.

Israel as the Arabs see it: the four constituencies

The Arabs viewed Israel as a foreign body transplanted onto Arab soil and saw its creation as a continuation of Western imperialism and colonialism. Even though the Jews are a people of the Book, Israelis were seen as oppressors and usurpers of Arab lands. As Israeli restrictions on access to Muslim holy places in Palestine grew, these views were further reinforced. The repeated defeats of the numerically superior Arabs at the hands of the Israelis dealt a severe blow to the Arab psyche and added further salt to their wounds. Seven decades since the establishment of the state of Israel, there is a sense of helplessness in many quarters in the Arab world that the situation cannot be altered.

The establishment of the state of Israel in 1948 was met by disbelief in the Arab world. Their inability to undo this through force of arms was a severe blow to Arab self-esteem. While damage to Egypt through the Suez crisis was limited, it demonstrated how Israel could be used in the region by Western powers. The comprehensive defeat of the Arab armies in 1967 and thereafter in 1973 and the peace treaties that Egypt and Jordan signed in its wake with Israel destroyed Arab illusions about removing the fact of Israel's existence from the region. Nevertheless, new actors continue to rise to articulate the Arab pain, fury and frustration which manifest through violent opposition to the state of Israel. While the Palestine Liberation Organisation (PLO) did emerge as a serious non-traditional threat to the Israeli state, it was not able to effect any change apart from indulging in some spectacular acts of terrorism. The Islamic Revolution in Iran led to the creation of another enemy sworn to the destruction of Israel.

The inability of the Palestinians in particular and the Arab world in general to effectively counter Israeli actions have further deepened their feelings of frustration.

Ambassador Sanjay Singh was Secretary (East), Ministry of External Affairs (MEA), New Delhi.

To name a few, these Israeli actions include the 1982 destruction in Sabra and Shatila by the Phalangist allies of Israel; the crushing Israeli response to the First (1987–1993) and the Second Intifada (2000–2005); the Lebanon Conflict of 2006; and the Gaza wars of 2007, 2008–2009, 2012 and 2014. While the mantle of violent opposition to Israel has passed from the PLO to groups such as Hamas and Islamic Jihad, among others, the rhetoric remains the same—from the West Bank to Gaza and from one generation to another. Despite decades of struggle by the Palestinians, there has been no material change on the ground. On the contrary, Israeli territorial ambitions and its settlements continue to expand.

This history has evoked different reactions from the four key constituencies in the Arab World—the ruling regimes, the clerics, the media and opinion-makers and the general mainstream or the 'street'. While Arab regimes were united in expressing vociferous opposition to Israel's creation initially, as the years went by, they have been engulfed by a sense of frustration owing to their inability to effect any meaningful change. The Arab attitude itself, meanwhile, has changed along with the changing strategic environment in the region. The Islamic Revolution in Iran in 1979 brought a new factor into play in regional politics: the Islamic regime, which wanted to alter the geo-political status quo. This posed a new threat to many regimes in the region, especially the monarchies. The Palestinian support to Saddam Hussein during the first Gulf crisis, when Iraq had occupied Kuwait, antagonised many in the Gulf Cooperation Council (GCC) countries.

The evolution of the Shia crescent after the Second Gulf War and, in recent years, the Obama administration's efforts to come to an accommodation with Iran on the nuclear issue have concentrated Arab minds in a manner such that Israel no longer remains the primary enemy. The 'Arab Spring' brought more immediate issues into focus. While many Arab regimes profess to support the Palestinian cause, and to heed the street, they largely do not intend to back their words with action.

The clerical establishment in the Sunni states largely takes its cue on political issues from the ruling establishment, and barring the Al Aqsa issue, it is no more concerned about the Palestinian question than the ruling regimes. Arab opinion-makers, especially the left-oriented ones and the media, remain strongly against Israel and its actions. This is unlikely to change. They influence the Arab street, but have other preoccupations at the moment, given the chaos affecting many parts of the region.

The opinion on the street, though fiercely anti-Israel in character, is fickle. On a given day, the Palestinian issue may be topmost on their minds, and on another day, something else. And then there is always Iran and its allies and proxies which keep reminding them of this as well as the looming geo-political threat. The view from the region towards Israel, therefore, is informed by the four elements delineated above—the regimes, the clerical establishment, the opinion-makers and the street—whose attitudes, while not being uniform, are broadly similar in being antithetical to Israel's place in the region. It is then not surprising that even after seven decades only two of the 22-member League of Arab States recognise Israel.

The West Asia region and India–Israel ties: the evolving trajectory

Pre-independence to Israel's creation

In analysing the view from West Asia of India–Israel ties, it would be useful to recount the history of India's evolving views on Israel and its ties with it. There have been many strands that have informed and continue to inform Indian policy. Having itself just achieved independence in 1947, India was opposed to colonisation in all its forms, and so empathised with the plight of the Palestinians, another colonised people. It viewed the creation of Israel as a continuation of the colonisation of Palestine in another form. Having suffered the agony of the communal divide, it was strongly averse to accepting religion as a basis for the creation of states. It was also apprehensive about Pakistan mobilising Muslim nations against India on the basis of Muslim sympathy. It countered malevolent Pakistani propaganda by being 'more loyal than the King' to the Palestinian cause. Further, as an aspirant to the leadership of the third world, India could not ignore Arab sentiments.

During the period of the Mandate (1922–1948), Indian political leadership had invested a considerable amount on Muslim issues and the struggle of the Arabs in general, and in Palestine in particular, and helped them materially and morally. Among those actively involved in promoting support in India for these causes were prominent Muslim leaders such as the Ali brothers. They were initially associated with the Indian National Congress and influenced the Congress and Gandhiji's thinking on the issue. Gandhiji, who when pressed did say that his understanding of the issue was limited, basically advocated that Palestine should be for the people of Palestine. Mohammad Ali Johar, a prominent leader of the Khilafat movement, who had strong relations with the Grand Mufti of Jerusalem Haj Amin al-Husseini, was a strong supporter of the Palestinian cause. There is a poem extolling his activities by the famous Egyptian poet Shawki. Johar died in London in January 1931 and was buried in Jerusalem. It is said that the Grand Mufti had him buried in Jerusalem in order to get Indian Muslims to support him at the 1931 General Islamic Congress in Jerusalem.

It was a combination of all these different strands which led India to oppose the partition of Palestine and the creation of the state of Israel at the United Nations (UN). Once Israel came into being in May 1948, there were two distinct views on it within the political elite of India. Maulana Abul Kalam Azad led the faction that was against the recognition of a state created on the basis of religion. On the other hand, there were others, including Sardar Vallabhbhai Patel, who advocated recognising this new reality. Prime Minister Jawaharlal Nehru argued that since the UN had recognised Israel, India must also do so but not establish diplomatic relations with it as that would be against its principles. India formally recognised Israel on September 17, 1950. India's stand was welcomed by all sections of Arab opinion-makers.

Intermittent diplomatic support

In keeping with its beliefs and principles, India extended support to Arab nationalist movements in Egypt and Algeria. Nehru took the Egyptian President Gamal Abdel Nasser to Bandung in 1955 in order to cement Afro-Asian solidarity. India extended support to Egypt during the Suez crisis in 1956. It is interesting to note that Israel was not invited to Bandung, perhaps due to the threat of an Arab boycott. Egypt, for its part, did not allow Portuguese ships to use the Suez Canal during India's action to expel them from Goa, a manifestation of the strongly held belief in parts of the Arab word that India and Indians were against colonialism and sided with the oppressed peoples of the world.

The first real test of the India–Arab relationship came during the 1965 India–Pakistan War. The Gulf States clearly supported Pakistan, as did its Central Treaty Organisation (CENTO) partner Iran. The Arab press also criticised the alleged supply of weapons by Israel to India. The Arab Republics however supported India. In 1967, following the 'Naqba'—the disastrous defeat of the Arab armies by Israel—India supported the Arabs. This was highly appreciated by the rulers, the street and the media. Yet in 1969, there was little support for India when, on Pakistani protests, it was requested to leave the meeting in Rabat which created the Organisation of Islamic Cooperation (OIC).

Again, during the 1971 Bangladesh War, the Arab world—except for Oman, Syria and Iraq—did not support India. Algeria remained neutral. Israel, on the other hand, did extend support to India. This negative reaction from the Arab world was not expected, and India realised that it would need to recalibrate its policies of support to the Arabs. Following the 1973 Arab Conflict with Israel, there was a marked shift in the worldview of some Arab countries. Egypt made an about-turn and established relations with Israel and shifted its allegiance from the Soviets to the US. It was consequently expelled from the Arab League. Jordan, too, followed Egypt's lead. The Arab world, the Arab street, media and regimes were divided. Indian relations with Egypt, its principal interlocutor in the Arab world, had turned lukewarm and its Palestinian policy in this context began losing some of its relevance.

India and the peace process

It was at this time that Yasser Arafat rose to world attention with his speech to the UN General Assembly in 1974. India, whose political establishment had been considerably influenced by Arafat, supported the UN providing this platform to him, at a time when many countries considered the PLO a terrorist organisation. In 1975, a PLO office was set up in New Delhi. In 1977, India was the first non-Arab country to recognise the PLO's authority as the sole legitimate representative of the Palestinian people. These moves were welcomed in the Arab world.

India also exhibited understanding of the First Intifada, launched in 1986. Following the proclamation of the establishment of the state of Palestine on November 15, 1988 at the extraordinary conference in Algiers, India was among the first few countries to recognise it. Indian support for the Palestinian cause also benefited from Indira Gandhi's empathy for the Palestinians and the close relationship that Arafat was able to establish with her. Rajiv Gandhi also continued in her footsteps. India consequently maintained a very positive image in the Arab world during the decades of the 1970s and 1980s.

The Iraqi invasion of Kuwait in 1990 divided the Arab world. In early 1991, the First Gulf War commenced. The US comprehensively routed the Iraqi Army and strengthened its hegemony over the Arab world. The US leveraged its victory in the Gulf War to launch anew the Arab-Israeli peace process. The Madrid Conference held on October 20 to November 1, 1991, brought Israelis and Palestinians to the same table. This led to an internal split in the Palestinian camp, with the rejectionist forces regrouping under the banner of Hamas. Relations with Israel, or lack of them, no longer remained the litmus test for good relations with the Arab world.

Recognition and its aftermath

By the end of 1991, the Soviet Union had collapsed, creating a unipolar moment and a completely different global environment, leaving the US as the sole hegemon. The Non-aligned Movement (NAM) and third world solidarity became less relevant, as well also the voice of NAM countries, including that of India. India needed to rethink its policies to deal with the US, an important component of which, given the domestic Jewish lobby in the US, would be India's relations with Israel. There was consequently a need to take another look at the policy India had been following vis-à-vis Israel since 1947 and make the necessary changes.

The logical outcome was that India established diplomatic relations with Israel in January 1992, launching India–Israel ties on a new trajectory. Interestingly, China also followed a similar path. Prior to establishing diplomatic relations with Israel, India took the Palestinian leadership into confidence. Arafat visited India and accepted that it was India's sovereign right to establish diplomatic relations with Israel and that Palestinians had no right to question this decision especially since they too were in talks with Israel. Palestinian interest was in the establishment of two states living side by side in peace. India's relations with Israel would help Indian efforts to assist in the establishment of the Palestinian state. This would also broaden the peace process beyond just the US.

The reaction from the Arab world was uniformly negative to India establishing diplomatic relations with Israel. The Arab street was shocked; the Arab media was sharply critical. The Arab leadership however was not overly bothered. Barring the Iranian clerical regime, others largely ignored the development. Iran, intent on assuming leadership of the Muslim world, was in the process of establishing strong ties with the rejectionist elements in the Palestinian camp. Yet, under President Ali Akbar Hashemi Rafsanjani, it followed a pragmatic policy and did not go beyond a point in criticising the Indian initiative. During this process, India kept the Arab regimes informed, briefing their envoys in Delhi and sending special envoys to their capitals to brief them on the logic of the step.

The Madrid Conference led to the Oslo Accords of 1993 and 1995 between Israel and the PLO, through which there was implicit recognition of the state of Israel. This led to the establishment of the Palestinian National Authority (PNA) with limited autonomy. Moreover, it was in the1990s that India initiated economic reforms and built up its own strengths. While it continued its policy of support to the Palestinian cause, it also slowly and surely built up its relations with Israel. These policies remained on parallel tracks, with relations with Israel strengthening but under the radar. It was recognised in the Arab world that India had changed.

The PLO and PNA continued to be appreciative of India's support, but the Arab street and media were not convinced and felt that India had changed its traditional role. Meanwhile, Pakistani propaganda was in full flow. It was largely at its instigation that the OIC repeatedly criticised India on the question of Kashmir and the treatment of Indian Muslims, citing the events in India such as the 1992 demolition of the Babri Masjid and the 1994 Mumbai riots. While member countries of the OIC individually told India bilaterally that they did not subscribe to the criticism, they did nothing to prevent it. This was naturally perceived poorly by India, which had been a strong supporter of Arab causes, and especially the Palestinian cause.

Decreasing salience of the regional factor in India's Israel policy

As its economic strength grew, India was ready to test the waters once again and be less circumspect about its relations with Israel. President Ezer Weizman became the first Israeli head of state to visit India in 1997, and Jaswant Singh the first Indian Foreign Minister to visit Israel in 2000. Israeli assistance during the Kargil War with

Pakistan in 1999 had already transformed it into a de facto strategic partner of India. This process culminated with the visit of Prime Minister Ariel Sharon to India in 2003. This elicited routine criticism from the West Asian region, but nothing that India could not live with. Interestingly enough, China did not receive similar criticism as it was argued that it had not been a traditional supporter and hence could not be seen as traitorous!

Meanwhile, the Israeli–Palestinian peace process continued and the Middle East Quartet was set up in 2002 following the start of the Second Intifada. Under a Saudi initiative, the Arab world itself came up with a peace plan in 2002, at the Beirut Summit of the Arab League, under which it offered Arab recognition to Israel under certain conditions. With the death of Yasser Arafat in 2004, India lost its principal interlocutor in Palestine, one who was aware of the great efforts that India had made to support the Palestinian cause.

The Second Intifada, Lebanon conflict and Gaza wars effectively divided the Palestinians into two warring camps. Indian relations were confined to the PNA. These developments further reduced the relevance of the Indian position of keeping relations with Israel delicately balanced with open criticism of Israeli treatment of the Palestinians. However, the lessening of India's relevance to the Palestinian cause also diminished the need for strident criticism of its actions by the Arabs.

In closing

The changing global environment and India's rapid economic development over the past two decades have increased its importance in the Arab world. Today, India stands on its own in the global firmament, and Palestine is no longer a major factor in Arab–India relations. The visit of King Abdullah of Saudi Arabia in 2006 as chief guest at the Republic Day effectively de-hyphenated India and Pakistan in the eyes of the Arab world. Pakistani propaganda has met with the law of diminishing returns. India–Israel relations have now entered a new phase of becoming de-hyphenated from both the Palestinian issue and, even more importantly, US–India relations.

The relationship has grown by leaps and bounds, and stands on its own today marked by high-level visits and increasing exchanges in the field of homeland security and defence. Prime Minister Narendra Modi met Prime Minister Benjamin Netanyahu on the side-lines of the UN General Assembly in 2014. India has also recalibrated its positions on resolutions criticising Israel. In 2015, Pranab Mukherjee became the first Indian president to visit Israel. He also became the first head of state to stay at Ramallah as a guest of the PNA. There was some comment that he did so as he was still steeped in Indian sentiments of the past. In November 2016, Israeli President Reuven Rivlin became the second Israeli head of state to visit India, a visit perhaps mainly noticed in India and Israel.

The 'Arab spring', the civil wars in Syria and Yemen and the Iran-P5 + 1 (the US, UK, France, Russia, China and Germany) nuclear accord have further changed the political landscape of the region, which is now suffering the consequences of Saudi–Iranian rivalry. Reportedly, China has offered to mediate between these two regional rivals, and they are considering the offer. This rivalry combined with the ambivalence exhibited by the Trump administration towards the two-state solution and the status of Jerusalem, along with refugee fatigue in Europe, have pushed the Palestinian problem to the back pages. The internecine warfare in the Palestinian camp also does not help their cause.

All this has allowed Netanyahu to block peace talks and even boycott events such as the Paris Palestine–Israel conference held in January 2017. The Arab street is also more focused presently on issues internal to their countries. In this new environment, there is little or no attention given by the region to India–Israel relations. Prime Minister Modi's visit to Israel in July 2017 will create few headlines in the region, except perhaps in Iran. However, it might negatively impact whatever sentiment for India that remains on the street. India will become another country for the region like China, important but not loved.

Disclosure statement

No potential conflict of interest was reported by the author.

Israel–China Ties at 25: The Limited Partnership

S. Samuel C. Rajiv

Abstract: Israel–China bilateral ties have witnessed significant growth since the establishment of full diplomatic relations in January, 1992. Both countries are currently investing their energies in realising the full potential of their on-going partnership in the innovation economy. Growing tourist linkages are another facet of the burgeoning relationship. While China has 'comprehensive strategic partnerships' with more than 30 countries, including with those in Israel's neighbourhood, like Egypt and Iran, the term 'strategic' is conspicuously absent in describing the nature of the bilateral ties by either Israel or China. The relationship is instead described as a 'comprehensive innovation partnership'. This article shows that three limiting factors continue to cast a shadow on the China–Israel partnership. These are: the conundrum of defence trade and security ties; China's long-standing support of the Palestinian cause in international forums, like the United Nations General Assembly (UNGA) and UN Human Rights Council (UNHRC)—multilateral bodies whose work is routinely described as a 'joke' and a 'circus' by Israel's top leadership; and China's growing stakes with the wider West Asia region, animated by arms, energy and infrastructure deals.

Introduction

Israel recognised the People's Republic of China (PRC) on January 9, 1950, among the first of the non-communist countries to do so. Full-fledged diplomatic relations were, however, not established until January 24, 1992. A panoply of factors were responsible for this, primarily relating to the 'negative influences of the international situation in general and of third parties in particular'.[1] These included, among others, the 1950 Korean War, which affected Sino-Israeli diplomatic negotiations in Moscow, the 1955 Bandung Conference, and China's subsequent association with the Arab-Palestinian campaign against Israel. Other analysts have noted that the 1956 Suez crisis led to the breakdown of contacts for over two decades.[2]

The fact that China and Israel were on opposite ends of the strategic divide during the Cold War did not help matters either. Israel was referred to as the 'Zionist Entity', 'running dog of US imperialism' and an 'imperialist dagger thrust into the heart of the Arab people'.[3] Positive movement in bilateral interactions occurred against the backdrop of the Chinese 'open-door' economic policy under Deng Xiaoping and the Egypt–Israel peace treaty. Diplomatic interactions between Israeli and Chinese officials in places like Paris, and at the United Nations (UN) in New York, set the stage for the eventual establishment of full diplomatic ties in January, 1992.

Political traffic since the establishment of full diplomatic relations has been decent, with visits from the Israeli side being more frequent. Prime Minister Benjamin Netanyahu visited China three times (in May, 1998, May, 2013 and

S. Samuel C. Rajiv is Associate Fellow, Institute for Defence Studies and Analyses (IDSA), New Delhi.

March, 2017), while Prime Minister Ehud Olmert visited in January, 2007. Israeli presidents have also been frequent visitors, starting with Chaim Herzog in December, 1992, Moshe Katsav (December, 2003) and Shimon Peres (July, 2008 and April, 2014). Peres was the President of the Council for the Promotion of Israel–China Relations since its founding in 1996 until his death in September, 2016. From the Chinese side, high-level visits have been less frequent, with President Jiang Zemin's visit in April, 2000 being the most high-profile. An important reason for his visit was to close the Phalcon deal. The deal was, however, cancelled a few months later on account of US pressure (see sections below).

Bilateral trade has grown from US$50 million in 1992 to more than US$10 billion in 2016. China is Israel's largest trading partner in Asia and the third-largest trading partner in the world, after the US and the European Union (EU). Israel sees cooperation with China (and other important countries in Asia, like India, South Korea and Japan, among others) as an essential element of its efforts to increase exports, generate jobs and boost its economic growth. Prime Minster Netanyahu's numerous statements to this effect in cabinet meetings, among other important occasions, amply illustrate this fact. In May, 2014, the Ministerial Committee on China Affairs, headed by Netanyahu, approved a plan to increase Israeli exports to China to US$5 billion, from about US$3 billion then.[4]

Cooperation in the high-tech/innovation sector has been one of the hallmarks of the Israel–China partnership. When Netanyahu visited Beijing in March, 2017, both sides announced a 'comprehensive innovation partnership'. It is pertinent to note that China has 'comprehensive strategic partnerships' with more than 30 countries, including with those in Israel's neighbourhood, like Egypt and Iran. The term 'strategic', however, is conspicuously absent in describing the nature of the bilateral ties by either Israel or China.

This article argues that this is because three limiting factors continue to cast a shadow on the China–Israel partnership. These are: the conundrum of defence trade and security ties; China's long-standing support of the Palestinian cause in international forums like the UN General Assembly (UNGA) and the UN Human Rights Council (UNHRC)—multilateral bodies whose work is routinely described as a 'joke' and a 'circus' by Israel's top leadership; and China's growing stakes in the wider West Asia region, animated by arms, energy and infrastructure deals. The article closes by examining the applicability, or otherwise, of these limiting factors, vis-à-vis Israel's relationship with its other key Asian partner, India. First, however, the article places in perspective some of the key elements of the Israel–China relationship. The issues that are examined include: the nature of cooperation in the high-tech/innovation sector; the education sector; the infrastructure sector; and people-to-people links.

Israel–China partnership: key elements

High-tech/innovation sector cooperation

Israel was one among the 20 countries, including, among others, the US, Japan and Finland, that were identified by the Chinese Ministry of Commerce (MOFCOM) in 2010 for focused efforts to undertake high-tech cooperation.[5] The Israeli Cabinet, in April, 2012, ratified an agreement to support joint ventures in the research and development (R&D) sector with China. Prime Minister Netanyahu even affirmed that Israel and China 'are a winning combination because we are two nations with magnificent traditions who also adopt modernism'.[6]

Netanyahu, in his May, 2013 visit to China, told Chinese Premier Li Keqiang that his country could be 'the perfect junior partner for China in its pursuit of economic excellence and competitive advantage, by offering our technological capabilities'.[7] After his visit, Netanyahu informed the Israeli Cabinet that the Chinese leaders were interested in 'three things: Israeli technology, Israeli technology and Israeli technology'. The China–Israel Innovation Development Fund was founded on November 17, 2014. The China–Israel Changzhou Innovation Park (CIP) Initiative was started to assist the efforts of Israeli companies to penetrate the Chinese market.[8]

China and Israel signed a three-year action plan on innovation cooperation (2015–2017) in January, 2015, when Israeli Foreign Minister Avigdor Lieberman visited Beijing and held the first meeting of the China–Israel Joint Committee on Innovation Cooperation. An Innovation Competition Award, worth US$1 million, was announced in February, 2015 with funding from Shengjing360 and Jerusalem Venture Partners (JVP) to encourage the most innovative start-ups.[9] During the visit of Chinese Vice Premier Liu Yandong to Israel in May, 2015, both countries signed a Memorandum of Understanding (MOU) to expand joint innovation cooperation. Liu was in Israel for the second meeting of the China–Israel Joint Committee on Innovation Cooperation.

The Chinese Communist Party (CPC), in October, 2015, made innovation one of the key concepts of a 2016–2020 Five Year Plan. Israel is only the second country, after Switzerland, to have such robust, institutionalised links in the innovation sphere with China. Switzerland and China established an 'Innovative Strategic Partnership' in April 2016. At the Pujiang Innovation Forum, held in November, 2015, Israel was the 'country of honour'. The first China–Israel Technology, Innovation and Investment Summit was held in Beijing in January, 2016, with over 100 Israeli companies and 2,000 Chinese investors participating.[10] For the first time in over 16 years, the GoforIsrael business conference was held in Shanghai, in September, 2016. China's Vice Minister of Science and Technology, Yin Hejun, affirmed that the 'golden age for Israel–China innovation cooperation has come'.[11] When Netanyahu visited Beijing in March, 2017, he chaired the third meeting of the China–Israel Joint Committee on Innovation Cooperation with Chinese Vice Premier Liu Yandong.

The Chinese MOFCOM indicated that China's non-financial direct investment into Israel in 2016 was US$190 million, up 46.2 per cent from the previous year.[12] About 40 per cent of all venture capital flowing into Israel came from China in 2015, according to Ziva Eger, chief executive of the Foreign Investments and Industrial Cooperation Division at the Ministry of Economy of Israel.[13] Chinese investments in the Israeli high-tech sector in 2014 amounted to US$300 million.[14]

According to the Israel Innovation Authority's 'Innovation in Israel 2016' report, Israel was placed at the 22nd position in the Global Innovation Index for 2015, out of 141 countries. While this was a significant position, given Israel's relatively small size and limited manpower resources, it was seven places lower than in 2014. A major challenge the report flags is the decrease in government spending on R&D. Israel therefore sees greater collaboration with countries like China as essential to maintaining its competitive edge in the innovation sector. The report affirms that China was becoming an 'innovation superpower' apart from being a manufacturing superpower.

The report indicated that Chinese investments in Israeli companies in 2015 totalled US$500 million, with more than 30 entities from China and the Hong Kong Special Administrative Region (SAR) having invested in Israel. It goes on to state that Israel has nine industrial R&D cooperation agreements with the Chinese Ministry of Science and Technology (MOST), spread across seven Chinese cities. The report, while waxing eloquent about the need to engage in innovation cooperation with China, also paradoxically highlights the fact that 'due to the growing presence of China and the United States in the [unmanned aerial vehicle (UAV)] market, there was increasing competition that threatens Israeli leadership in the field of military robotics (e.g. in the field of UAVs)'.[15]

China's huge investment capabilities (foreign exchange reserves in excess of US$3 trillion at the end of 2016) are no doubt a major magnet. There have, however, been some challenges to Chinese efforts to get a controlling stake in Israeli companies. Reports note that the Israeli Finance Ministry has rejected several Chinese bids to buy insurance companies, for instance, due to reputational and financial risks.[16] The lack of transparency on macro-economic factors was among reasons cited that prevented Israeli companies from making informed decisions. While the Beijing Xinwei Technology Group agreed to buy Spacecom Technologies (which operates Amos communication satellites) for US$285 million in August, 2016, analysts believed the move could face regulatory hurdles going forward.[17] The negotiations, however, collapsed in January, 2017 in the wake of the failure of the launch of the Amos-6 satellite and a revaluation of the company to US$190 million. Israeli analysts further warn that China's economy was slowing down and that Israel 'should not get used to Chinese money' as China is cracking down on the flight of capital out of the country.[18]

Education sector

The Israel Science Academy Liaison Department first established offices in 1990, even prior to the establishment of formal, full-fledged diplomatic ties. China established Israel's first Confucius Institute at Tel Aviv University (TAU) in 2007. Educational cooperation encompasses scholarships that both countries provide to the other's students/researchers to facilitate research activities. Prime Minister Netanyahu, for instance, launched a programme to provide scholarships to 250 Chinese students every year, on the occasion of the 20th anniversary of the establishment of diplomatic relations, in January, 2012. The Tsinghua-TAU XIN Centre was set up in September, 2013 as an international hub for high-tech innovation. At the meeting of the Forum of Presidents of Israel–China Higher Education Institutions in March, 2016, Ben Gurion University and Jilin University signed an agreement to establish a joint centre for entrepreneurship and innovation.[19]

Technion's Israel Institute of Technology and China's Shantou University are building a new academic complex, the Guangdong Technion Israel Institute of Technology (GTIIT). Hong Kong real-estate baron Li Ka-shing provided a donation of US$130 million to the joint venture.[20] The US$130 million grant by the Li Ka-shing Foundation (LKF) was described as the 'largest ever and the most generous in the history of the Israeli higher education'. Shantou is one of the special economic zones (SEZ) in South China's Guangdong province. At the ground-breaking ceremony of the Institute, in December, 2015, Israeli Science and Technology Minister Ofir Akunis affirmed that he saw 'a strategic importance in strengthening and deepening our relations with China in all aspects: economically, technologically and scientifically'.[21] The President of GTIIT, Li Jiange, stated that the joint venture with Israel was an important effort to make the region the 'Silicon Valley' of South China.

Technion, one of Israel's oldest and most prestigious technology institutes, was chosen from among 74 potential partners.

What is interesting to note is that Li Ka-shing's Horizon Ventures invested in the Israeli Global Positioning System (GPS) navigation start-up, Waze, in 2011, while on a visit to Israel for meetings at Technion. Waze was subsequently bought for over US$1 billion by Google in 2013, and the profits from that sale were a part of the donation by Li to Technion.[22] The Institute is set to offer courses in cutting-edge fields like aerospace engineering, beginning from 2020. Nobel Laureate Aaron Ciechanover is Vice Chancellor (Research) at the University, and the Chairman of the Technical Council is Gideon Frank, who was former chief of the Israel Atomic Energy Commission (IAEC) from 1993–2007.

Cooperation in the infrastructure sector

The Shanghai International Port Group (SIPG) Company Limited won the bid in March, 2015 to operate Haifa port for 25 years, starting from 2021. Israeli Transport and Intelligence Minister Yisrael Katz asserted that the involvement of the SIPG was 'an expression of confidence in the State of Israel on the part of a superpower'. The company will invest US$2 billion to build and upgrade existing port infrastructure.[23] Earlier, in June, 2014, the China Harbour Engineering Company Limited won a bid to build the Ashdod port, with an investment of US$1 billion. The Chinese company submitted the lowest bid to win the contract.

Another ambitious project that would involve Chinese participation to succeed is the Red-Med railway link, from Eilat on the Red Sea to the port of Ashdod on the Mediterranean Sea. The freight railway line is expected to cost anywhere between US$6 and US$13 billion. It has, however, not yet secured funding or final approvals. Analysts note that many imponderables exist—including the inability of the Eilat port to handle larger-capacity cargo ships—and point out the need to involve Jordan's port of Aqaba to make the project a success.[24]

When the Israeli Government decided, in September 20, 2015, to seek the services of 20,000 Chinese construction workers, there was criticism of the deal.[25] The deal, finally signed in January, 2017, is expected to give a boost to Israel's housing sector.[26] As of 2016, about 3,500 Chinese construction workers were working in Israel. Israel meanwhile is a founding member of the Asian Infrastructure Investment Bank (AIIB).

People-to-people links

Growing tourist linkages are an important facet of the bilateral ties. While 70,000 Chinese tourists visited Israel in 2015, Israel hopes to soon be attracting 100,000. A 10-year multiple visa entry agreement was signed in January, 2016, making Israel the third country, after the US and Canada, to have such an agreement with China.[27] Negotiations for the agreement commenced in November, 2015. Israel invested ₪ 20 million (about US$5.5 million) to promote tourism in China in 2016. Hainan Airlines started three direct flights per week from Hainan to Tel Aviv. Given that China became the biggest source of global tourists in 2012, and is expected to have 200 million tourists abroad annually by 2020, Israel wants to have a slice of the pie as well.[28] In 2016, 122 million Chinese travelled abroad, spending close to US$110 billion.[29]

Israeli non-governmental organisations, like Save A Child's Heart (SACH), active since 1999, are another important element of the people-to-people links; SACH was awarded the Friendship Award by the Chinese Government in September, 2010. An Israeli computer science professor got the same award in 2013. The first Israel–China cultural festival in San Francisco was held in July, 2012. In September, 2016, the Chinese People's Association for Friendship with Foreign Countries kicked off its world tour from Israel and Palestine.

Limiting factors in the Israel–China partnership

Defence trade/security ties conundrum

China was a significant recipient of Israeli military technology, even prior to the establishment of full diplomatic relations, with business tycoon-cum-arms dealer Shaul Eisenberg being a key player.[30] According to some analysts, until 1992, Israel sold US$3–4 billion-worth of arms to China.[31] It is widely acknowledged that arms exports were an important part of Israel's playbook to enhance diplomatic leverage, as well as cater to the export-driven imperatives of its domestic arms industry.[32] The advanced military technology that Israel allegedly sold to China from the mid-1970s onwards included air-to-air missiles (Python-3), fighter aircraft technology (flowing from the Lavi fighter programme terminated by Israel in 1987), anti-tank missiles (Mapatz), thermal imaging tank sights, and technical information regarding Patriot missile technology, among other things.[33]

Washington adopted a soft attitude towards most such transfers, in the context of the Cold War (when the Chinese were a counter-weight to Soviet power). It, however, urged caution during the post-Cold War era in sharing sophisticated military technology that had been co-developed with the US, especially in the context of rising tensions with China over Taiwan.[34] Matters came to a head when Israel was forced to cancel the 1996 deal, worth more than US$1 billion, for the sale of four Phalcon Airborne Early Warning (AEW) aircraft in July, 2000. Prime Minister Ehud Barak, in a letter to Chinese President Jiang Zemin from Camp David, Maryland, 'expressed sorrow that Israel … will not be able, under the current circumstances, to continue in the implementation of the Phalcon project'. He, however, reiterated that Israel 'will continue to look for ways to implement the deal, in understanding with the United States, if the circumstances will change'.[35]

Israel had to pay a penalty of US$350 million for cancelling the contract, inclusive of the US$190 million China had already paid for realising the contract.[36] In the aftermath of the Phalcon fiasco, incidents like Chinese fighter jets, equipped with Israeli Python III air-to-air missiles, troubling US reconnaissance flights annoyed US defence officials.[37] The US urged Israel to stop all military sales to China in early January, 2003. China reacted strongly, asserting that 'no country has a right to interfere in the developing military trade cooperation between China and Israel'.[38] US concerns subsequently peaked over the possible supply of spare parts for Israeli-made Harpy drones. China imported nearly 100 such drones in 1994 (the US knew about the deal), but when Beijing requested upgrades to the drones in 2003/2004, it was resolutely opposed by the US and Taiwan, which felt the drones could be a force multiplier in the event of an armed conflict over the Taiwan Straits.[39] Taiwan and the US, in fact, began to worry about the Israeli drones in the Chinese inventory when the People's Liberation Army (PLA) used the drones in a massive exercise facing the

Taiwan Straits in July, 2002. The US felt that these drones could be used to target US and Taiwanese command and control facilities with impunity.

Despite this, high-level military consultations resumed in March, 2004, when an Israeli Ministry of Defence (MoD) delegation visited Beijing. Some analysts note that Israel's success in cementing a strong strategic relationship with India, as evidenced by a plethora of high-tech defence deals in the aftermath of the Kargil War, and in the context of the 9/11 attacks (including for Barak point-defence systems and Phalcon Airborne Warning and Control System [AWACS]), probably paradoxically gave Israel the confidence to resume defence dialogue with Beijing.[40] Washington, however, was still in no mood for military ties between Israel and China. The US reacted strongly to the possibility of Harpy upgrades by suspending cooperation with Israel on long-range military development projects, including for the cutting-edge F-35 Joint Strike Fighter (JSF).[41] On account of such US pressure, Israel did not go through with the Harpy upgrades. The US and Israel then reached an agreement on August 16, 2005 requiring Israel to adopt stricter export control restrictions, akin to the Wassenaar Arrangement, on the sale of such military hardware.[42] Veteran China analyst Yitzhak Schichor concluded that, in the aftermath of the Harpy fiasco, Israel's defence industries 'lost' the China market for the 'foreseeable future'.[43]

Israel continued its efforts at testing the waters, however, given China's need for niche technology due to the continuing EU arms embargo that was imposed in the wake of the Tiananmen Square massacre in 1989, and to feed the growth of the export-driven Israeli arms industry. On July 25, 2008, President Shimon Peres, ahead of a visit to China for the Beijing Olympics, described the country as the 'future of the world', and said that he saw 'great importance in the strengthening of the relations between Israel and China and in promoting economic, cultural and security ties'.[44] During the visit of Israeli Navy Chief Eliezer Marom in December, 2010, Chinese Defence Minister Liang Guanglie urged that both countries should increase their 'inter-military links', a sentiment reciprocated by Marom.[45] The first-ever port visit by a Chinese Navy flotilla, however, occurred nearly 20 months later, in August, 2012, in the context of 20 years of the establishment of diplomatic ties.[46] Reports noted, though, that Israel trained Chinese anti-terrorist armed police ahead of the Beijing Olympics, which critics noted was an 'export of occupation police tactics'.[47]

The nature of interactions between the national security establishments of both countries gained momentum during 2011–2012. Defence Minister Ehud Barak visited China in June, 2011. Iranian nuclear concerns and counter-terrorism cooperation dominated the discussions.[48] Barak's visit was followed by the visit of the Chief of the General Staff of the PLA, General Chen Bingde, in August, 2011. A statement from the Chinese Defence Ministry indicated that Chen's visit would 'deepen under-standing, enhance friendships, expand consensus and promote cooperation' with Israel.[49] Chen visited the Israeli Defence Forces (IDF) Urban Warfare Training Centre, among other institutions. While Iran was the topmost concern for Chen's Israeli interlocutors, reports noted that Israel was also concerned about Chinese-made rockets in the hands of Palestinian militants in Gaza.[50]

A delegation of People's Armed Police (PAP) underwent training at the Israel Border Police's training establishment in December, 2011. The visit generated angst among human rights watchers, as PAP units are involved in policing Tibet and the Uyghur region, and were alleged to have used live ammunition to suppress Tibetan protesters in 2008.[51] Israeli Chief of Staff Benny Gantz visited China in May, 2012, with Iran again dominating the discussions. The *People's Daily* noted that the reciprocal visits of high military officials were in the context of the 20th anniversary of the establishment of diplomatic ties.[52] Prior to Gantz, Barak was the first highest-ranking military official to have visited China, in July, 1994, when he was the IDF Chief of Staff.

In light of the increasingly robust nature of cooperation between Israel and China in the field of innovation and high-technology, Israeli officials deny any restrictions or pressure from third parties, like the US, on high-tech 'civilian' exports/collaboration with China. Israeli Economy Minister Naftali Bennet, in July, 2013, insisted that there was no restriction on high-tech cooperation with China, adding that 'in security areas, there's restriction all over the world. It's not unique'.[53] Analysts, however, note that, given the dual-use applications of many high-tech solutions, Israel would have to be wary of such cooperation.

Furthermore, many cutting-edge Israeli start-ups have been established by alumni of elite IDF units, like Unit 8200, which invariably have to share their unique skills with their Chinese investors. The Chinese have invested in Israeli companies like Beyond Verbal Communication Limited, which specialises in voice analytics software. Reports note that the company's main product is the Cloud, a network of balloons that provides internet access and data analysis, like Google's Project Loon, which could also be used for surveillance purposes by government agencies.[54] The example illustrates the inherently dual-use nature of such technologies.

A critical arena in which this tension could play out pertains to UAVs. Israel, along with the US, is a world leader in such technologies. Chinese companies, however, are making rapid progress. Drone maker DJI, for instance, has cornered about 70 per cent of world civilian demand, with a market value of around US$10 billion less than 10 years since its founding.[55] Other reports also note that China was gaining market share in military drones, with models like the Wing Loong, which are cheaper (costing about US$1 million as opposed to US$30 million for the US-made Reaper).[56]

Reports further note that China has sold military drones to countries like the United Arab Emirates (UAE), Egypt, Nigeria and Pakistan.[57] To be sure, Israel is not in the market to supply military drones to Pakistan, while it seems to be having a cosy 'above-the-radar' relationship currently with countries like the UAE, even taking part in multilateral joint military exercises, which involved the UAE Air Force in Greece (INIOHOS 2017), and the US (Red Flag 2016). However, the proliferation of cheaper Chinese military drones in its neighbourhood would only add to security uncertainties in the region. One of the significant deals concluded during the visit of Saudi King Salman to Beijing in March, 2017 (a week ahead of Netanyahu's visit) pertained to the manufacturing of CH-4 armed UAVs, making the Kingdom of Saudi Arabia only the third country, after Pakistan and Myanmar, to have a local production facility for the killer drone.[58] Further, if Chinese drones dramatically improve their capabilities in the wake of high-tech innovation collaboration with Israel, it could potentially reduce business opportunities in other world markets.

Beijing's arms transfers to countries in the West Asian region have been another long-standing issue of concern in Israel–China ties. Israel was worried when China sold CSS-2 Intermediate Range Ballistic Missiles (IRBMs) to Saudi Arabia in the late 1980s. The accuracy of these missiles was, paradoxically, reported to have been improved, with Israeli assistance, by China.[59] Apart from Saudi Arabia, China has been a significant arms, as well as strategic technology, supplier to countries like

Iran.[60] At the same time, Israel's arms transfers to countries in China's neighbour-hood, with which Beijing has a history of antagonistic relationships, further adds a complicating dimension to the Israel–China defence conundrum. Taiwan, for instance, produced Dvora fast-attack patrol boats and Gabriel anti-ship missiles under licence from Israel.[61]

Reports noted that China was unhappy about the forward deployment of Israeli-sourced, long-range (130 km) artillery rocket launchers by Vietnam on the Nansha Islands in mid-2016.[62] Vietnam also received the Israeli-made Spyder air-defence missile system at about the same time.[63] In order to deter Beijing's increasing encroachments in the South China Sea, reports note that Vietnam is currently eyeing the 250-km-range Delilah air-launched cruise missile.[64] Israel and Vietnam estab-lished a formal framework for defence cooperation in March, 2014 when a senior Vietnamese security minister visited Tel Aviv.[65] Other Southeast Asian countries that are benefiting from Israeli military technology include the Philippines, Singapore, Thailand and even Myanmar, of late.[66]

China and Palestine

The Chinese Foreign Ministry, in 1987, stated that 'China has yet to establish diplomatic relations with Israel in order to support the just struggles by Arab and Palestinian peoples against the aggressive and expansionist policy of the Israeli regime'.[67] While analysts note that the Cold War and the US factor were far more important constraints on China establishing diplomatic links with Israel prior to 1992, the statement nevertheless places in perspective the ideological justification for China's support of the cause of Palestine. The PRC began to celebrate 'Palestine Solidarity Day' annually from 1965. In March, 1965, the Palestine Liberation Organisation (PLO) was allowed to open a 'quasi-diplomatic mission' in Beijing, the first in a non-Arab country.[68] In the aftermath of the 1967 rout the Arabs received at the hands of the Israelis, Mao Tse-tung was convinced that guerrilla warfare was the way to go for the Palestinians to achieve their objectives.[69] China, therefore, embarked on providing military support to the Palestinians. During 1965–1972, Palestinian organisations, like the People's Democratic Front for the Liberation of Palestine (PDFLP) and the Popular Front for the Liberation of Palestine (PFLP), apart from the (PLO), received guerrilla warfare training from the PLA. Small arms were provided to these organisations as well.[70]

After 1992, even as the Israel–China partnership has witnessed growth, China has been active in extending diplomatic and economic support, and has opposed Israeli policies pertaining to the construction of settlements or the Gaza blockade. The Chinese Foreign Ministry Spokesperson, in February, 2011, expressed 'deep regrets' and 'opposition' to Israel's approval of 1,100 new homes in East Jerusalem, and urged Israel to resume negotiations with Palestine as soon as possible.[71] China, in December, 2012, expressed 'serious concern over the announcement of settlement construction in the E1 area, and Israel's suspension of transfers of tax payments to the Palestinian side'.[72] In April, 2013, China's Permanent Representative to the UN, Li Baodong, blamed Israel's settlement activities as 'the direct reason behind the stagna-tion of the peace talks'.[73] Ambassador Wu Haitao, on December 16, 2016, charged that construction of Israel's settlements 'undermined the prospects of the two-State solution'.[74] Further, China bans its workers from working on Israeli settlement construction.

As for the Gaza blockade, China, in June, 2010, urged Israel to 'take effective steps to break the blockade on Gaza to avoid the Palestine–Israel peace talks and the situation in the region from being further interfered' with.[75] As for economic support, during Operation Cast Lead, for instance, China offered US$1 million emergency aid to Palestine.[76] During the visit of Chinese Commerce Minister Chen Denming to Israel and Palestine in March, 2011, China offered 'in-kind assistance' of US$5.5 million to the Palestine National Authority (PNA).[77] China has also supported the PNA's request for full UN membership. The Chairman of the National Committee of the Chinese People's Political Consultative Conference (CPPCC), Jia Qinglin, in a meeting with the Secretary General of the PNA in Beijing in November, 2010, reiterated that China 'always supports the Palestinian people to fight for their legitimate rights and unswerving efforts for establishing an independent state'.[78] An editorial in the *Global Times* of September, 2011 insisted that China's support does not mean 'hostility towards Israel' and that China had the right to express its views on such major issues.[79]

Further, while China is not part of the Quartet on the Middle East Peace Process (made up of the US, EU, UN and Russia), it has consistently put forward proposals to address the issue. President Xi Jinping's four-point proposal of May, 2013 is a case in point.[80] Foreign Minister Wang Yi's 'three stops' (stop violence, settlement expansion, Gaza blockade) and 'three explorations' (peacemaking efforts, follow-up measures, incentive mechanisms for peace) of June 2016 is another formulation. Four of China's senior diplomats have, since September, 2002, functioned as Special Envoys on the Middle East issue, and have actively engaged in diplomatic consultations across the region and beyond.

For China, the Palestinian issue remains at the 'core' of the Middle East issue. President Xi Jinping, while welcoming the PNA President, Mahmoud Abbas, to Beijing in May, 2013 (at the same time as Netanyahu was visiting Beijing), reiterated that the non-resolution of the 'core' issue of the Palestinians, which has brought deep suffering to the Palestinian people, remains an important reason for 'extended turbulence' in the region.[81] Prime Minister Li Keqiang, in his meeting with the visiting Israeli prime minister in May, 2013, insisted that 'the Palestinian issue is at the core of factors influencing peace and stability in the Middle East' and that 'China expects Israel and Palestine to work together …'[82] At the UNGA, on December 23, 2016, Ambassador Wu described the 'question of Palestine' as the 'underlying cause of the situation in the region'.[83] Xi told Netanyahu, on March 20, 2017, that peaceful co-existence between the Israelis and Palestinians would not only benefit both of them, but the entire region.

It is pertinent to note that such Chinese views of the Palestinian issue as the 'core' of the regional problem are in direct opposition to the views of the Israeli government. Prime Minister Netanyahu, at the UNGA in September 2016, for instance, insisted that the 'true core of the conflict' is the 'persistent Palestinian refusal to recognise the Jewish state in any boundary'. He further added that 'this conflict is not about the settlements. It never was'.[84] Netanyahu slammed the UNGA for passing 20 resolutions against Israel in 2015 and a 'grand total of three' against the rest of the world. He termed the work of the UNHRC as a 'joke' and of the UN Educational, Scientific and Cultural Organisation (UNESCO) as a 'circus' for allegedly denying the connection between the Jewish people and the Temple Mount.

Netanyahu was referring to the UNESCO resolution passed on April 15, 2016 that criticised Israel for allegedly blocking access to Muslim holy places on the Temple Mount. The resolution used the Muslim name describing the Temple Mount

(Al-Haram al-Sharif), which Israel contended was in disregard to the Jewish people's historical links to the place, which was the site of the Second Jewish Temple, destroyed in 70 AD. UNESCO passed two other resolutions on October 13, 2016, and May 2, 2017, accusing Israel, the 'Occupying Power', of 'illegal demolitions' and 'intrusive work' near the area.[85] China voted in favour of all the three resolutions. The Chinese positive vote did not go down well with the Israelis. Former National Security Advisor Yaacov Amidror, who accompanied Netanyahu on his May, 2013 visit to China, criticised the Chinese vote as a 'sign of weakness', saying that such decisions 'potentially opened the door to similar UN resolutions in the future, undercutting its historic right to the South China Sea, and perhaps even Tibet'.[86]

China's West Asian stakes

In 2005, China imported 55.36 million tons of crude oil from Arab countries, 43.7 per cent of the country's total oil imports. By 2014, China was importing over 52 per cent of its energy needs from the region.[87] China's energy investments in the region have been termed 'dragon nests' by analysts, who point out that, by 2035, West Asia is set to provide over 70 per cent of the country's energy needs.[88] Foreign Minister Li Zhaoxing, in June, 2006, summarised 50 years of Sino-Arab relations as involving 'mutual trust, mutual benefit and mutual assistance'.[89] China has 'strategic partnerships' with the Arab League, Turkey, the UAE and Qatar; a 'strategic partnership for long-term friendship' with Saudi Arabia; and a 'comprehensive strategic partnership' with Egypt.[90] Algeria, Sudan, Jordan and Iraq also have 'strategic cooperative partnerships' with China, as pointed out by Xi in his *Al Ahram* op-ed, ahead of his state visit to Egypt in January, 2016.[91]

President Xi's visits to Saudi Arabia, Egypt and Iran in January, 2016 symbolise a rising power's efforts to cement its interactions with critical countries in the region. In the *Al Ahram* op-ed, Xi affirmed that China–Arab relations 'were thriving'. He pointed out that trade between China and Arab countries exceeded US$251.1 billion in 2014, and that China had provided Arab countries with a:

> total of 25.4 billion RMB yuan in economic assistance, trained over 20,000 people in different professions … Eleven Arab countries have become approved destinations for Chinese tourists. There are now 183 weekly flights between the two sides, and every year, 1.02 million people travel back and forth between China and Arab countries.[92]

China–Saudi Arabia two-way trade in 2014 amounted to US$69 billion. More than 100 Chinese enterprises have contractual projects in Saudi Arabia, with a combined contract value of over US$50 billion.[93] Xi described Saudi Arabia as a 'brotherly' state, and acknowledged with gratitude the US$60 million assistance provided by Riyadh during the Sichuan earthquake of 2008.[94] King Salman, as noted earlier, was in Beijing a week prior to Netanyahu's March, 2017 visit, when massive deals, worth US$65 billion, were signed, spanning energy, culture, education and technology. It is pertinent to note that both countries' relations have witnessed significant momentum, given that they only established ties in July, 1990.

The trade between China and Iran, which established bilateral ties in 1971, was US$52 billion in 2014. It was US$21 billion in 2010.[95] Xi urged Iran to pursue 'win–win outcomes and common prosperity' ahead of his visit to Tehran, the third leg of his West Asia tour.[96] Beijing and Tehran vowed to take forward their bilateral trade to over US$600 billion over the course of the next decade (2026) and agreed on a 'comprehensive strategic partnership'. One growth area in Iran–China bilateral ties (apart from increasing cooperation in the energy sector) could be military relations. Reports suggest that China could become an important avenue for Iran to meet its defence requirements, including, among other things, fighter aircraft.[97] The aftermath of the Iran nuclear deal has seen enhanced interactions between the national security establishments of the two countries.

Other mega infrastructure projects that China has been involved in the region include highway projects in Algeria and rail projects in Saudi Arabia, apart from its grand, contemporary efforts to make the region part of its Belt and Road Initiative (BRI). China sees the BRI partnerships with the West Asian region as an essential element to boosting economic development, which 'is both the root and solution to solving thorny issues in the conflict-torn region'.[98] Even prior to the BRI, analysts note that China's interactions with the countries in West Asia not only provided 'rich dividends to its economy, trade, investments, energy, defence exports …' but also garnered Arab diplomatic support, at forums like the UNGA and UNHRC, on issues ranging from Taiwan to blunting charges of human rights abuses.[99]

Apart from having huge stakes in the countries of the region, some of which have been delineated above, China has exhibited support and 'sympathy' for parties on the other side of the divide from Israel. This is true not just with the Palestinians, but *vis-à-vis* Syria on the issue of the Golan Heights, among others. Foreign Minister Wang Yi informed Lebanese Foreign Minister Gebran Bassil in June, 2014 that China 'shows deep sympathy and understanding towards the problems and situations facing Lebanon'. The 'problems' that Bassil indicated to Wang included those relating to terrorism, Syrian refugees, Lebanon–Israel conflicts and Palestine–Israel conflicts.[100]

A Chinese delegation, led by the former Deputy Foreign Minister, Yang Fuchang, visited Hezbollah's Tourist Landmark of the Resistance, a jihadi museum in Tuffah, South Lebanon, in April, 2013.[101] Chairman of the CPPCC National Committee Jia Qinglin visited the Golan Heights on November 1, 2010. He insisted that 'China unswervingly supports the just cause of the Syrian government and people to safeguard their national sovereignty and territorial integrity, backs Syria to resume the exercise of sovereignty there, and supports Syria's long-time efforts for peace in the Middle East'.[102]

Relevance of the limiting factors *vis-à-vis* the Israel–India partnership

Undoubtedly, India's support of the Palestinian cause remains unshaken, and New Delhi is routinely critical of Israeli policies on settlements, and its frequent military interventions in the Gaza Strip, among other issues. Nevertheless, India's behaviour has seen a perceptible shift under the Narendra Modi government on issues such as co-sponsoring resolutions critical of Israel at the UNGA. While India continues to support such resolutions, it has in recent times desisted from co-sponsoring some of them (such as the resolution on 'Right to Self Determination of the Palestinian People'). Furthermore, India also abstained on the October, 2016 and May, 2017 UNESCO resolutions that Israel felt were delegitimising its historical links to the Temple Mount. India (along with other countries, such as France) had voted in favour of the April, 2016 resolution, though, with reports indicating that Israel's Ministry of Foreign Affairs (MFA) had expressed strong displeasure with their votes. Both Paris and New Delhi subsequently abstained in the October, 2016 and May, 2017 votes.

The Chinese positive vote in favour of the UNESCO resolutions, as has been pointed out, did not go very well with Israel's sensitivities.

While China's commercial and energy stakes in the West Asian region are huge, India has far more organic linkages in its 'proximate neighbourhood', given the presence of the eight million diaspora (with the maximum percentage living in Saudi Arabia). This adds enormous strength to India's interactions with the region. China's UN Security Council permanent membership will continue to accentuate its positions on issues relating to the disputes of the region. Corruption issues linked to some of the Chinese infrastructure projects in the region have further dampened its soft-power profile. Also, India does not supply military equipment to countries at the opposite ends of the strategic divide in the region, like Saudi Arabia and Iran.

The most crucial limiting factor in the Israel–China partnership, the defence and security cooperation conundrum, is not only absent, but such cooperation is the most dynamic part of the India–Israel equation. Given that arms sales have historically been an important part of the Tel Aviv-headquartered Ministry of Defence's efforts to enhance the country's diplomatic influence and leverage, the inability of the two sides to overcome this conundrum will continue to hamper the optimum growth of the bilateral ties. Despite this, the 'comprehensive innovation partnership' that the two countries are so robustly pursuing potentially gives China access to cutting-edge Israeli technology, with dual-use applications. This could play out to Israel's disadvantage, as regards arenas of its niche technological expertise, such as UAVs and surveillance technologies. While Israel will have to be wary of the Chinese behemoth eating into its market spaces pertaining to such technologies, Israel's long-standing defence partners, like India, meanwhile cannot discount the possibility of such technology being passed on to China's 'all-weather friend' Pakistan.

In closing

Netanyahu, at the 20th anniversary of the establishment of diplomatic ties in January, 2012 remarked that the friendship between the two sides can only further deepen: 'We've barely scratched the surface of Israeli-Chinese relations. I have no doubt that in the coming years we'll see a dramatic expansion of these ties.'[103] Netanyahu further remarked that Israeli prime ministers normally attended the national days of only one country (the US), and hoped that they would make it a custom to attend the national days of two countries (the US and China) from then on. Apart from President Reuven Rivlin attending the 65th anniversary celebrations of the establishment of the PRC in October, 2014 at the Chinese Embassy, Netanyahu's hopes of the seniormost Israeli political leadership attending Chinese diplomatic events regularly does not seem to have materialised.[104]

China and Israel have indeed forged mutually beneficial ties in many fields, as shown above; however, this article has shed light on the still significant limiting factors that continue to constrain the Israel–China partnership. While Israel will have to continue to live with the fact that China has far greater economic incentives and diplomatic use of the Arab world, the view from Beijing will continue to be clouded by the fact that Israel is firmly ensconced in the American strategic orbit. In the meantime, however, China will be happy to lap up the benefits conferred by the 'comprehensive innovation partnership' with a key technology powerhouse like Israel.

Acknowledgements

The author wishes to acknowledge the critical and constructive comments provided by three anonymous reviewers that helped in refining the article.

Disclosure statement

No potential conflict of interest was reported by the author.

Notes

1. Yitzhak Schichor, 'Hide and Seek: Sino-Israeli Relations in Perspective', *Israel Affairs*, 1(2), Winter 1994, p. 189.
2. Chen Yiyi, 'China's Relationship with Israel, Opportunities and Challenges: Perspectives from China', *Israel Studies*, 17(3), Fall 2012, pp. 3–5.
3. Zev Sufott, 'The Crucial Year 1992', in Jonathan Goldstein (ed.), *China and Israel 1948–1998: A Fifty Year Retrospective*, Praeger, London, 1999, p. 107. Sufott was appointed Israel's first Ambassador to China in 1992. He was sent to the US by the Israeli Government to study the Chinese language in 1956. Also see Han Xiaoxing, 'Sino-Israeli Relations', *Journal of Palestine Studies*, 22(2), Winter 1993, p. 66.
4. 'Israel–China Task Force to be Launched at First China–Israel Cooperation Conference', Prime Minister's Office (PMO), March 30, 2015, at http://www.pmo.gov.il/English/MediaCenter/Spokesman/Pages/spokechina300315.aspx# (Accessed March 30, 2017).
5. 'Opinions on Implementing a Proactive Strategy to Promote the Importation of Machinery and Electronic Products During the 12th Five-Year Plan Period', Ministry of Commerce (MOFCOM), March 30, 2011, at http://english.mofcom.gov.cn/article/policyrelease/domestic policy/201105/20110507553462.shtml (Accessed March 25, 2017).
6. 'Israeli Government Approves Agreement to support joint R&D Ventures with China', *Global Times*, April 2, 2012, at http://www.globaltimes.cn/content/703045.shtml (Accessed March 30, 2017).
7. 'Prime Minister Benjamin Netanyahu's Visit to China', Consulate of Israel in Hong Kong & Macau, May 9, 2013, at http://embassies.gov.il/hong-kong/NewsAndEvents/Pages/PM-Netanyahu-welcomed-in-Beijing-by-Chinese-PM-Li-Keqiang-.aspx (Accessed March 30, 2017).
8. See China–Israel Changzhou Innovation Park (CIP) Initiative, at http://www.matimop.org.il/cip.html (Accessed April 4, 2017).
9. 'Chinese Company Launches Innovation Contest to Tech Companies in Israel', MOFCOM, February 5, 2015, at http://english.mofcom.gov.cn/article/newsrelease/counselorsoffice/wes ternasiaandafricareport/201502/20150200889790.shtml (Accessed April 4, 2017).
10. 'Tel Aviv to Host China–Israel Investment Summit', *Globes English*, June 9, 2016, at http://www.globes.co.il/en/article-tel-aviv-to-host-China-Israel-investment-summit-1001131131 (Accessed April 4, 2017).
11. 'China, Israel Embraces Golden Age for Innovation Cooperation', *Global Times*, January 6, 2016, at http://www.globaltimes.cn/content/962216.shtml (Accessed April 4, 2017).
12. 'Regular Press Conference of the Ministry of Commerce', MOFCOM, March 24, 2017, at http://english.mofcom.gov.cn/article/newsrelease/press/201703/20170302540791.shtml (Accessed March 30, 2017).
13. 'China, Israel Embraces Golden Age for Innovation Cooperation', No. 11.
14. Song Shengxia, 'China–Israel Ties on the Rise', *Global Times*, March 1, 2015, at http://www.globaltimes.cn/content/909569.shtml (Accessed April 4, 2017).
15. See 'Innovation in Israel 2016', at http://innovationisrael-en.mag.calltext.co.il/?article=8 (Accessed August 25, 2016).
16. Efraim Chalamish, 'China–Israel Economic Renaissance', *Jerusalem Post*, March 30, 2017, at http://www.jpost.com/Opinion/China-Israel-economic-renaissance-A-tale-of-two-realities-485703 (Accessed April 4, 2017).
17. Shelly Appelberg and Michael Rochvarger, 'Chinese Firm Agrees to Buy Israel's Spacecom for US$285 Million', *Haaretz*, August 25, 2016, at http://www.haaretz.com/israel-news/busi ness/1.738532 (Accessed April 4, 2017).

18. David Rosenberg, 'Why China Is on a Shopping Binge in Israel', *Haaretz*, August 25, 2016, at http://www.haaretz.com/opinion/.premium-1.738709 (Accessed April 4, 2017).

19. Lidar Gravé-Lazi, 'Israeli and Chinese Universities to Establish Entrepreneurship Center', *Jerusalem Post*, March 31, 2016, at http://www.jpost.com/Business-and-Innovation/Israeli-and-Chinese-universities-to-establish-entrepreneurship-center-449862 (Accessed April 4, 2017).

20. 'New technology Institute for Shantou', MOFCOM, November 11, 2013, at http://english.mofcom.gov.cn/article/counselorsreport/europereport/201311/20131100386665.shtml (Accessed April 10, 2017).

21. 'Launch of First Israeli University in China', Technion – Israel Institute of Technology, December 16, 2015, at http://www.technion.ac.il/en/launch-of-first-israeli-university-in-china-five-thousand-in-attendance-for-groundbreaking-of-guangdong-technion-israel-institute-of-technology/ (Accessed April 10, 2017).

22. It was not reported however what percentage of the US$130 million donation of the LKF came from the profits that Horizon Ventures made as a result of the sale of Waze to Google. Notwithstanding profits from that particular deal, however, the LKF by 2013 had made donations worth nearly US$800 million to Shantou University. See 'Technion – Israel Institute of Technology Comes to China with US$130 Million from Li Ka-shing Foundation', Technion – Israel Institute of Technology, October 2, 2013, at http://www.technion.ac.il/en/2013/10/technion-israel-institute-of-technology-comes-to-china-with-us130-million-from-li-ka-shing-foundation/ (Accessed April 10, 2017).

23. 'Port Project Marks New Achievement in China–Israel Infrastructure Cooperation', MOFCOM, June 3, 2015, at http://english.mofcom.gov.cn/article/counselorsreport/europereport/201506/20150601000991.shtml (Accessed March 30, 2017); 'Port Project Marks New Achievement in China–Israel Infrastructure Co-op', *China Daily*, May 29, 2015, at http://africa.chinadaily.com.cn/business/2015-05/29/content_20857011.htm (Accessed March 30, 2017).

24. Mordechai Chaziza, 'The Red-Med Railway: New Opportunities for China, Israel, and the Middle East', *BESA Centre Perspective Paper No. 385*, December 11, 2016, at https://besacenter.org/perspectives-papers/385-chaziza-the-red-med-railway-new-opportunities-for-china-israel-and-the-middle-east/ (Accessed March 30, 2017).

25. 'Israel Rights Groups Attack Plan to Import 20,000 Chinese Workers', *Financial Times*, September 20, 2015, at https://www.ft.com/content/1f0cdc62-5f9a-11e5-9846-de406ccb37f2 (Accessed March 30, 2017).

26. Herb Keinon, 'Israel–China Deal Paves Way for Thousands of Chinese Construction Workers in Israel', *Jerusalem Post*, January 4, 2017, at http://www.jpost.com/Israel-News/Politics-And-Diplomacy/Israel-China-deal-paves-way-for-thousands-of-Chinese-construction-workers-in-Israel-477439 (Accessed March 30, 2017).

27. Yu Haijie, 'China–Israel Visa Deal Has No Political Bent', *Global Times*, April 7, 2016, at http://www.globaltimes.cn/content/977522.shtml (Accessed March 25, 2017).

28. Niv Elis, 'Israel Eases Visa Rules for Chinese Tourists', *Jerusalem Post*, December 2, 2015, at http://www.jpost.com/Business-and-Innovation/Israel-eases-visa-rules-for-Chinese-tourists-436065 (Accessed March 25, 2017).

29. Ma Jingjing, 'Chinese Abroad to Surpass 6m during Spring Festival', *Global Times*, January 24, 2017, at http://www.globaltimes.cn/content/1030550.shtml (Accessed March 25, 2017).

30. P.R. Kumaraswamy, 'The Military Dimension of Israel–China Relations', *China Report*, 31(2), 1995, p. 237. Kumaraswamy notes that President Chaim Herzog travelled to China in December, 1992 on a state visit on Eisenberg's private aircraft. Yoram Evron, 'Between Beijing and Washington: Israel's Technology Transfers to China', *Journal of East Asian Studies*, 12, 2013, pp. 508–509. Evron notes that Eisenberg's private aircraft was used to conduct defence trade with China prior to 1992 to maintain strict secrecy; See also Yossi Melman and Ruth Sinai, 'Israeli-Chinese Relations and Their Future Prospects: From Shadow to Sunlight', *Asian Survey*, 27(4), April 1987, p. 395.

31. Stephen Blank, 'China, Israel March in Step Again', *AsiaTimes*, March 26, 2004, at http://www.atimes.com/atimes/China/FC26Ad02.html (Accessed April 5, 2017); Kumaraswamy, though, concurs with the view that the figures could be exaggerated, given that Israel primarily sold technology and avionics, and not military hardware. See his P.R. Kumaraswamy, No. 30, p. 244.

32. Yoram Evron, No. 30, pp. 506–507.

33. Duncan Clarke, 'Israel's Unauthorized Arms Transfers', *Foreign Policy*, 99, Summer 1995, p. 103; Yoram Evron, No. 30, pp. 509–510; See also Yitzhak Schichor, 'Israel's Military Transfers to China and Taiwan', *Survival*, 40(1), Spring 1998, p. 70.

34. P.R. Kumaraswamy, 'Israel–China Arms Trade: Unfreezing Times', Middle East Institute, July 16, 2012, at http://www.mei.edu/content/israel-china-arms-trade-unfreezing-times (Accessed April 10, 2017).

35. 'Statement by a Spokesman for PM Barak on Israel–China and the Phalcon System', Ministry of Foreign Affairs (MFA), July 12, 2000, at http://mfa.gov.il/MFA/PressRoom/2000/Pages/Statement%20by%20a%20Spokesman%20for%20PM%20Barak%20on%20Israel-%20C.aspx (Accessed April 10, 2017).

36. Amnon Barzilai, 'Israel, China Agree on Compensation for Canceled Phalcon Deal', *Haaretz*, March 13, 2002, at http://www.haaretz.com/israel-china-agree-on-compensation-for-canceled-phalcon-deal-1.50512 (Accessed April 10, 2017).

37. Chris Plante, 'Chinese F-8s Carried Israeli Missiles', CNN, April 17, 2001, at http://edition.cnn.com/2001/US/04/17/china.plane.weapons/ (Accessed April 10, 2017).

38. Cited in Wade Boese, 'Israeli Arms Exports to China of Growing Concern to US', *Arms Control Today*, 33(2), March 2003, p. 30.

39. Specifically, the upgrades included the addition of sensors which would have enabled the drones to detect even radars that were turned off. See Scott Wilson, 'Israel Set to End China Arms Deal under US Pressure', *The Washington Post*, June 27, 2005, at http://www.washingtonpost.com/wp-dyn/content/article/2005/06/26/AR2005062600544.html (Accessed April 10, 2017).

40. Stephen Blank, 'Arms Sales and Technology Transfer in Indo-Israeli Relations', *Journal of East Asian Studies*, 19(5), Spring/Summer 2005, p. 233.

41. Carol Migdalovitz, 'Israel: Background and Relations with the United States', CRS Report for Congress, June 6, 2008, at https://digital.library.unt.edu/ark:/67531/metadc700549/m1/1/high_res_d/RL33476_2008Jun06.pdf, p. 32 (Accessed April 10, 2017).

42. Miles A. Pomper, 'US, Israel Reach China Arms Deal', *Arms Control Today*, 35(7), September 2005, p. 34.

43. Yitzhak Schichor, 'The US Factor in Israel's Military Relations with China', *China Brief*, 5(12), May 24, 2005, at https://jamestown.org/program/the-u-s-factor-in-israels-military-relations-with-china/ (Accessed April 25, 2017).

44. 'Israeli President Looking Forward to Seeing Games', *China Daily*, July 25, 2008, at http://www.chinadaily.com.cn/olympics/2008-07/25/content_6875146.htm (Accessed April 10, 2017).

45. 'China Vows to Enhance Bilateral Ties with Israel', *China Daily*, December 14, 2010, at http://europe.chinadaily.com.cn/2010-12/14/content_11697145.htm (Accessed April 20, 2017).

46. 'Chinese Navy Ships Visit Israel's Haifa Port', Xinhua, August 4, 2012, at http://news.xinhuanet.com/english/china/2012-08/14/c_123578558.htm (Accessed April 2, 2017).

47. Alex Pevzner, 'US Loses by Blocking Sino-Israeli Ties', *Global Times*, October 25, 2010, at http://www.globaltimes.cn/content/740429.shtml (Accessed April 2, 2017).

48. Yaakov Katz, 'Ban on China Arms Sales in Place despite Barak Visit', *Jerusalem Post*, June 12, 2011, at http://www.jpost.com/Diplomacy-and-Politics/Ban-on-China-arms-sales-in-place-despite-Barak-visit (Accessed April 1, 2017).

49. 'Chinese Military Chief Visits Israel for First Time', *USA Today*, August 14, 2011, at https://usatoday30.usatoday.com/news/world/2011-08-14-military-chief-israel-visit_n.htm (Accessed April 1, 2017).

50. Ibid.

51. Joseph Federman and Christopher Bodeen, 'China–Israel Ties Alarm Human Rights Advocates', *The Washington Times*, May 29, 2012, at http://www.washingtontimes.com/news/2012/may/29/china-israel-ties-alarm-human-rights-advocates/ (Accessed April 15, 2017).

52. 'Israel's Chief of General Staff Visits China', People.cn, May 19, 2012, at http://en.people.cn/90883/7821507.html (Accessed April 1, 2017).

53. 'Israel Calls for Closer Cooperation with China', *China Daily*, July 5, 2013, at http://www.chinadaily.com.cn/business/2013-07/05/content_16736586_2.htm (Accessed April 5, 2017).

54. 'Space-tech Outfit on Shopping Spree', MOFCOM, September 19, 2016, at http://english.mofcom.gov.cn/article/counselorsreport/europereport/201609/20160901395986.shtml (Accessed April 25, 2017).

55. 'After Decades of Innovation Catch-up, China Moves to the Fore', MOFCOM, December 24, 2015, at http://english.mofcom.gov.cn/article/counselorsreport/europereport/201512/20151201217723.shtml (Accessed April 15, 2017).

56. 'China gaining market share in military drones', MOFCOM, September 26, 2013, at http://english.mofcom.gov.cn/article/newsrelease/counselorsoffice/westernasiaandafricareport/201309/20130900325545.shtml (Accessed April 15, 2017).

57. Sarah Kreps, 'China Swooping in on Military Drone Market', CNN, April 1, 2016, at http://edition.cnn.com/2016/04/01/opinions/china-drone-sales-kreps/ (Accessed April 15, 2017).

58. Minnie Chan, 'Chinese Drone Factory in Saudi Arabia First in Middle East', *South China Morning Post*, March 26, 2017, at http://www.scmp.com/news/china/diplomacy-defence/article/2081869/chinese-drone-factory-saudi-arabia-first-middle-east (Accessed April 15, 2017).

59. P.R. Kumaraswamy, No. 30, pp. 240–241.

60. See John Garver, *China and Iran: Ancient Partners in a Post-Imperial World*, University of Washington Press, Seattle, 2006, pp. 139–200.

61. P.R. Kumaraswamy, No. 30, p. 244; Yitzhak Schichor, No. 33, pp. 72–73.

62. Mo Jingxi and Chen Weihua, 'China Faults Vietnam on Islands', *China Daily USA*, August 11, 2016, at http://usa.chinadaily.com.cn/china/2016-08/11/content_26442083.htm (Accessed April 10, 2017).

63. 'Vietnam Receives First Israeli-made SPYDER Air Defense Missile System', *Defence Blog*, July 18, 2016, at http://defence-blog.com/news/vietnam-receives-first-israeli-made-spyder-air-defense-missile-system.html (Accessed April 10, 2017).

64. Tyler Rogoway, 'Vietnam Eyes Israel's Delilah Standoff Missile, and F-16s Could Be Next', *The Drive*, March 10, 2017, at http://www.thedrive.com/the-war-zone/8219/vietnam-eyes-israels-delilah-standoff-missile-and-f-16s-could-be-next (Accessed April 10, 2017).

65. Alvite Singh Ningthoujam, 'South East Asia: The Emerging Market for Israeli Arms', *ISSSP Reflections No. 16*, May 19, 2014, at http://isssp.in/south-east-asia-the-emerging-market-for-israeli-arms/ (Accessed April 10, 2017).

66. Alvite Singh Ningthoujam, 'Southeast Asia Can't Get Enough of Israel's Weapons', *The National Interest*, June 12, 2016, at http://nationalinterest.org/feature/southeast-asia-cant-get-enough-israels-weapons-16550?page=show (Accessed April 10, 2017).

67. Han Xiaoxing, No. 3, p. 63.

68. Yitzhak Schichor, No. 1, p. 191.

69. William W. Haddad and Mary Foeldi-Hardy, 'Chinese-Palestinian Relations', in P.R. Kumaraswamy (ed.), *China and the Middle East: The Quest for Influence*, Sage, New Delhi, 1999, p. 45.

70. Ann Gilks and Gerald Segal, *China and the Arms Trade*, Croom Helm, London, 1985, pp. 210–212.

71. 'EU, US, China Criticize Israel on New Housing Units in East Jerusalem', Radio Free Europe/Radio Liberty, September 28, 2011, at http://www.rferl.org/a/eu_us_critical_of_new_housing_units_in_jerusalem/24342331.html (Accessed April 5, 2017).

72. 'China Urges Israel to Remove Obstacles to Peace Talks: UN Envoy', *Global Times*, December 20, 2012, at http://www.globaltimes.cn/content/751320.shtml (Accessed April 5, 2017).

73. 'China Calls for Action on Lasting Peace in Middle East', *Global Times*, April 25, 2013, at http://www.globaltimes.cn/content/777377.shtml (Accessed April 5, 2017).

74. 'Statement by Ambassador Wu Haitao at the Security Council Briefing on the Palestinian Question', Foreign Ministry of Peoples Republic of China (FMPRC), December 16, 2016, at http://www.fmprc.gov.cn/mfa_eng/wjb_663304/zwjg_665342/zwbd_665378/t1427775.shtml (Accessed April 5, 2017).

75. 'China Urges Israel to Break Blockade on Gaza', *Global Times*, June 1, 2010, at http://www.globaltimes.cn/content/537572.shtml (Accessed April 5, 2017).

76. 'China Offers US$1 Million Emergency Aid for Palestine', *China Daily*, December 30, 2008, at http://www.chinadaily.com.cn/china/2008-12/30/content_7354915.htm (Accessed April 5, 2017).

77. 'China to Expand Economic Ties with Israel', *China Daily*, March 3, 2011, at http://www.chinadaily.com.cn/m/hebei/2011-03/03/content_12111685.htm (Accessed April 5, 2017).

78. 'China Urges Peaceful Coexistence of Palestine, Israel', *China Daily*, November 26, 2010, at http://www.chinadaily.com.cn/china/2010-11/26/content_11617486.htm (Accessed April 5, 2017).

79. 'US Stands against Public Will in Mideast', *Global Times*, September 21, 2011, at http://www.globaltimes.cn/content/676205.shtml (Accessed April 5, 2017).

80. 'Chinese President Makes Four-point Proposal for Settlement of Palestinian Question', *Global Times*, May 6, 2013, at http://www.globaltimes.cn/content/779577.shtml (Accessed April 5, 2017).

81. 'China Supports Palestinian People: President Xi', *Global Times*, May 6, 2013, at http://www.globaltimes.cn/content/779573.shtml (Accessed April 5, 2017).

82. 'Chinese Premier Meets Israel PM, Urging Cooperation', *Global Times*, May 9, 2013, at http://www.globaltimes.cn/content/780373.shtml (Accessed April 5, 2017).

83. 'Statement by Ambassador Wu Haitao at the Security Council after Voting on the Draft Resolution on the Palestinian Question', FMPRC, December 23, 2016, at http://www.fmprc.gov.cn/mfa_eng/wjb_663304/zwjg_665342/zwbd_665378/t1427773.shtml (Accessed April 5, 2017).

84. 'PM Netanyahu's Speech at the United Nations General Assembly', PMO, September 22, 2016, at http://www.pmo.gov.il/english/mediacenter/speeches/pages/speechun220916.aspx (Accessed April 10, 2017).

85. 'Full Text of UNESCO's Contentious Resolution on Jerusalem and the Countries That Voted', *Haaretz*, October 18, 2016, at http://www.haaretz.com/israel-news/1.747982 (Accessed April 10, 2017).

86. Yacoov Amidror, 'Lessons of UNESCO's Vote', *Israel Hayom*, October 28, 2016, at http://www.israelhayom.com/site/newsletter_article.php?id=37483 (Accessed April 10, 2017).

87. 'China: Country Profile', US Energy Information Administration (EIA), at https://www.eia.gov/beta/international/analysis.cfm?iso=CHN (Accessed April 12, 2017).

88. Manochehr Dorraj and James English, 'The Dragon Nests: China's Energy Engagement of the Middle East', *China Report*, 49(1), 2013, pp. 43–67.

89. Le Tian, 'China, Arab Nations Sign Action Plan', *China Daily*, June 2, 2006, at http://www.chinadaily.com.cn/cndy/2006-06/02/content_606604.htm (Accessed April 12, 2017).

90. Zhao Jun and Hu Yu, 'On China's New Era Anti-Terrorism Governance in the Middle East', *Yonsei Journal of International Studies*, 7 (2), Fall/Winter 2015, pp. 274–275, at http://theyonseijournal.com/wp-content/uploads/2016/01/Jun-Yu-Chinas-Anti-Terrorism-Governance-1.pdf (Accessed April 12, 2017).

91. Xi Jinping, 'Let China-Arab Friendship Surge Forward like the Nile', FMPRC, January 20, 2016, at http://www.fmprc.gov.cn/mfa_eng/wjdt_665385/zyjh_665391/t1333118.shtml (Accessed April 14, 2017).

92. Ibid.

93. 'Regular Press Conference', MOFCOM, March 23, 2017, at http://english.mofcom.gov.cn/article/newsrelease/press/201703/20170302540791.shtml (Accessed April 12, 2017).

94. Xi Jinping, 'Be Good Partners for Common Development', FMPRC, January 18, 2016, at http://www.fmprc.gov.cn/mfa_eng/wjdt_665385/zyjh_665391/t1332852.shtml   (Accessed April 12, 2017).

95. See *China Statistical Yearbook*, National Bureau of Statistics of China, various years, at http://www.stats.gov.cn/english/ (Accessed April 12, 2017).

96. Xi Jinping, 'Work together for a Bright Future of China-Iran Relations', FMPRC, January 21, 2016, at http://www.fmprc.gov.cn/mfa_eng/wjdt_665385/zyjh_665391/t1334040.shtml (Accessed April 12, 2017).

97. Joel Wuthnow, 'Are Chinese Arms about to Flood into Iran?', *National Interest*, January 13, 2016, at http://www.nationalinterest.org/feature/are-chinese-arms-about-flood-iran-14887?page=2 (Accessed February 10, 2016).

98. 'Why the Belt and Road Initiative Has Exceeded Expectations', *China Daily*, March 28, 2017, at http://www.chinadaily.com.cn/business/2017-03/28/content_28704780.htm (Accessed April 12, 2017).

99. Srikanth Kondapalli, 'China's Relations with West Asia', in Srikanth Kondapalli and Emi Mifune (eds.), *China and Its Neighbours*, Pentagon Press, New Delhi, 2010, p. 269; Mao Yufeng, 'China's Interests and Strategy in the Middle East and the Arab World', in Joshua Eisenman, Eric Heginbotham and Derek Mitchell (eds.), *China and the Developing World: Beijing's Strategy for the Twenty-First Century*, M.E. Sharpe, London, 2007, pp. 118–119.

100. 'Wang Yi Meets with Minister of Foreign Affairs and Emigrants Gebran Bassil of Lebanon', MOFCOM, June 9, 2014, at http://english.mofcom.gov.cn/article/newsrelease/counselorsoffice/bilateralexchanges/201407/20140700666122.shtml (Accessed April 10, 2017).

101. Mordechai Chaziza, 'Beijing Seeks Balancing Role in Middle East Conflicts', *Global Times*, May 7, 2013, at http://www.globaltimes.cn/content/779936.shtml (Accessed April 10, 2017).

102. 'Top Chinese Political Advisor Pledges Support to Syria, Arab Nations', *Global Times*, November 2, 2011, at http://www.globaltimes.cn/content/588577.shtml (Accessed April 2, 2017).

103. 'Israel, China Celebrates 20 Years of Diplomatic Relations', *Global Times*, January 25, 2012, at http://www.globaltimes.cn/content/693259.shtml (Accessed April 2, 2017).

104. Prime Minister Ariel Sharon visited the home of the then Indian Ambassador, Raminder Jassal, on September 20, 2004, a year after his path-breaking India visit. Since then, reports of visits by senior Israeli political leadership if any to Indian Embassy events are not in the open domain. A contributing factor could have been the conscious decision by both sides to play down the strategic aspects of cooperation between the two countries.

Index

Note: **Bold** page numbers refer to tables and page numbers followed by "n" denote endnotes.